FINAL FANTASY REBIRTH VII

""UNVEILING THE EPIC JOURNEY"

BY

SUZUKI ANNAISHA

Copyright © 2024 **SUZUKI ANNAISHA**

All rights reserved. This book is copyright and no part of it may be reproduced, distributed, or transmitted in any form or by any means, including photocopying, recording, or other electronic or mechanical methods, without the prior written permission of the publisher, except in the case of brief quotations embodied in critical reviews and certain other noncommercial uses permitted by copyright law.

Printed in the United States of America Copyright 2024

© **SUZUKI ANNAISHA**

Table of Contents

INTRODUCTION 12

CHAPTER ONE 14

FALL OF A HERO 14

    Reach the Crash Site: 15

    Explore Nibelheim: 16

    Follow Tifa: 18

    Go Through the Facility: 21

    Find Another Route to the Reactor: 23

    How to Beat Materia Guardian: 26

    Investigate the Reactor: 28

    Search for Sephiroth: 29

    Follow Tifa: 30

    Materia Locations: 31

CHAPTER TWO 32

DEEPER INTO DARKNESS 32

    Gear Up: 32

Evade the Shinra Soldiers: 34

Explore the Grasslands: 35

Finding Piko: 37

Chadley Returns: 39

Chocobo Riding Practice: 40

Through the Swamp: 41

How to Defeat Midgardsormr: 42

CHAPTER THREE 46

DEEPER INTO DARKNESS 46

Explore the Mines: 47

How to Get Past the Broken Ladder and Elevator: 49

How to Defeat Rude and Elena: 50

How to Escape the Depths: 52

How to Defeat Mythril Golem: 55

Catch Up With the Others: 56

CHAPTER FOUR 58

DAWN OF A NEW ERA 58

Explore the Junon Region: 58

How to Defeat Terror of the Deep: 61

Check on Yuffie: 63

Dolphin Mini-Game: 65

Infiltrate Upper Junon: 66

Parade Mini-Game: 67

NOTE: 69

After the Parade: 69

How to Defeat Roche: 71

CHAPTER FIVE 73

BLOOD IN THE WATER 73

To play cards: 73

To go to the Deck: 74

How to Defeat Jenova Emergent: 77

CHAPER SIX 80

FOOL'S PARADISE 80

Exploring Costa del Sol: 80

    Get Ready for the Beach: 82

    Aerith & Tifa: 84

    How to Defeat Grasptropod: 85

    Beach Time: 87

    Yuffie Strikes Again: 88

CHAPTER SEVEN 89

THOSE LEFT BEHIND 89

    Onward to Mt. Corel: 89

    How to Defeat Custom Valkyrie: 92

    Corel Mako Reactor: 94

    Through the Mines: 95

    How to Defeat Gigatrice: 101

    Setting Their Path: 103

CHAPTER EIGHT 105

ALL THAT GLITTERS 105

    Welcome to the Gold Saucer: 105

    Retro Boxing: 106

Get Some Rooms: 107

Explore the Gold Saucer: 109

Find the Culprit: 110

Feeding Piko: 111

Joining the Race: 115

Back on the Trail: 116

How to Beat Dyne: 117

How to Beat Anuran Suppressor: 119

How to Escape From Shinra: 120

Find Biggs: 121

CHAPTER NINE 123

THE PLANET STIRS 123

Getting to the Reactor: 123

Investigating the Reactor: 126

Restoring Power to the Door: 128

Raising the Water Level: 130

Defeating Specimen H1024: 133

Fast Travel with Chocobos: 134

How to Beat Crimson Mare Mk. II: 137

Remembering the Past: 138

Taking Flight: 140

CHAPTER TEN 142

WATCHER OF THE VALE 142

Welcome to Cosmo Canyon: 142

The Planetarium: 144

Follow Bugenhagen: 146

The Trial Begins: 148

Pass the Gates: 150

Defeating Gi Nattak: 153

Following Gi Nattak: 156

CHAPTER ELEVEN 160

THE LONG SHADOW OF SHINRA 160

Homecoming: 160

Finding the Inspector: 162

How to Bypass the Locked Fence: 165

How to Defeat Diabolic Variant: 167

Onward and Downward: 169

Cait Sith to the Rescue: 170

How to Defeat Yin & Yang: 177

How to Beat Forgotten Specimen: 179

The Coffin: 181

How to Beat Galian Beast: 182

How to defeat Roche: 184

Investigate the Smoke: 185

CHAPTER TWELVE 187

A GOLDEN KEY 187

When You're Grounded, Take to the Water: 187

Track Down Dio: 189

Loveless: 191

Prepare for the Tournament: 193

Encountering Rude and Elena Again: 195

Defeating Rufus: 196

Finding Cait Sith: 198

CHAPTER THIRTEEN 200

WHERE ANGELS FEAR TO TREAD 200

Setting Sail North: 201

Journey to the Temple: 202

Navigating the Maze: 204

How to Defeat the Red Dragon: 207

Splitting Up the Party: 209

The Other Half: 212

How to Defeat Ironclad: 215

How to Defeat Rude and Reno: 216

Back to Aerith: 217

How to Beat Elena and Tseng: 219

A Series of Trials: 221

How to Defeat Demon Gate: 226

Run: 227

CHAPTER FOURTEEN ... 229

END OF THE WORLD ... 229

The Illusion of Choice: ... 229

Follow Aerith: ... 230

Follow the Whispers: ... 231

How to Defeat Jenova Lifeclinger: ... 233

How to Defeat Sephiroth: ... 236

How to Beat Sephiroth Reborn: ... 237

INTRODUCTION

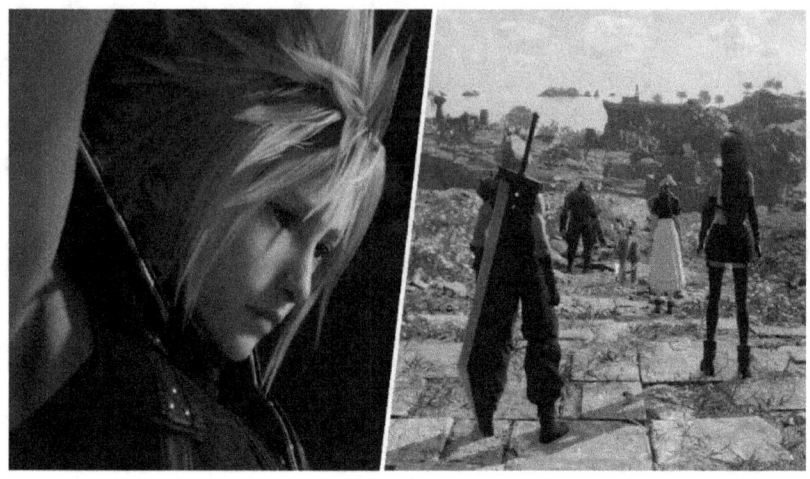

Final Fantasy 7 Rebirth, like many modern video games, does a great job of explaining its main features. It has tutorials and tips on the screen to help players understand what to do. If you've played the 2020 version of the game, you'll find it easy to adapt to the changes in Rebirth. But if you're new to Final Fantasy or the Final Fantasy 7 remake, you might need some help. This part of Game Rant's Final Fantasy 7 Rebirth guide is made for beginners. It has guides on how to play, tips and tricks, and answers to common questions.

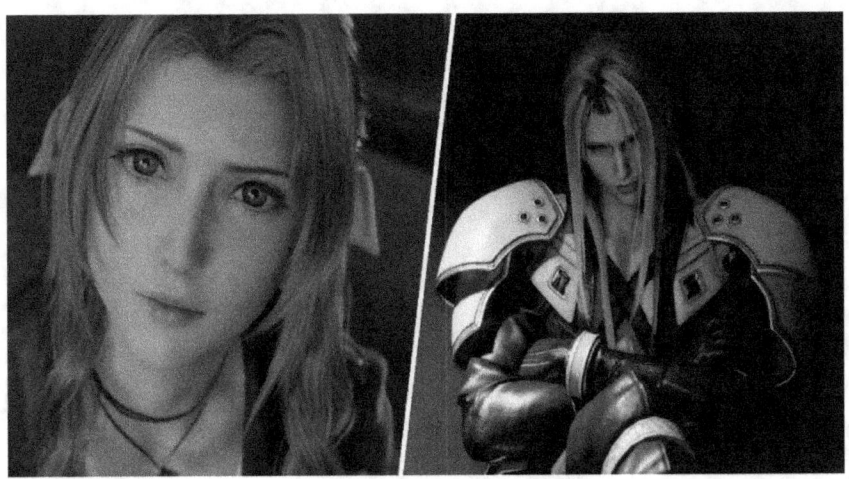

Though there are a few small changes, the main story of Final Fantasy 7 Rebirth should feel familiar to fans of the original game. It picks up where the previous part of the remake project left off, with Cloud and the party in a small town near Midgar. From there, they'll journey to the forgotten capital, facing lots of exciting action along the way. In Game Rant's Final Fantasy 7 Rebirth walkthrough, we'll cover all 14 chapters and provide guides for specific puzzles and decisions players will face.

CHAPTER ONE

FALL OF A HERO

The remake of Final Fantasy 7 was a huge project, and you can tell how much effort went into both Final Fantasy 7: Remake and Final Fantasy 7: Rebirth. After the ending of Final Fantasy 7: Remake, nobody knows what comes next in the story. But now, with the release of Rebirth, players can find out what happens next for Cloud and his friends.

Though there are many changes, some parts of the story remain the same. You can't redo Final Fantasy 7 without talking about what happened in Nibelheim five years ago. That's where Final Fantasy 7: Rebirth starts in its first chapter, "Reach the Crash Site."

Reach the Crash Site:

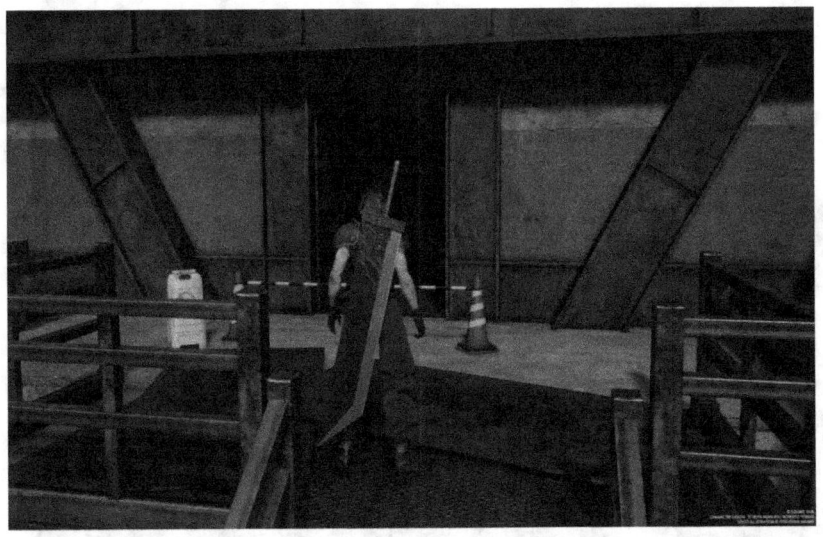

Once you've chosen your preferred difficulty, take a moment to relax and enjoy the beginning of Final Fantasy 7: Rebirth. Even if you've already tried the demo, make sure to watch all the cutscenes, as there are some new ones.

Once the cutscenes are over, head towards the stairs in front of you. The path is simple, so there's no need to explore. You won't find any items in crates during this part. Once you leave Midgar, jump over the blockage and approach the Shinra soldiers.

Now, it's time for combat. In this part, you only have two actions: Attack and Combo Charge. Attack the soldiers and use Combo Charge when it's available. After defeating the reinforcements, another cutscene will play, and the prologue will come to an end.

Explore Nibelheim:

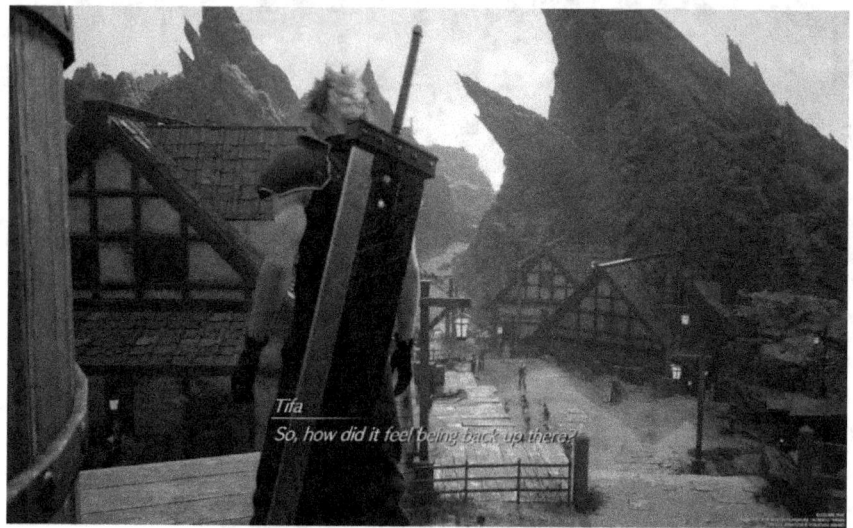

Now, the first chapter begins. After the cutscenes, you'll briefly control Sephiroth in a one-sided fight against a monster. When the next set of cutscenes finish, you'll take control of Cloud as he explores Nibelheim.

When you reach the door leading to Cloud's old house, you'll have the choice to enter or leave. After visiting Cloud's mom, head towards the ladder that goes to the top of the iconic windmill in the village to start another cutscene.

Opposite the windmill is Tifa's house. You can go inside to hear some comments from Cloud's companions as he tells the story, especially Tifa's complaints if you enter her room. If you approach the piano in Tifa's room, you'll have the option to play a piano mini-game. Although you can choose to walk away from the piano, the story will only continue if you sit down to play. Regardless of whether you play a tune or just press buttons randomly, the story will move forward.

In Tifa's parents' bedroom, there's also a chest containing an Ether, so don't forget to grab that before leaving the house. Go inside the Nidhogg Hotel and approach the man with the red cape to trigger a cutscene. There's nothing to buy at the inn or the general store, so head upstairs and approach Sephiroth to start another cutscene.

Follow Tifa:

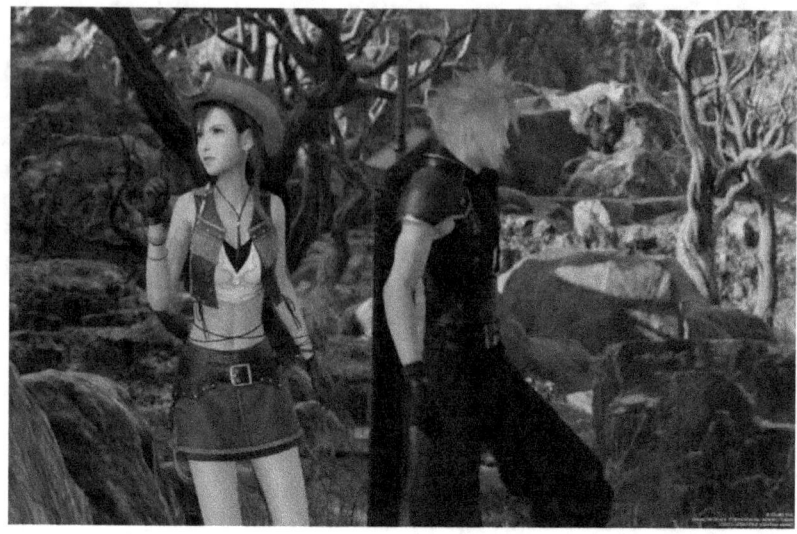

Once you're back in control of Cloud, stick close to Tifa. Smash any boxes you come across, as they might contain useful items like mega-potions. But, your leisurely stroll is cut short when you encounter some monsters along the path. This time, you'll have access to the full combat system of Final Fantasy 7: Rebirth. This means you can use actions, items, and magic. The enemies you face aren't too tough, so take this chance to learn how to use your abilities and get comfortable moving around.

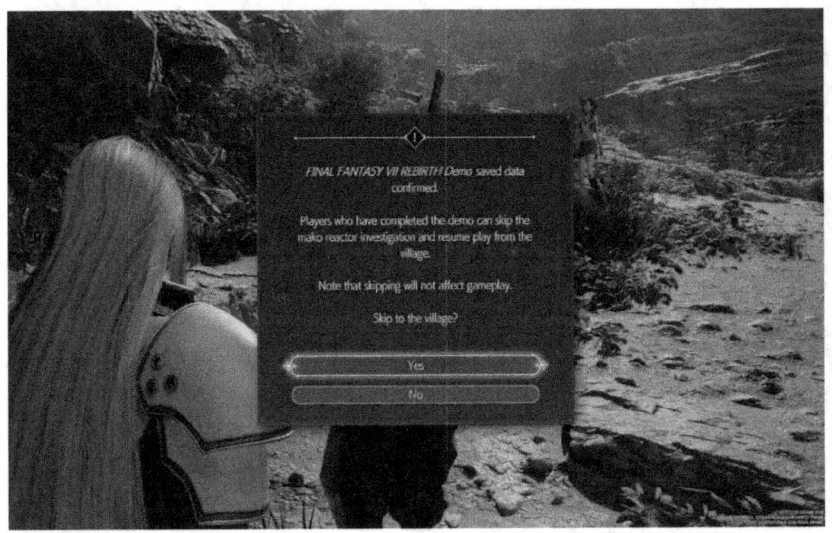

NOTE:

- If you've played the demo, a window will pop up asking if you want to skip ahead to where the demo ended. There's no penalty for either choice, so pick what suits you best.

Continue following Tifa and battle any enemies you come across. You'll receive tutorials on combat mechanics like guarding and locking onto enemies. Once the tutorials are over, you'll take the lead in dealing with the monsters. Head towards the blue diamond marked with an exclamation point, battling any monsters you encounter along the way. You'll also find a chest containing potions as you progress.

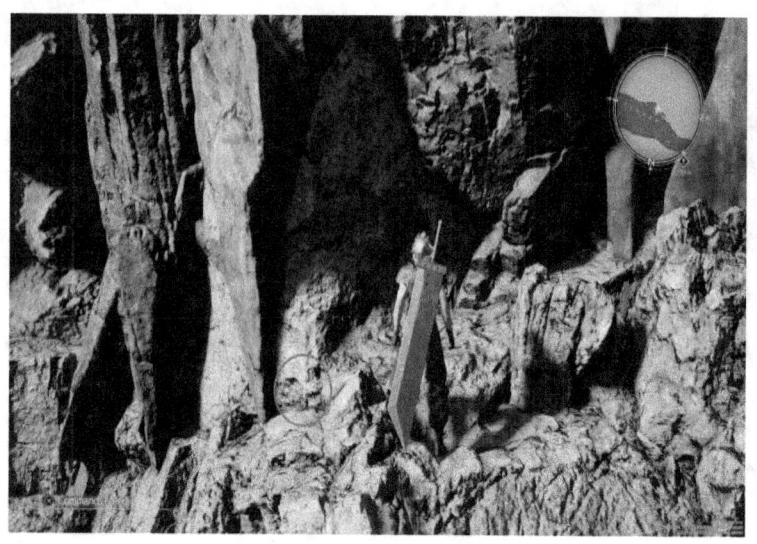

After ascending a set of stairs, you'll notice some green materia on a ledge to your left. To reach it, approach the rock wall and press the circle button to climb up and grab the wind materia. Proceed towards the dead end, then return to Tifa. Follow her through the narrow crevice as she leads you to an old Shinra facility. Wait for Sephiroth to open the door, then enter.

Go Through the Facility:

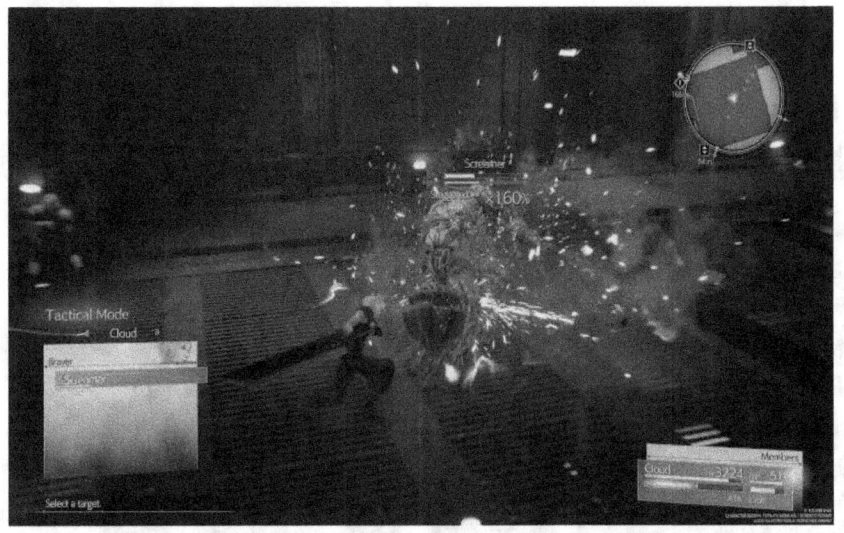

Climb the stairs and step onto the elevator. On the next floor, you'll face a big monster called Screamer. It has a hammer attached to its arm and swings it around, making it challenging to hit without getting hit yourself. Wait for your opportunity to attack and fill up your ATB bar. If you block perfectly, Screamer will stumble, giving you a chance to land some hits and maybe stagger it.

Once the boss is staggered, use your abilities and deal as much damage as you can. If your ATB gauge is filled enough, you might be able to inflict significant damage while it's staggered. Once you defeat Screamer, continue onward. Before moving on, head north towards the rails and jump over them. Go left to find a chest containing ether.

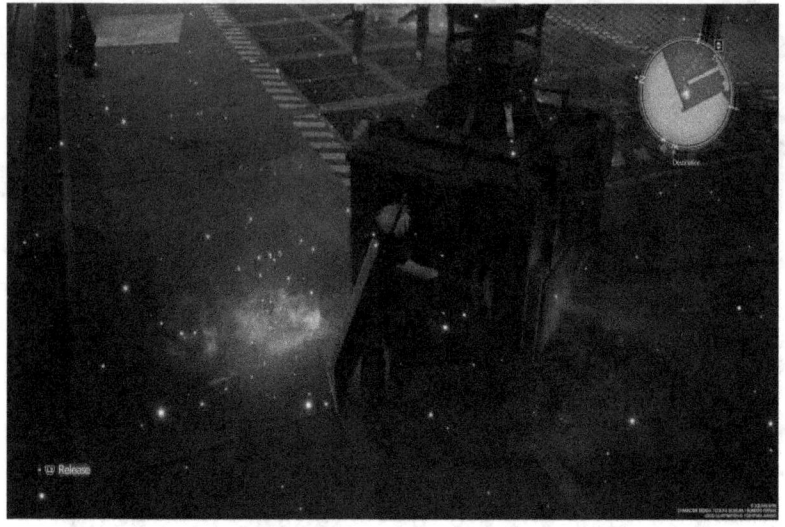

Ascend the stairs to another elevator. When you interact with the terminal, it'll inform you that the elevator can't be used until you clear out the Mako gas. Go past the fence on the right and hold down L2 to operate the vacuum. Keep the vacuum over each Mako gas cloud until it disappears. Once all three clouds are gone, the elevator door will open, leading outside to another path. Walk across the bridge until a cutscene begins.

Find Another Route to the Reactor:

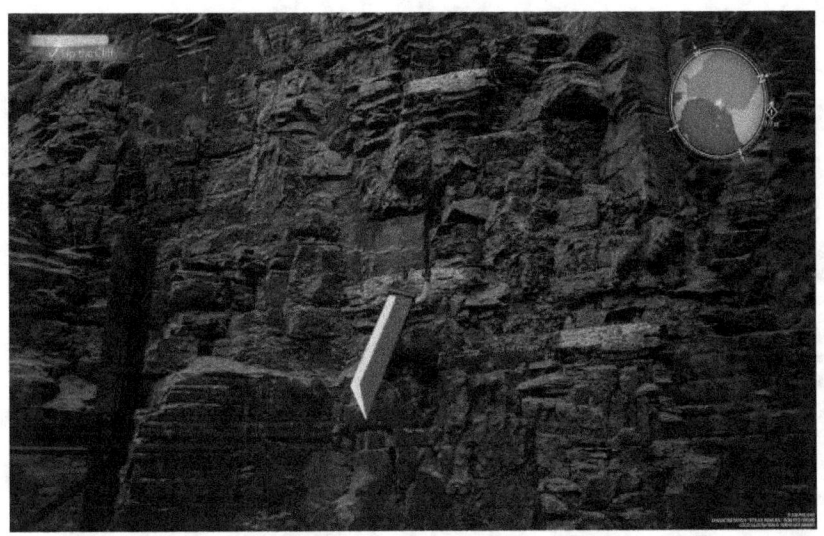

After an unexpected lightning strike, you'll need to find a different path to reach the reactor. Following the cutscene, Sephiroth will join the party and participate in battles. Climb the painted rock walls and collect the purple material next to the rest area. Then, you'll receive a tutorial on switching between characters during battle. Enter the cave and proceed to the large open space below.

After the cutscene, head north towards the other side of the cave. If your MP is running low, you can break the small Mako shards along the walls to restore it. Once outside the cave, climb up the three ledges and then the rock wall beyond. The path ahead is mostly clear and easy to follow.

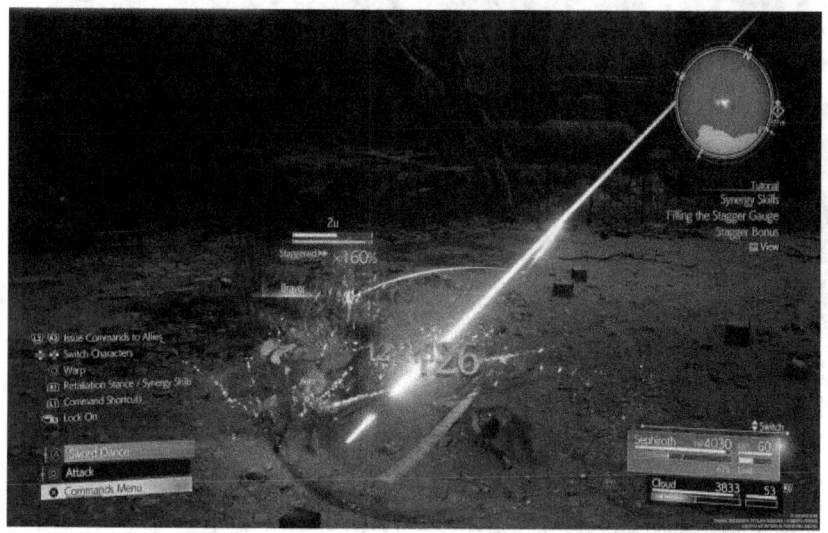

When you notice a path on the left leading to a small ledge, descend and pick up the blue materia. Climb back up the rock wall to continue towards the reactor. Upon entering an open area, you'll be attacked by Zu, which serves as a tutorial for Synergy Skills. Using Synergy Skills repeatedly on Zu will stagger it, making it easier to damage.

Ascend the stairs and turn left to reach some climbable rocks. At the top of the metal structure, you'll find a purple materia. Then, go right and climb several ladders. But before proceeding, go left and up the stairs to discover a blue materia. From there, head straight towards the ladder on the other side of the platform, but be sure to smash all the boxes on the left first.

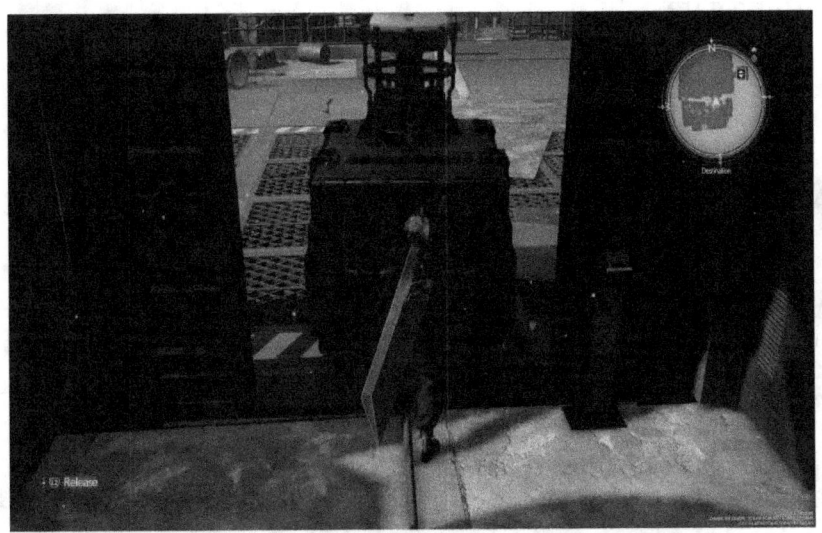

Upon reaching the top of the ladder, you'll encounter another locked elevator. Similar to before, you'll need to use the vacuum to clear out the Mako gas. The challenging part is that the vacuum doesn't have enough range to reach everything. To solve this, approach the gate and hold down the triangle button to open it. After clearing out all the gas clouds, use the elevator.

Upon exiting the elevator, be sure to go through the open gate directly ahead and turn right. There will be a chest on the other side of the fence containing an elixir. Next to the rest area is a ladder leading to another chest with another elixir. Utilize the rest area to heal your party, then ascend the stairs. Also, remember to save your game, as a boss fight awaits on the other side of the gate.

How to Beat Materia Guardian:

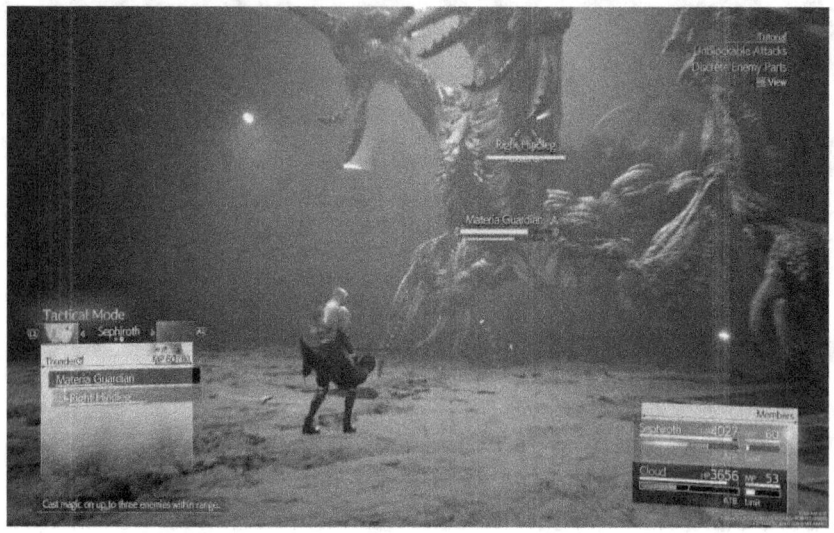

This initial boss battle also serves as a tutorial. Early on, you'll learn about attacks that can't be blocked, marked with a red triangle and exclamation point. When you see one, move away from the enemy quickly. You'll also receive a lesson on attacking specific parts of an enemy to either weaken it or stop its abilities.

For example, if a party member gets grabbed by the Materia Guardian, you can target the arm and attack to free them and apply pressure. As you chip away at the boss's health, an in-combat cutscene will play as it jumps onto the wall. Use magic and target one of the legs to pressure the Materia Guardian and bring it back down into melee range. At this point, staggering the boss won't take much effort. Keep dealing damage until it's down.

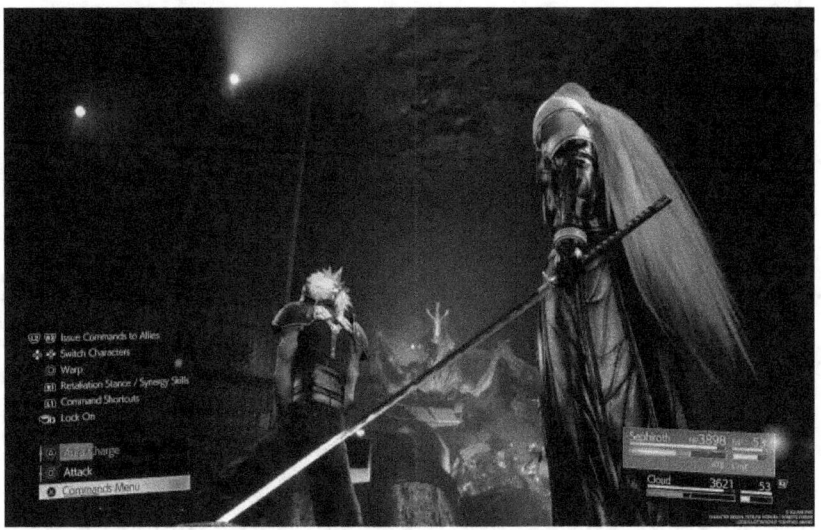

As the Materia Guardian's health decreases, another in-combat cinematic will occur. Once the battle resumes, open the command menu and use the Double Helix synergy ability. Then, stay on the offensive, and the boss will soon be defeated.

Investigate the Reactor:

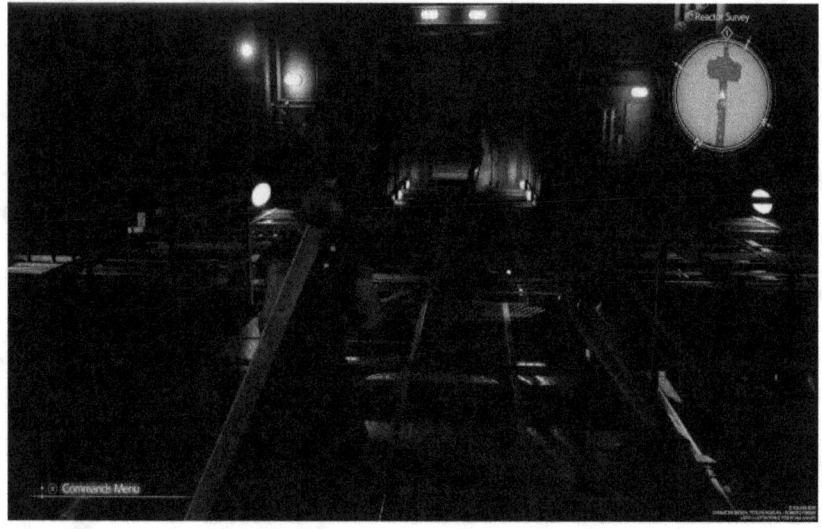

After the cutscene ends, ascend the stairs to enter the reactor. Go right to find an elevator that takes you deeper into the reactor. Follow the path ahead until you find a door that's been broken open. Enter the room to trigger another cutscene, then step back outside to locate the pressure valve. Hold down L2 and R2 as Cloud turns the wheel, release them, and then hold them down again. Keep repeating this until the main objective updates.

Search for Sephiroth:

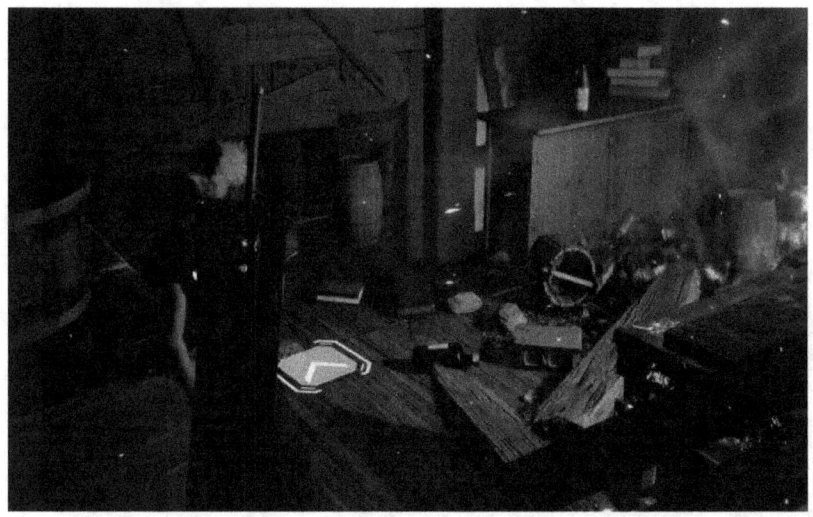

Return to the room to start several more cutscenes. Once you're back in control of Cloud, descend the stairs and leave the inn. Follow the group of three villagers heading towards Shinra Manor. Inside, go left to find an elevator leading to the basement. Traverse the next room to find Sephiroth in the library, triggering another cutscene.

After the cutscenes, return to the village. Due to an injury, you won't be able to run. Keep following the path until it's blocked by flaming rubble. Turn around and go left to find another way to Cloud's house. Enter the nearby burning building and crawl through the space. Follow the path ahead to reach the house and trigger another cutscene. When you regain control of Cloud, press either L2 or R2 as they appear on the screen. Keep doing this until you trigger another cutscene.

Follow Tifa:

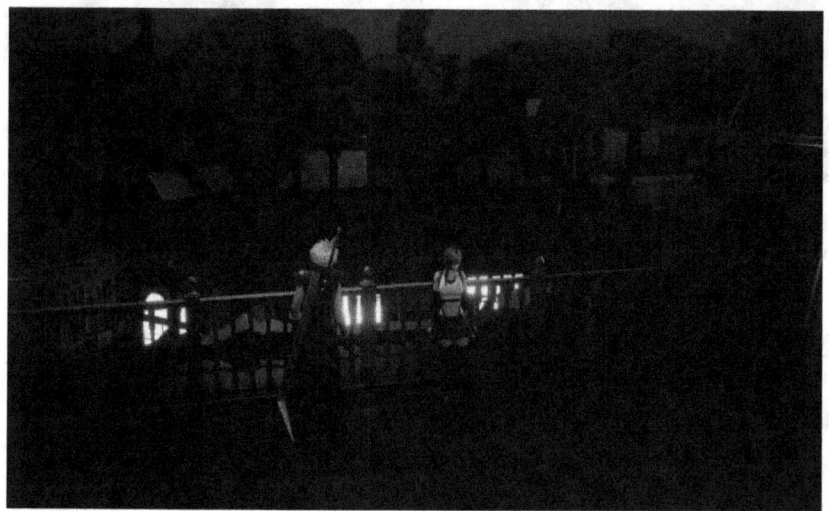

After a series of lengthy cutscenes, you'll find yourself controlling Cloud in the present day. Approach the door, open it, and talk to Tifa. Follow her upstairs to the balcony. After that scene, return to the room to rest, concluding the current chapter.

Materia Locations:

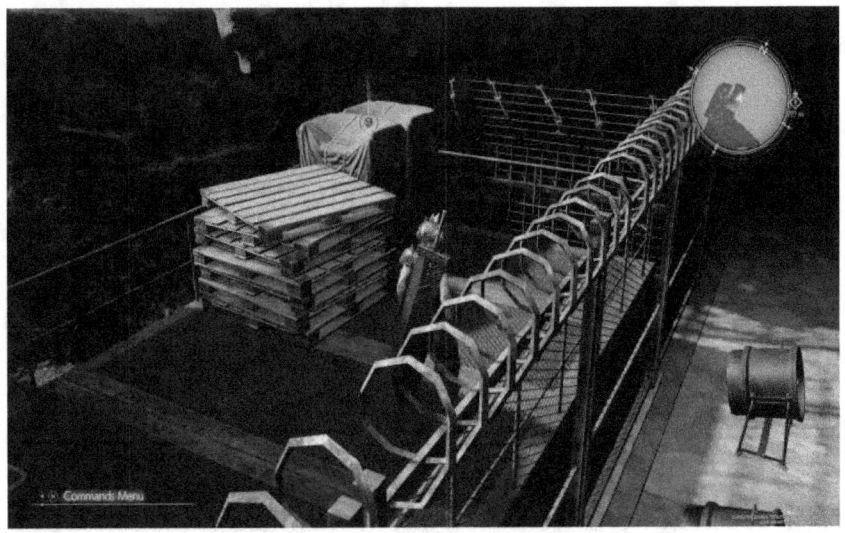

If you're looking for specific materia from this chapter, here are the locations we found:

- **Green Materia:** Located on a ledge near the dead end that Tifa warns you about.
- **Purple Materia:** Found right next to the first rest station.
- **Blue Materia:** Situated on a ledge just before the encounter with the Zu.
- **Another Purple Materia:** Located on a metal platform shortly after the Zu fight.

CHAPTER TWO

DEEPER INTO DARKNESS

Final Fantasy 7: Rebirth continues where Final Fantasy 7: Remake left off, delving deeper into Cloud's history with Sephiroth and setting the stage for the journey ahead. As you enter the second chapter, the game introduces its open-world element, the Grasslands. There's a vast expanse to explore, so take your time and savor the adventure as A New Journey begins.

Gear Up:

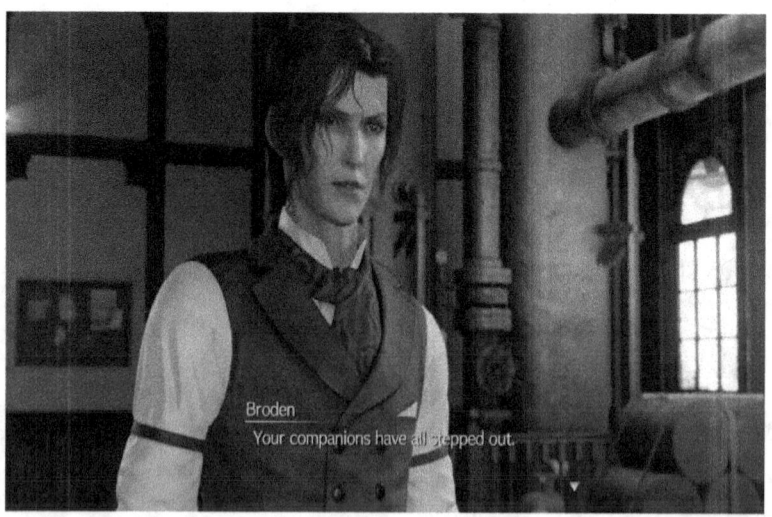

At the beginning of the second chapter, it's important to note that this is your chance to claim any DLC or bonuses from pre-ordering or purchasing the Deluxe Edition. Simply go to the Systems tab in the main menu and select DLC/Bonuses to claim what's available. Once you're ready to continue with the story, leave the room to watch a cutscene where you receive a starter deck for the Queen's Blood mini-game.

When you approach Broden on the first floor, he'll pass along a message from Barrett. As you leave the inn, Red XIII will join your party, and you'll receive a brief tutorial on Party Level. Your initial tasks in this chapter are to visit the weapons vendor and head to the bookstore to learn more about Folios. The order in which you tackle these tasks doesn't matter since both are crucial. You'll also encounter your companions around town, and your responses to them can strengthen your relationship with them.

If you've completed the two errands mentioned earlier and agreed to meet Aerith at the clock tower, your next objective will be to find her there. Head to the clock tower and follow Aerith up the steps. This triggers a cutscene, disrupting the peaceful morning in Kalm.

Evade the Shinra Soldiers:

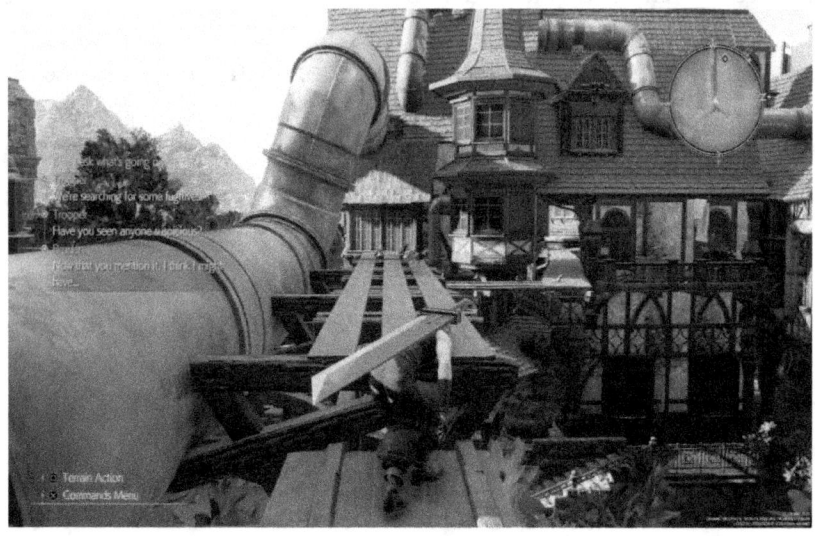

Follow Aerith back down to the first floor and use the pole as a shortcut to get outside. After the ensuing cutscene, follow Broden until he instructs you to climb over the nearby Shinra soldiers. At the top of the ladder, move along the narrow platform. When you reach the end, use the pole to descend and rejoin Broden. Follow him into the inn and then use the secret passage to regroup with the rest of the party.

The Air-Raid Shelter is a narrow tunnel, with the only notable feature being a chest at the end of the hallway, just past a narrow crevice. Loot the chest, then catch up with the group at a set of double metal doors leading out to the Grasslands.

Explore the Grasslands:

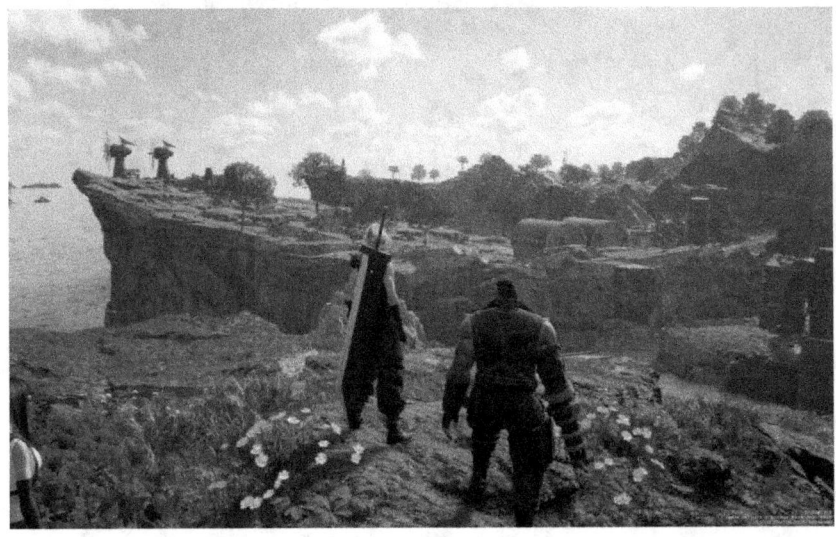

Now, in Final Fantasy 7: Rebirth, the game opens up, offering a vast area to explore. While you could head straight to the next objective, it's worth taking some time to wander around. You might stumble upon materials like iron ore, which can be handy for crafting items. East of Kalm, you'll stumble upon a Waterwheel with a stash you can loot. If you loot all the chests at a stash location, you'll unlock a trophy.

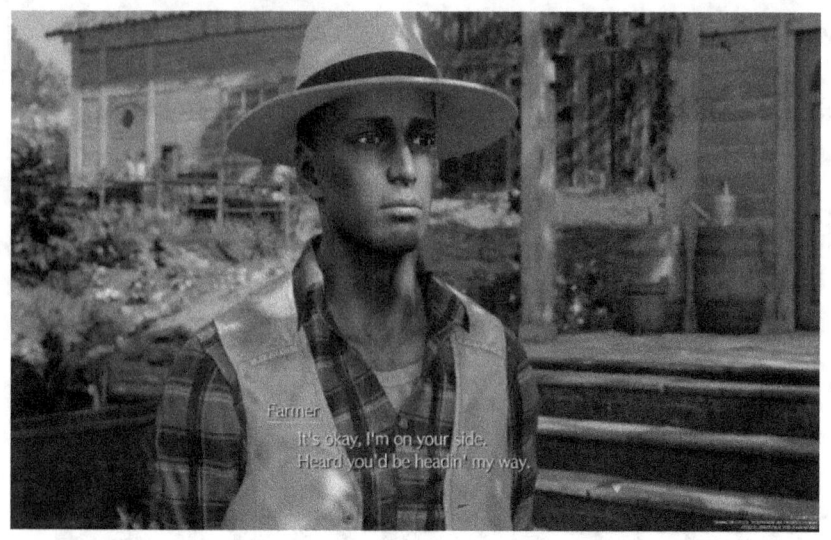

To continue with the story, make your way to Oliver's Farm, marked by the orange circle when you first entered the Grasslands. Chat with the farmer, who will mention a hiding spot from Shinra in a swamp to the southwest. After a cutscene, the map will update with the location of Bill's Chocobo Ranch. Before leaving, make sure to loot the nearby chest for a Sleek Saber for Cloud.

Upon arrival at the ranch, have a chat with Bill to trigger a cutscene. Then, head to the barn and talk to Billy. However, getting a Chocobo and journeying to Junon won't be a walk in the park. Firstly, you'll need to track down a runaway Chocobo. In the back of the barn, there's a chest containing a Timeless

Rod, an upgrade for Aerith. When you're ready, speak to Chloe to receive Gyshal Greens.

Finding Piko:

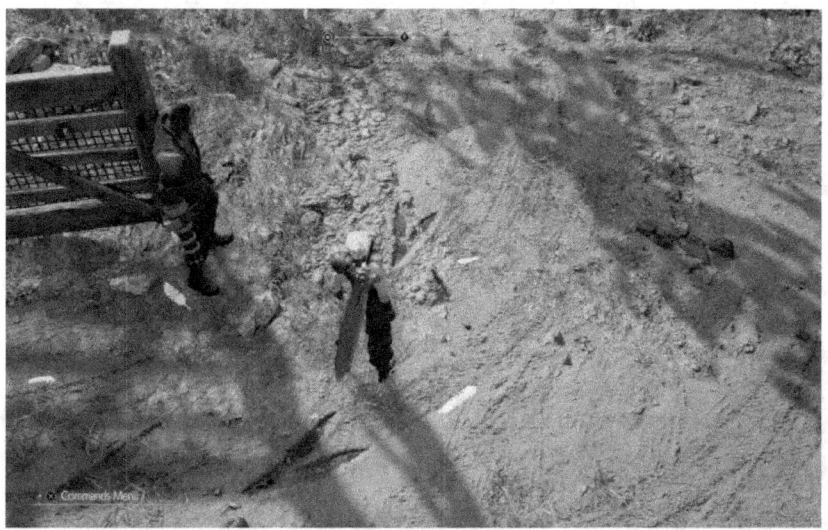

Leave the ranch and look down and to your left. Among the Chocobo feathers, you'll spot tracks in the mud. Follow the trail closely until you trigger a cutscene and a subsequent mini-game. To advance the story, you must sneak up to Piko without being spotted by him or the other Chocobo. If you fail, you can retry by holding down the triangle button.

To start, swiftly move towards the tall grass in front of you where the Chocobo is. Roll into the grass and stay behind this Chocobo, as it won't turn around. The second wild Chocobo further ahead is the one to watch out for, as it moves around and can easily spot you if your timing is off. Wait for its back to be turned before rolling into the next patch of tall grass. If you reach this point, you'll reach a checkpoint in the mini-game.

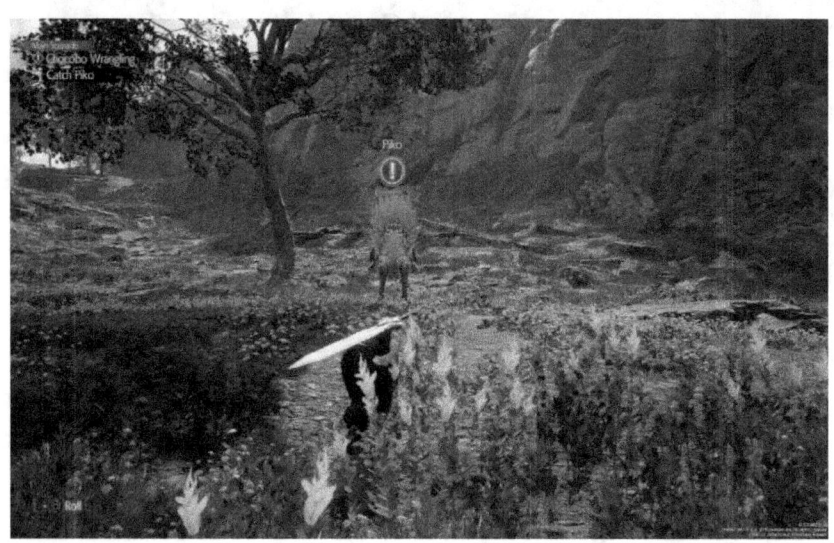

Once the second Chocobo has turned away, swiftly roll into the grass to approach Piko. You'll reach a second checkpoint, and both wild Chocobos will doze off. Grab one of the nearby rocks and toss it behind Piko. While Piko's back is turned, carefully approach him and press the Triangle button once you're close enough to capture him. After the cutscene, head back to the ranch.

Chadley Returns:

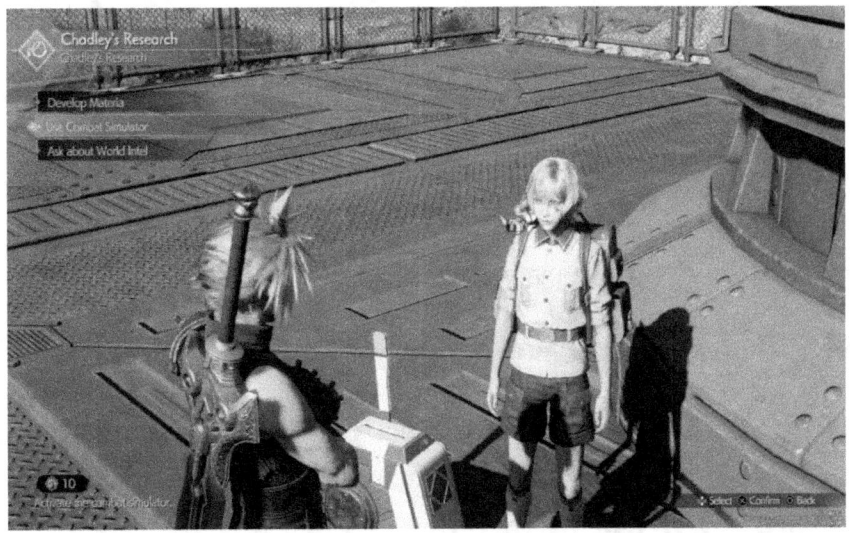

Enter the barn to trigger a cutscene, then head outside to meet a familiar face from Final Fantasy 7: Remake. Chadley will guide you through activating towers scattered across the Grasslands and beyond. Follow Chadley to activate the first tower. For those who know open-world games, these towers serve a similar purpose to viewpoints in Assassin's Creed or Tallnecks in the Horizon series, revealing information about the area on your map.

NOTE:

- You'll also earn Party EXP each time you activate a tower, so aim to activate as many as possible.

Chadley will also introduce the combat simulator and materia creation. It's a good idea to check out the combat simulator first. Chadley will offer a mission to unlock the Titan Materia and basic training missions for other materia rewards. When you're ready to move forward, check on Piko at the barn.

Chocobo Riding Practice:

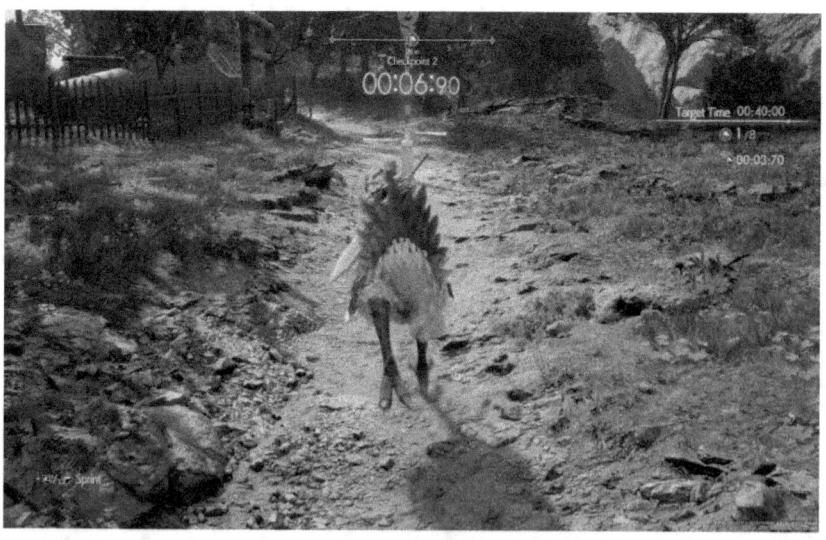

Follow Billy and summon Piko by pressing R1. Then, talk to Billy again to start a mini-game where you'll learn the basics of riding a Chocobo. Your task is simple: pass through each checkpoint and reach the finish line. Successfully completing the race allows you to advance the story.

After completing this mini-game, you'll gain the ability to return to Kalm and take on side quests. Throughout the second chapter of Final Fantasy 7: Rebirth, there are numerous side quests to discover, and exploring off the main path is always rewarding. Additionally, you'll unlock fast travel at this point.

Through the Swamp:

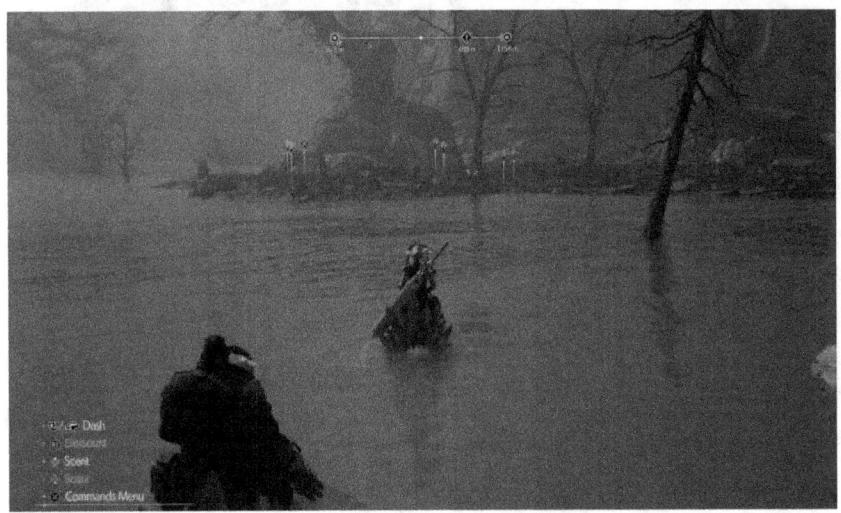

When you're ready to continue with the story, head to the swamp and mount your Chocobo. Move towards the water and start swimming southwest. Keep going until you spot a hooded figure on the other side. Before approaching, be sure to loot the chest on the right, containing a High Caliber Rifle for Barrett. Once done, hop back on your Chocobo and continue southwest through the swamp. However, ensure your party is prepared before reaching your destination, as the notorious Midgardsormr awaits.

How to Defeat Midgardsormr:

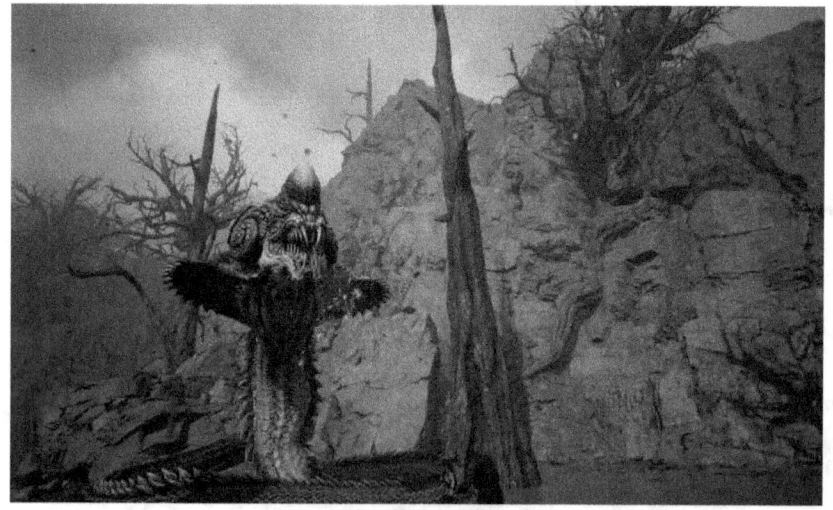

Midgardsormr remains a tough adversary in Final Fantasy 7, just as it was in the original game. When it unleashes its regular attacks, your best bet is to either guard or dodge. Pay close attention to its Devour move; when it initiates this, step back or guard, as it packs a heavier punch than its usual attack. If you have Assess equipped, use it once your ATB gauge is filled.

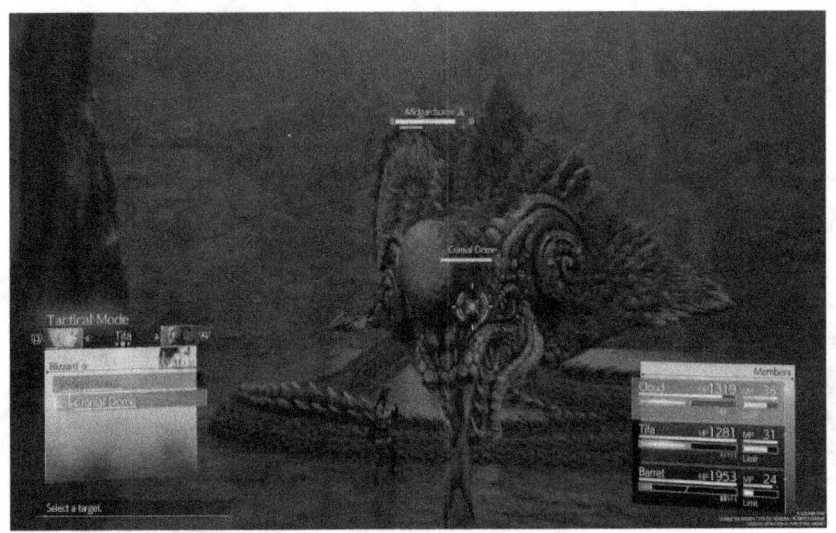

This massive serpent is weak against ice but resistant to fire. Activate Synergy Skills to apply pressure to Midgardsormr. As its health drops below 90%, one of your allies will suggest targeting its head. Watch out for Midgardsormr casting Toxic Waters; move onto dry land until the water clears to avoid this. Once the water returns to its normal color, it's safe to re-engage.

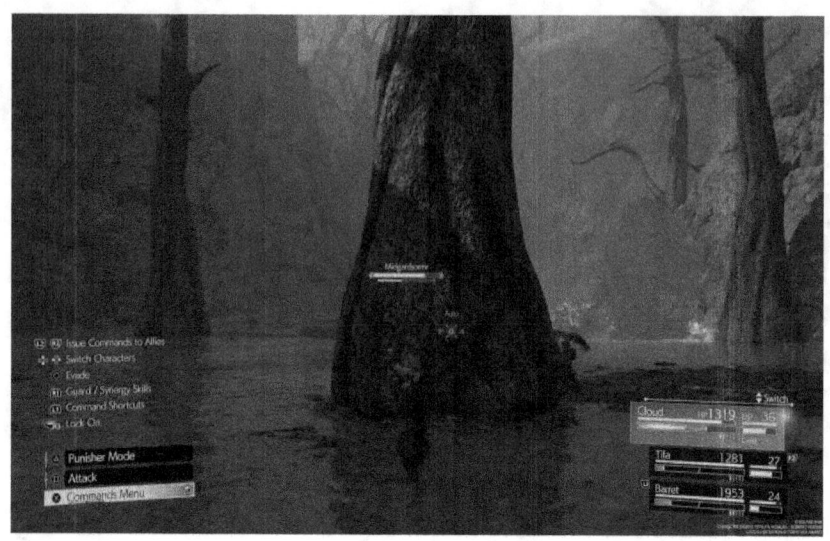

If you hit Midgardsormr's head with Blizzard, it triggers an in-battle cinematic. Quickly move away because Midgardsormr is preparing for a fire breath attack. Take cover behind one of the trees to evade this assault. Once the danger has passed, resume using Synergy Skills to increase the pressure on Midgardsormr. After a while, Midgardsormr will dive into the water and resurface, grabbing one of your party members. This member will be swallowed and temporarily removed from the battle. However, if you deal enough damage to Midgardsormr, it will eventually spit the character back out.

Continue dealing damage to the boss and focus your attacks on its head whenever possible. As Midgardsormr takes more hits, another in-battle cinematic will trigger, causing the trees to catch fire. By this point, the boss's health will be significantly reduced, making it easier to defeat. Once you enter the tunnel on the far side of the swamp, the third chapter will begin. If you have any unfinished tasks in the Grasslands, you can always return even after starting the next chapter.

CHAPTER THREE

DEEPER INTO DARKNESS

After completing the second chapter of Final Fantasy 7 Rebirth, the game takes a break from its open-world exploration. In the third chapter, "Deeper Into the Darkness," you'll venture into the Mythril Mines to find a way to the other side. Cloud and his companions follow mysterious figures dressed in black robes, their only lead in the search for Sephiroth.

Although this chapter is more straightforward compared to the last one, there's still plenty to explore and challenges to face. Here's what to expect as you delve "Deeper Into the Darkness."

Explore the Mines:

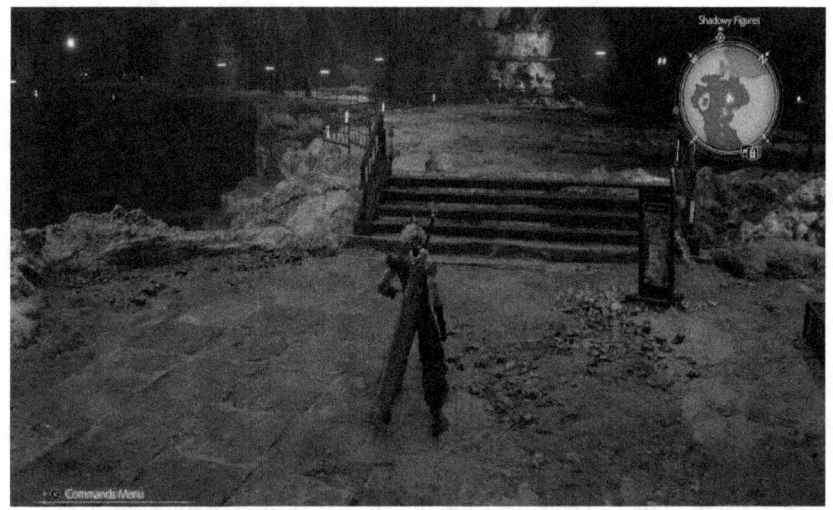

Once the cutscene ends, enter the mines. Further inside, you'll find a rest area and a vending machine for your convenience. Make use of these facilities as needed. When you're ready to proceed, continue until you encounter a group of robed individuals. As you approach, a cutscene will trigger, temporarily separating Barret and Red XIII from the party.

NOTE:

- While Barret and Red XIII are away, you won't be able to fast travel temporarily. Keep this in mind if you're not ready to proceed yet.

Follow the tunnel until you reach a set of damaged stairs, leading to a secluded area of the map. On the other side, look to your left at the bottom of the steps to find some blue materia. Then, descend the ladder and deal with the two lurking monsters below. Before descending the nearby ladder, be sure to open the purple chest and obtain the sylph gloves.

Once you've descended another ladder, cross the tunnel and loot the chest. Then, turn back and head west toward the tunnel marked with the "Workers" sign above it. In this next area, you'll encounter an Ogre. While not as formidable as Midgardsormr, the Ogre can still inflict significant damage. It's vulnerable to fire damage, so use any fire-based magic or abilities to defeat it quickly.

How to Get Past the Broken Ladder and Elevator:

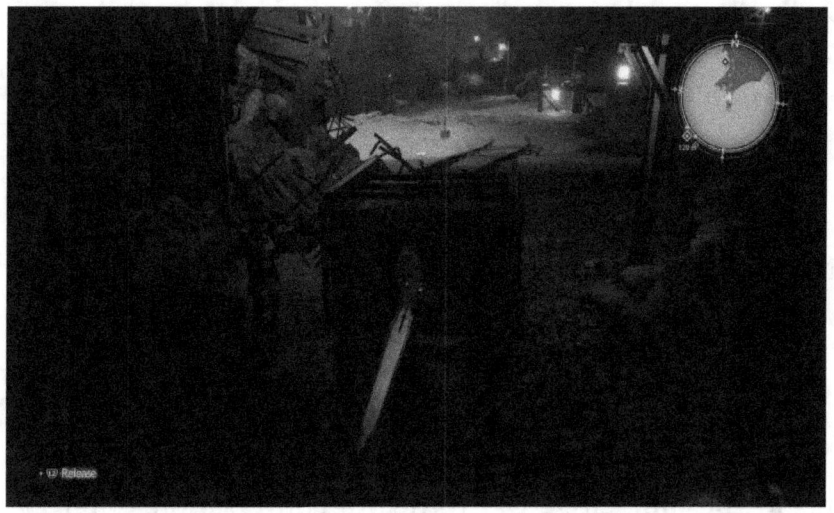

Continue through the tunnel and follow the tracks of the mine cart. Eventually, you'll come across a large mine cart blocking the path ahead. Hold down L2 and pull it further back into the tunnel. Once you've moved the cart past at least two sets of support beams, there will be enough space to proceed. After a short cutscene, head left across the bridge and confront the monsters on the other side.

Right where you battled the monsters, you'll find a ladder and an elevator, both unfortunately broken and unusable. Loot the chest beside the elevator, then proceed left toward what appears to be a dead end. Pass along the left side of the mine cart and push it along the tracks toward the broken ladder. Once you spot the blue symbol atop the mine cart, you can use it to climb past the broken ladder and onto the platform above.

On the opposite side and up the stairs, there are two Ogres waiting. Once you've dealt with them, climb the ladder and move along the sloped platform. Follow this path until you reach a rest area with vending machines. Ascend the stairs, stand in the blue circle to overhear a conversation. After the scene, prepare for a boss fight.

How to Defeat Rude and Elena:

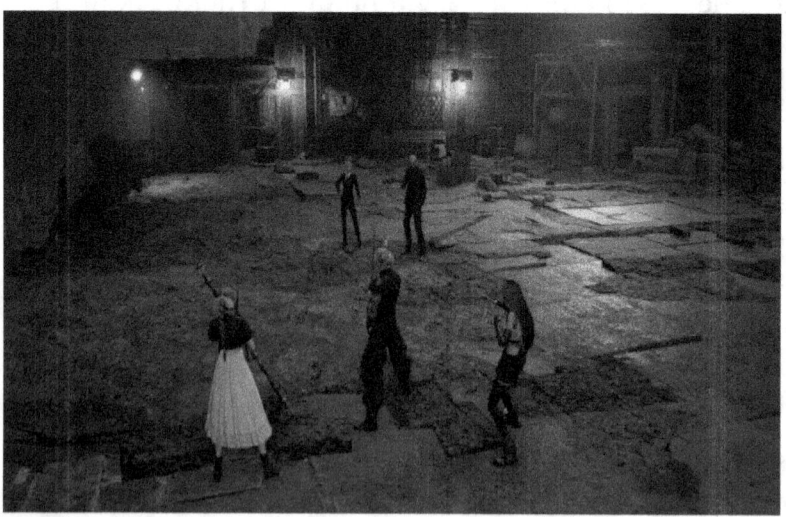

Rude primarily employs close combat attacks, while Elena switches between close combat and throwing daggers from a distance. Occasionally, she leaps into the air and throws stun grenades to the ground; avoid these as they cannot be blocked. Rude also sporadically unleashes Spirit Geyser, causing yellow energy clouds to shoot up from random spots. Dodge this attack as well.

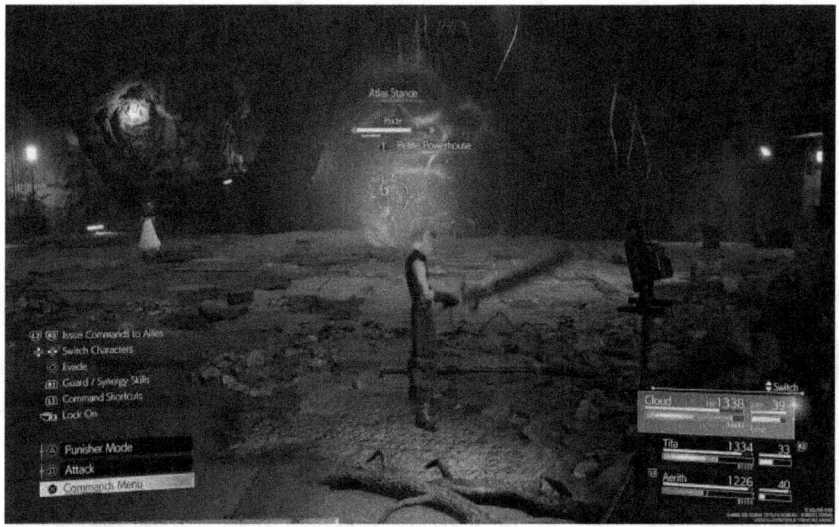

Rude is vulnerable to air damage, while Elena is weak against lightning. Keep battling them, dodging their moves until a cinematic sequence begins in battle. At this point, Elena and Rude will assume Atlas Stance and use Petite Powerhouse. During this phase, Elena cannot be targeted. Once she finishes charging, she strikes all three party members. Focus on staggering either Rude or Elena, as staggering both simultaneously is challenging.

Once one of them is staggered, use Limit Breaks or Synergy on them to deal as much damage as possible. The fight becomes much easier once one of them has been defeated.

How to Escape the Depths:

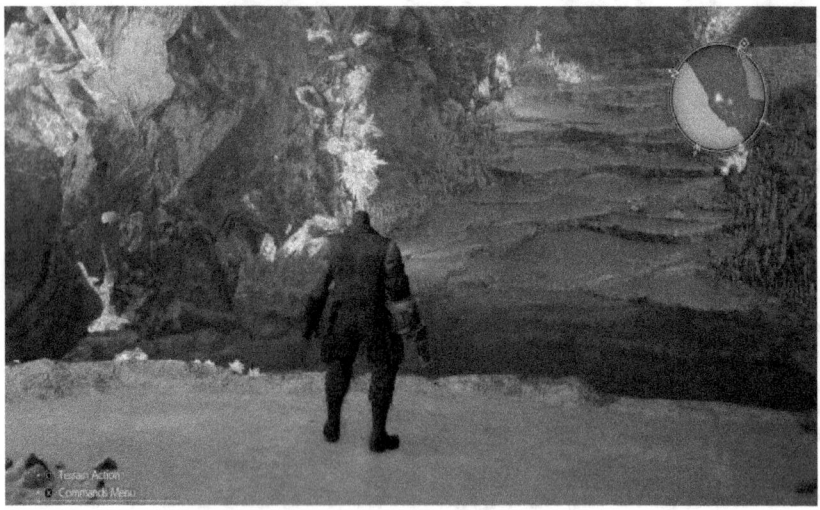

After the cutscene, you'll control Barret and Red XIII as they search for a way out from the depths. Head toward the vending machine and don't miss the Renegade's Collar from the nearby chest. There's also a rest area beside the vending machines.

As you explore, keep an eye out for a blue circle with an arrow, guiding you to crystals Barret can blast with his gun. Follow the path northeastward, swim across the water, climb the ledges, and head east. Use Barret's gun to break the rocks once you reach the top.

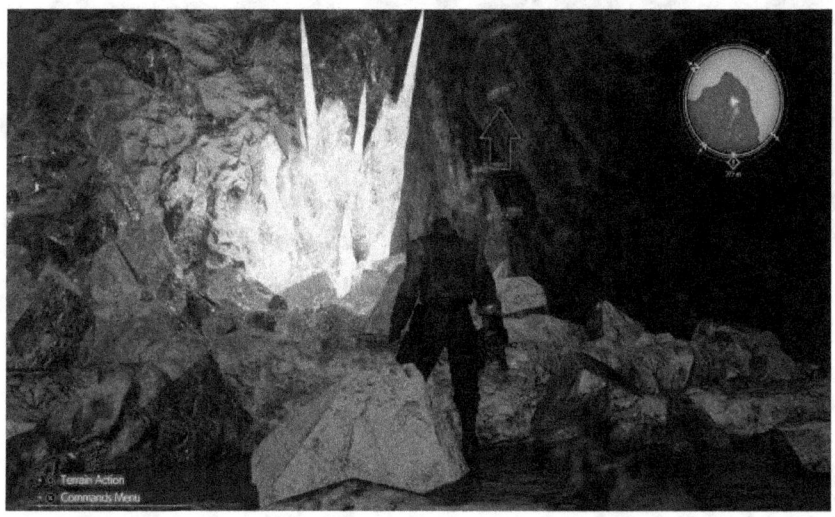

Look for another climbable tree to ascend higher. Traverse through the tunnel, defeating any enemies along the way. Keep an eye out for a chest containing Beast Bones inside the tunnel. Eventually, you'll reach a dead end with a lever next to two mine cart tracks.

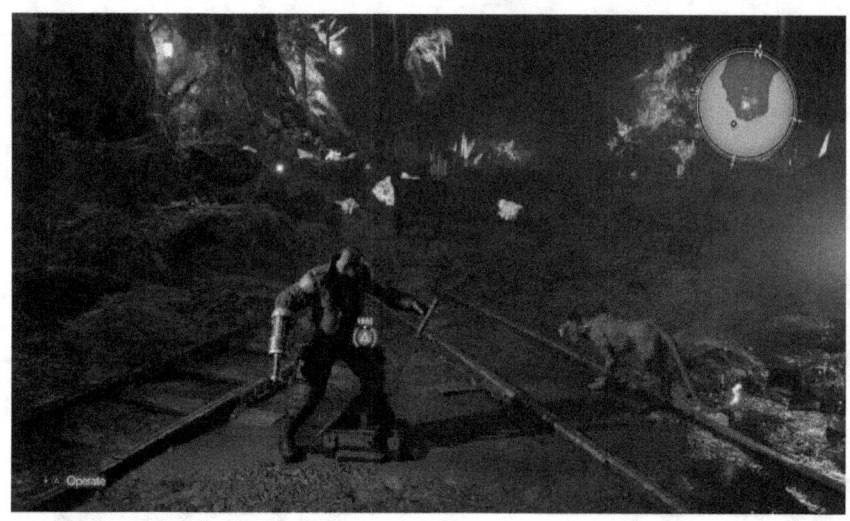

Use the lever to switch the tracks, allowing you to reach a previously inaccessible ledge. Move the cart to grab a chest with a bulletproof vest. Break the rock blocking the path with Barret's gun and proceed through the narrow tunnels, dealing with an Ogre along the way.

Approach the cliff to trigger a cutscene. Afterward, free the stuck ladders with Barret's gun, climb up, and enter the room with the mine cart. Use the lever to open the gate and push the cart out. Destroy the rock blocking the path and continue pushing the cart.

At another lever spot, push the cart to the end of the track and change its direction with the lever. Push it until a cutscene activates and a bridge rises for Cloud and the others. Return to the room where the cart was, and Aerith will open the gate blocking your path. Grab the lightning materia on your way out and prepare for what's ahead in the wide, open area.

How to Defeat Mythril Golem:

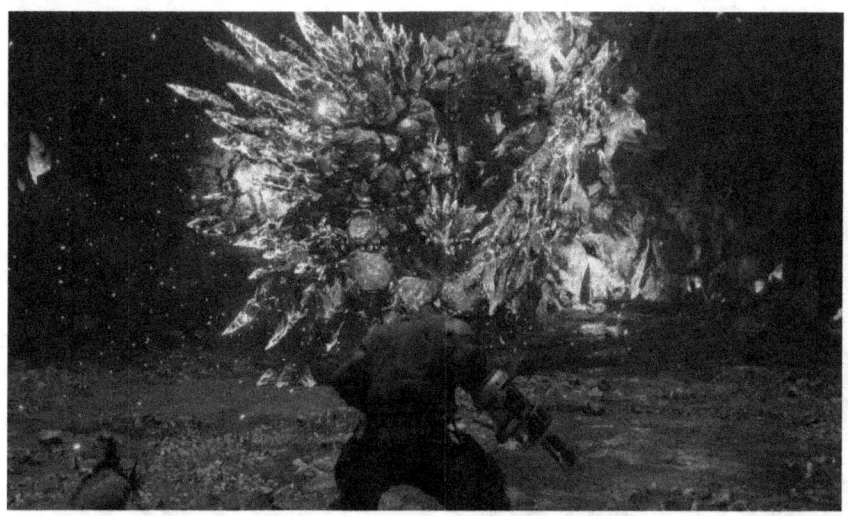

At the start of the battle, focus your attacks on the Mythril Golem's head until its health runs out. Dodge its arm swipes by moving away. Once the head is gone, the boss becomes easier to stagger. Take advantage of this by dealing as much damage as possible while it's staggered.

When the Mythril Golem recovers, its head will regenerate. Watch out for glowing rocks that drop and explode. New targetable parts appear as the fight progresses: the spine and the right arm. Destroying these weakens the boss's abilities.

Focus on destroying the head again to stagger the Mythril Golem. Save powerful abilities like Limit Breaks for when it's staggered to deal maximum damage. Repeat the cycle until the boss is defeated.

Catch Up With the Others:

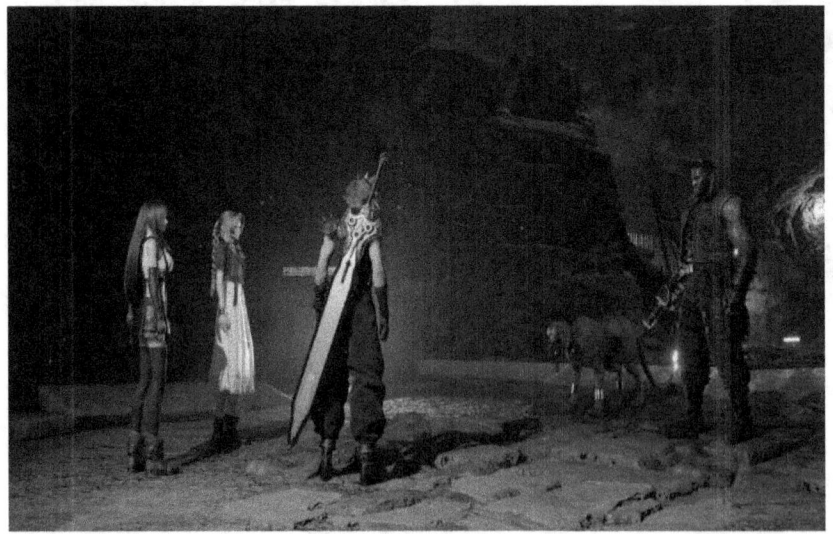

Cross the new bridge and grab mythril ore from a nearby chest. Reunite with your party triggering another cutscene. Proceed through the tunnel ahead, dealing with any ogres you encounter. As you ascend, daylight floods in from the exit, signaling your escape. Once outside, approach the black-robed figures to start the fourth chapter.

CHAPTER FOUR

DAWN OF A NEW ERA

After traversing the Mythril Mines in the third chapter of Final Fantasy 7 Rebirth, the next chapter immerses you in another expansive area to explore. Much like the previous chapter, the Junon Region offers numerous activities to engage in. Besides acquiring Phoenix, there are also various side quests available for those seeking a break from the main storyline. However, if you're eager to progress to Chapter 4: Dawn of a New Era, here's what awaits you.

Explore the Junon Region:

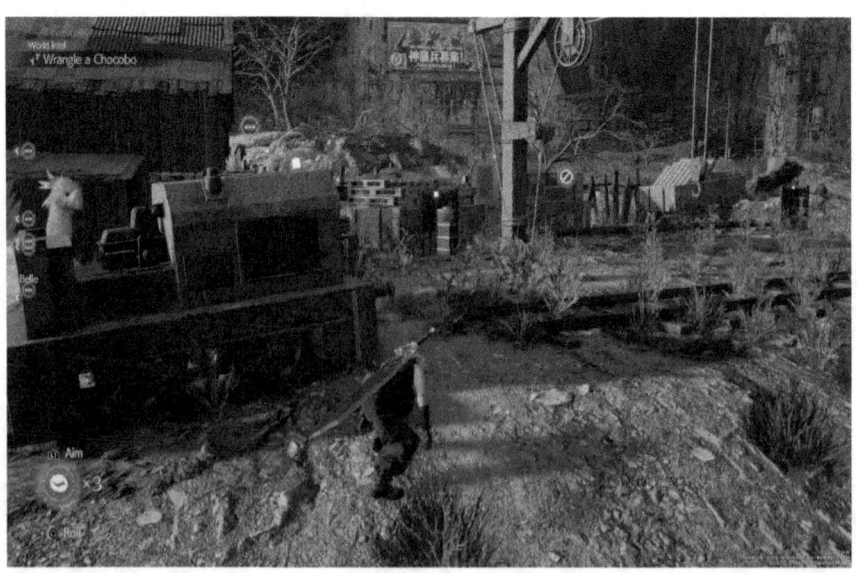

Similar to the previous chapter, you have the freedom to roam a vast territory. Instead of the Grasslands, you'll now explore the Junon Region. Before heading to Junon itself, consider activating the scattered towers throughout the area to gain insights into the surroundings. There's one southwest of the Mythril Mines exit and another to the east.

These towers also help locate a spot where you can tame a Chocobo specifically for the Junon Region. Given that the Junon Mountain Chocobo can scale certain cliff faces, it's advisable to tame one early in this chapter. Once you've thoroughly explored and feel ready to progress, head northwest towards Junon. As you near the town, a cutscene will unfold.

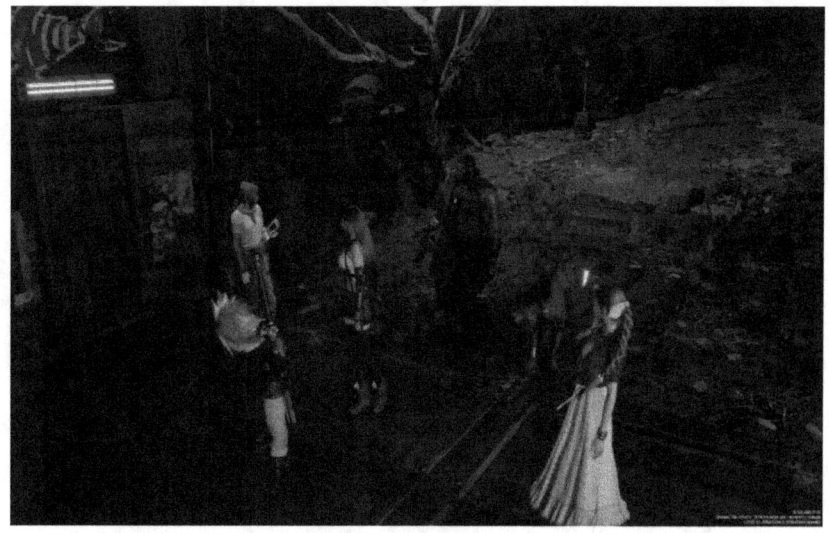

Enter the town, where the group disperses to gather information about the black-robed figures and transportation options. Several shops are available for stocking up on supplies if necessary. To advance the story, engage in conversations with Tifa, Barret, and Aerith. Then, locate the inn marked by a fish sign and speak with the innkeeper. Finally, head towards the docks to investigate a distress call.

NOTE:

- Be sure you're prepared to advance the storyline before entering the inn, as fast travel will be temporarily unavailable.

How to Defeat Terror of the Deep:

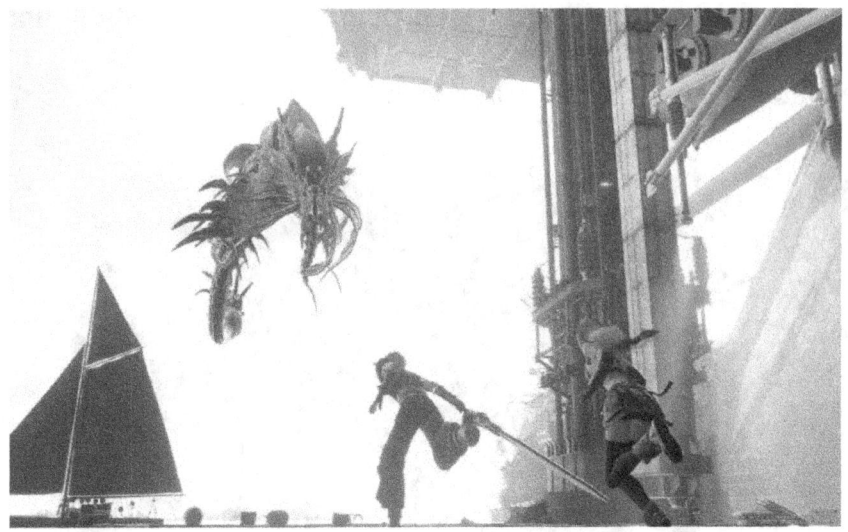

Upon arriving at the dock, a cutscene will play out. After it concludes, you'll confront the Terror of the Deep. Be wary of its primary attack, Water Cell, which ensnares one of your party members in a water sphere, rendering them immobile. Unfortunately, there's no way to evade this attack. To release your comrade, you must employ magic on the water.

Ensure you have at least one party member capable of ranged attacks, as the Terror of the Deep is exceptionally challenging (if not impossible) to hit with melee strikes at the beginning of the battle. Utilize Assess whenever feasible to discern the boss's weakness and swiftly stagger it, facilitating easier damage for the rest of the party. As a water-dwelling creature, the Terror of the Deep is susceptible to electricity. Therefore, when not freeing party members, employ lightning-based assaults.

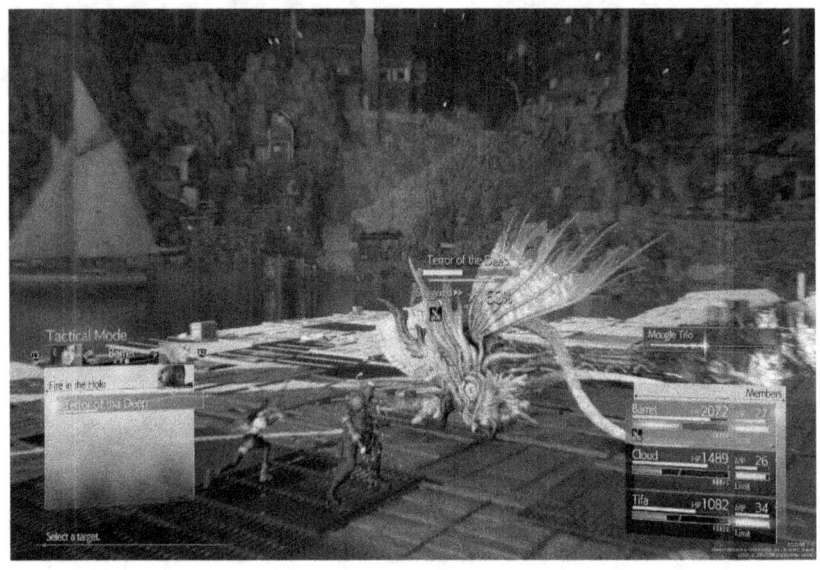

As you accumulate Limit Breaks and Synergy Abilities, it's prudent to reserve them for when the boss draws nearer in the later phases of the encounter. You'll notice this shift when an in-battle cinematic unfolds. A massive water tornado will emerge at the arena's center, with water spurting from nearby grates. When the boss is within melee range, pressuring and staggering it becomes more manageable.

Once the Terror of the Deep is staggered, unleash all your stored power, as you won't need to concern yourself with water cells for a while. With sufficient Limit Breaks and Synergy at your disposal, it's feasible to vanquish the Terror of the Deep in a single stagger.

Check on Yuffie:

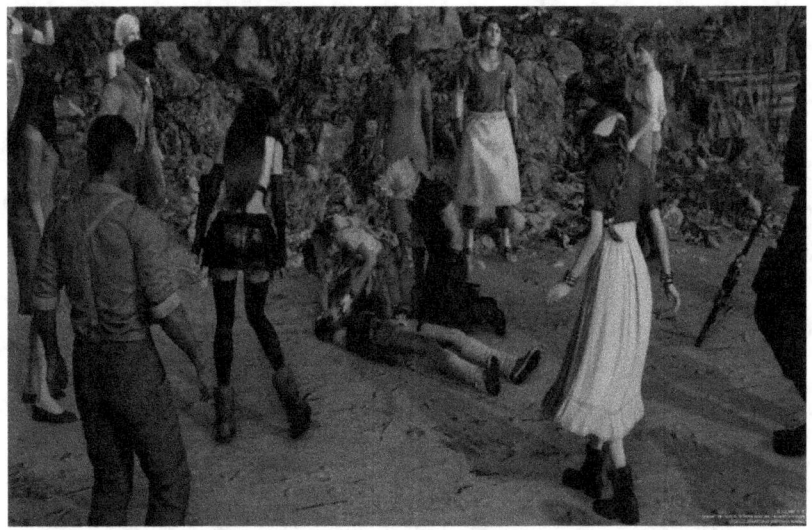

Yuffie, the girl aboard the boat, endured significant harm in the previous cutscene. Swim back to shore to assess her condition. Following the cutscene, return to the town center to trigger another one. Subsequently, proceed to the inn to rest and advance the storyline.

On your way to your room, eavesdrop on the conversation behind Aerith's door. After she closes it, knock and re-enter to retrieve the chest containing a weapon upgrade for her. Additionally, take the opportunity to converse with everyone, potentially strengthening your rapport with them. However, don't deliberate too long, as there's a time constraint.

Cloud's room is situated on the second floor. When ready to proceed, enter this room, prompting another cutscene for the following day. Upon its conclusion, depart Cloud's room and swiftly descend downstairs and exit the inn. Following a brief cutscene, fast travel will once again become available. Additionally, several side quests in the Junon Region will unlock. When adequately prepared to advance, proceed to the docks and converse with Priscilla.

NOTE:

- Ensure readiness before engaging with Priscilla, as you'll be confined to Upper Junon for a while.

Dolphin Mini-Game:

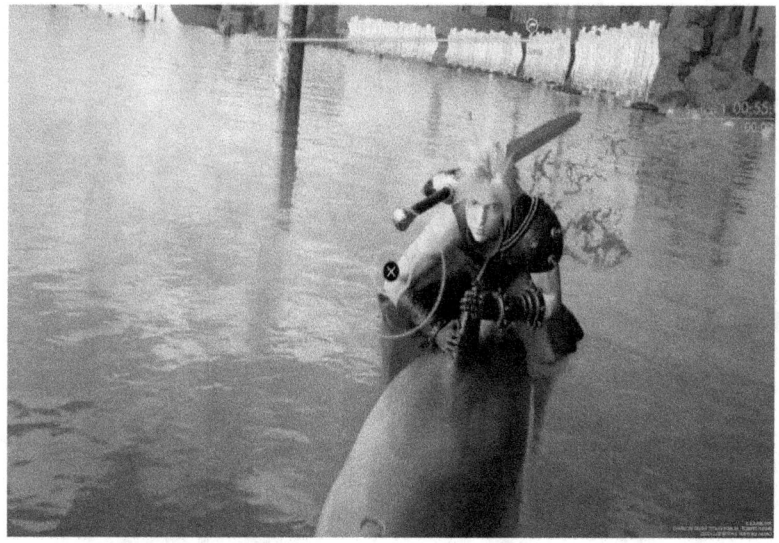

Take a dive into the water and follow the dolphin's lead. While swimming, you'll kick off a mini-game eventually. Your goal is to complete the course before time runs out. To speed up, hit as many balls in the water as you can. Watch out for obstacles though, as they'll slow you down. Once you reach the end, get ready for some quick-time events. Nail these to ace the mini-game and keep the story flowing.

Infiltrate Upper Junon:

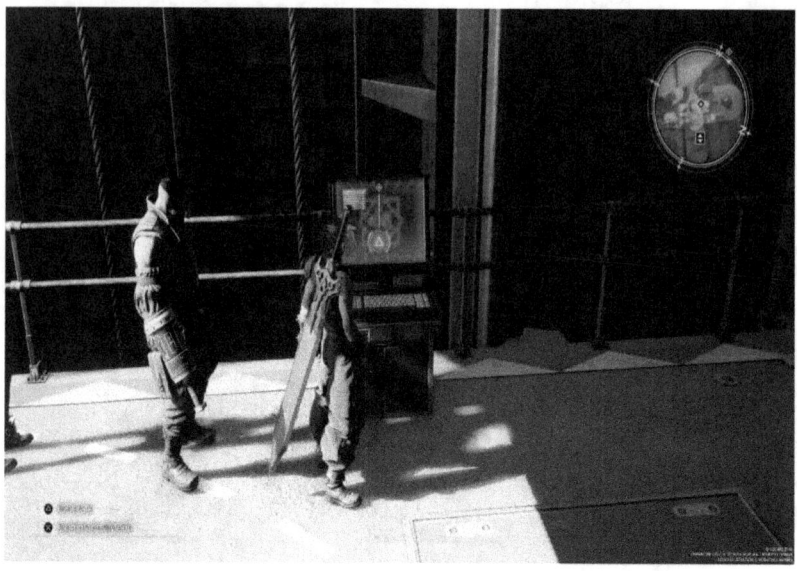

Climb up the platform and step into the control room. Utilize the controls and the right stick to lower the tanker for the rest of the crew to hop on. After the boarding cutscene, raise the tanker once more. When you're back in control of Cloud, exit the room and join your pals. Walk down the hallway's end and snag the chest near the vending machine. Don't fret about the Shinra soldiers; they're not giving you any hassle.

Ascend the stairs and veer left. Dash past the Shinra soldiers and head left toward the terminal. Activate it to descend into the city. Following the cutscene, cross the hallway and enter the compact room with the terminal. Use it to fire up the elevator. Once you hit the bottom, a cutscene unfolds, bidding farewell to Barret and Red XIII from the crew. Tag along with Tifa and Aerith, where you'll stumble upon some handy spare uniforms. Exiting the room kicks off another cutscene and mini-game.

Parade Mini-Game:

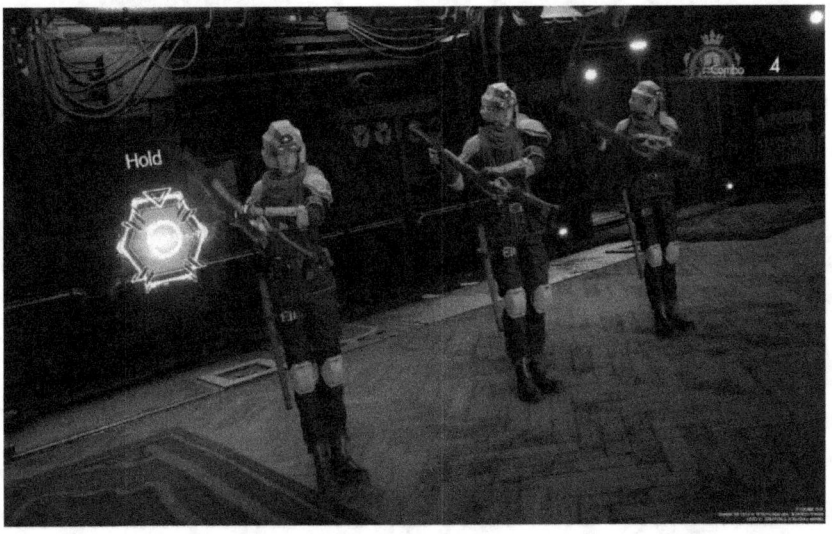

Post-cutscene, you'll get a chance to rehearse for the parade. This mini-game is a simple rhythm challenge. Tap the red button in sync with the beat. If it's yellow, keep tapping repeatedly. Hold down the button for blue cues. Practice away until you feel confident. Once you're through, you'll be promoted to parade captain.

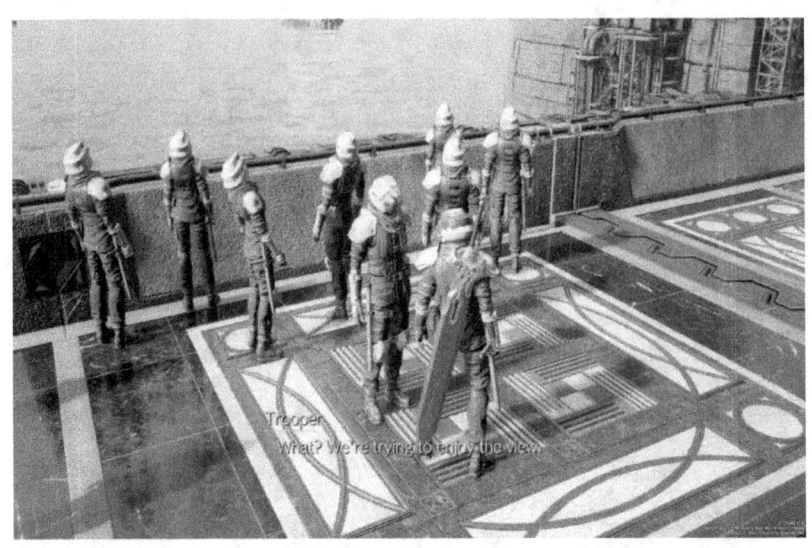

To push the story forward, scout the Seventh Infantry members across the city, including the shops. You only need to find five groups to progress, but hunting down everyone earns you a trophy. When you're set to move on, chat with the Commander (rocking a red hat and coat).

Before confirming readiness, tweak your Parade Formation. The order affects the mini-game difficulty, with tougher setups racking up more points. Practice until you're polished before kickstarting. Aim for a top-notch score of 100,000 points for the best outcome.

NOTE:

- Points tally up after each round, letting you keep tabs on your progress.

After the Parade:

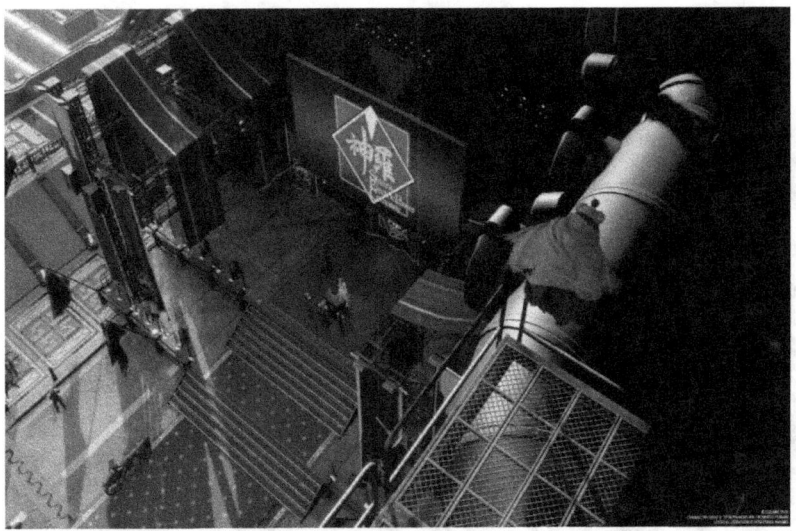

After the cutscenes wrap up, you'll take charge of Yuffie. Climb up the scaffolding ahead and ascend the ladder. To progress, traverse along the clock to reach the other side of the scaffolding. Keep climbing until you reach the top, where another cutscene kicks in, followed by a mini-game.

Follow the instructions for the mini-game, aligning your circle with the target until it gleams gold. Then, hit the X button.

Repeat this until yet another cutscene rolls in. Once it wraps, you'll be back in control of Cloud and a squad of Shinra soldiers who are on your side. Keep an eye on their health during the fight, patching them up as necessary, and continue forward, taking down more Shinra soldiers.

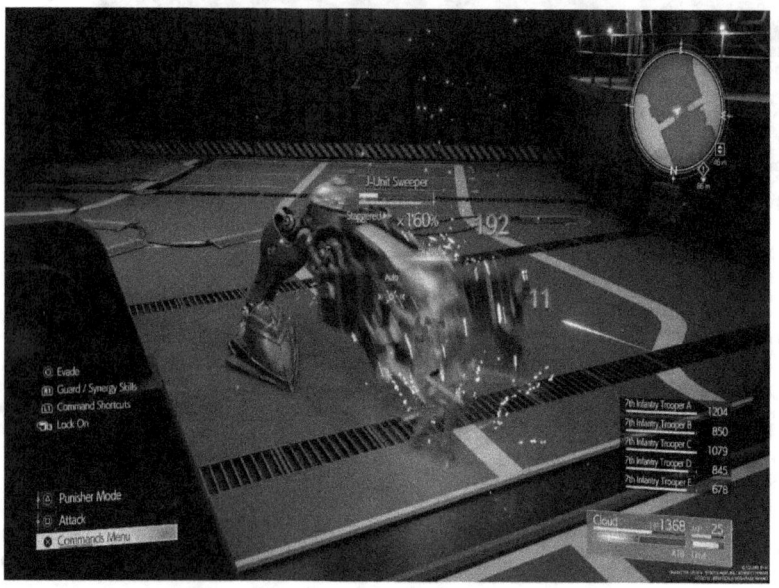

As you ride the elevator, you'll encounter a hefty mech. Crush it, and another one will spring to life. Shinra Soldiers will also pop up on the balcony. Once all foes are dispatched, hop on the next elevator to push ahead. At the end of this section, you'll spot vending machines. Resting here will patch up the soldiers tagging along with you. Make sure everyone's in top shape before entering the next zone, where a boss showdown awaits.

How to Defeat Roche:

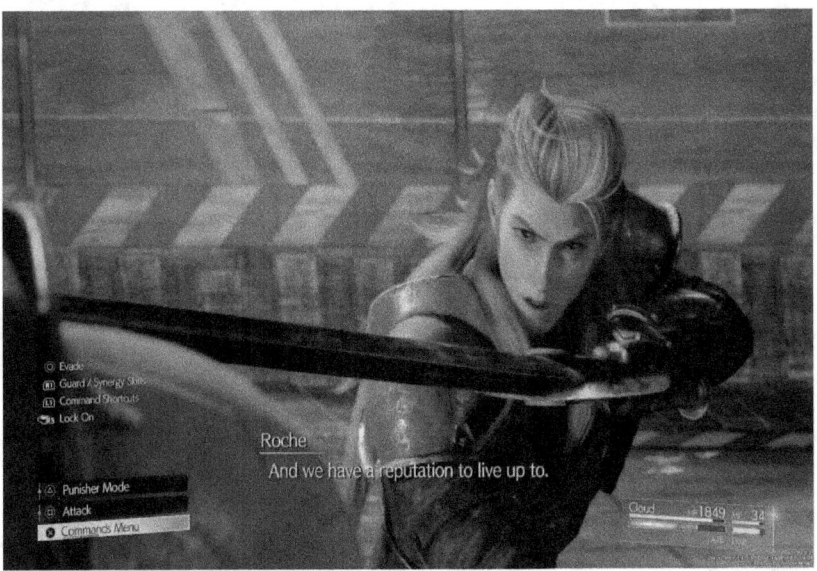

You'll square off against Roche while he's tearing up the scene on his motorcycle, though you won't have one of your own. Block and dodge his attacks, then unleash abilities or magic that packs a fiery punch since he's susceptible to it. Knock him off balance to make landing blows easier, and he'll go down swiftly. After the boss brawl, make your way through the gap in the wall toward the elevator. Following a cutscene, ride the elevator to reunite with the rest of your crew. Crossing the bridge triggers yet another cutscene, bringing the current chapter to a close.

CHAPTER FIVE

BLOOD IN THE WATER

In the Final Fantasy 7 Rebirth game, each chapter is different in length. Some are long, letting you explore different places freely, while others are short. Chapter five, called "Blood in the Water," is very short. It follows Cloud and his friends after the events in Junon. They continue chasing mysterious figures dressed in black, hoping to find Sephiroth. This chapter is about their journey to Costa del Sol, which is not as nice as they expected.

To play cards:

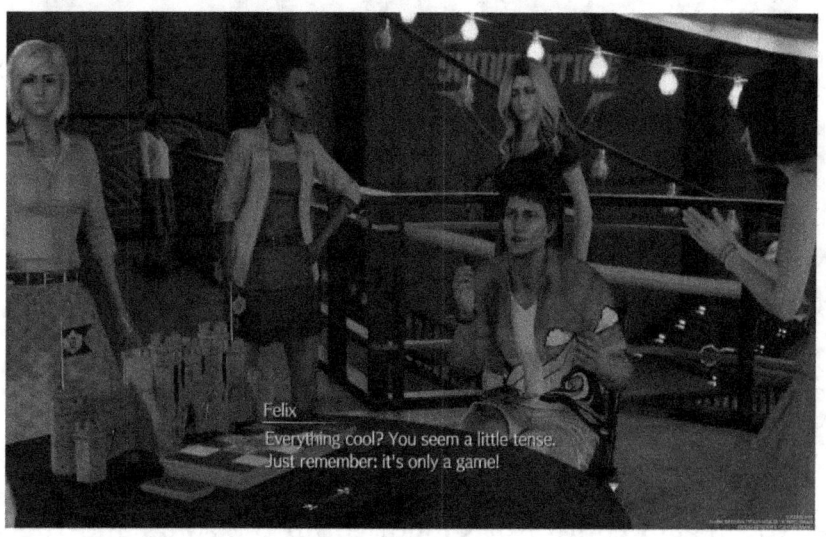

After you regain control of Cloud, go up the stairs and then down the hallway. There's another set of stairs leading to a place where a cutscene starts. Then, talk with your friends. To continue the story, you must join and play in the Queen's Blood tournament. Winning or losing doesn't matter; you can still go on with the story. If you don't want to play in the Queen's Blood tournament, you can choose to quit from the start. Once the bonus match at the award ceremony is over, go back to your room and rest.

To go to the Deck:

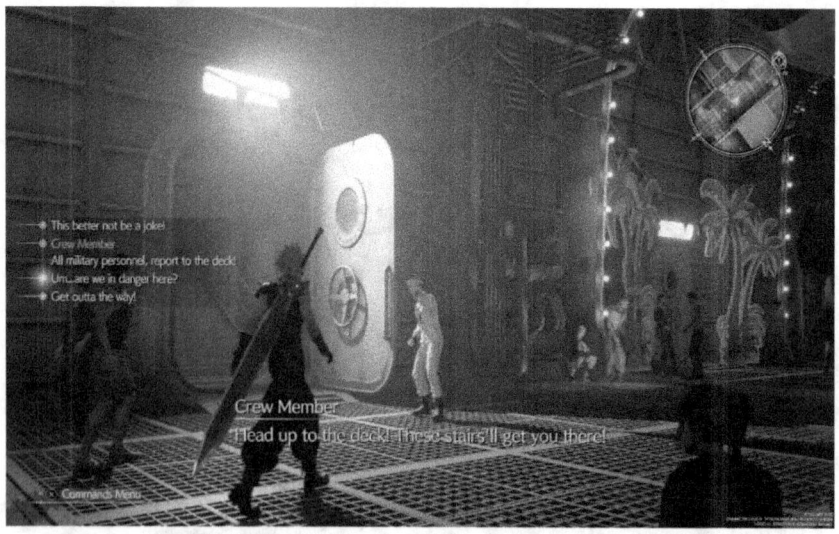

After you regain control of Cloud, go up the stairs and then down the hallway. There's another set of stairs leading to a place where a cutscene starts. Then, talk with your friends. To continue the story, you must join and play in the Queen's Blood tournament. Winning or losing doesn't matter; you can still go on with the story. If you don't want to play in the Queen's Blood tournament, you can choose to quit from the start. Once the bonus match at the award ceremony is over, go back to your room and rest.

The crew tells you how to find the deck where the captain is. There are some monsters, called fiends, on the ship that need to be taken care of. You can only use Cloud, Red XIII, and Aerith for this. Head to the sundeck and deal with the fiends there. After defeating several waves of enemies, including the ones inside, head down the stairs near where a crew member is hiding. On the lower floor, Tifa will join your party again. Run down the hallway and fight the two Necrotic Entities that show up. They don't have any weaknesses, so just focus on putting pressure on them and staggering them. Once they're defeated and the cutscene ends, follow Barret's voice. Go downstairs to enter the cargo hold. In the open space there, you'll have to fight another Necrotic Entity along with a Daemonic Entity.

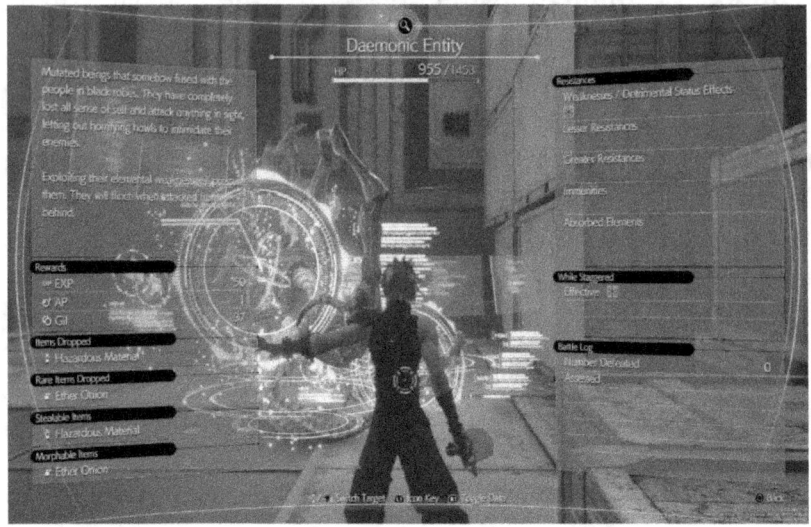

Unlike the Necrotic Entity, the Daemonic Entity is vulnerable to ice attacks. After defeating them, go left to grab the chest containing gloves for Tifa. Then, head up the stairs on the right and cross the platform to reach an area with more Daemonic Entities. Move under the boxes to find a path forward where you'll encounter another Necrotic Entity and a Shrieker, similar to the Screamer from the first chapter. The Shrieker doesn't have weaknesses, but it takes less damage from the front when it swings its mace. Once you've dealt with them, climb the stairs toward the engine room. Take advantage of the vending machines and rest station before proceeding to the next room. When you descend the stairs and meet up with Barret, get ready for a boss fight.

How to Defeat Jenova Emergent:

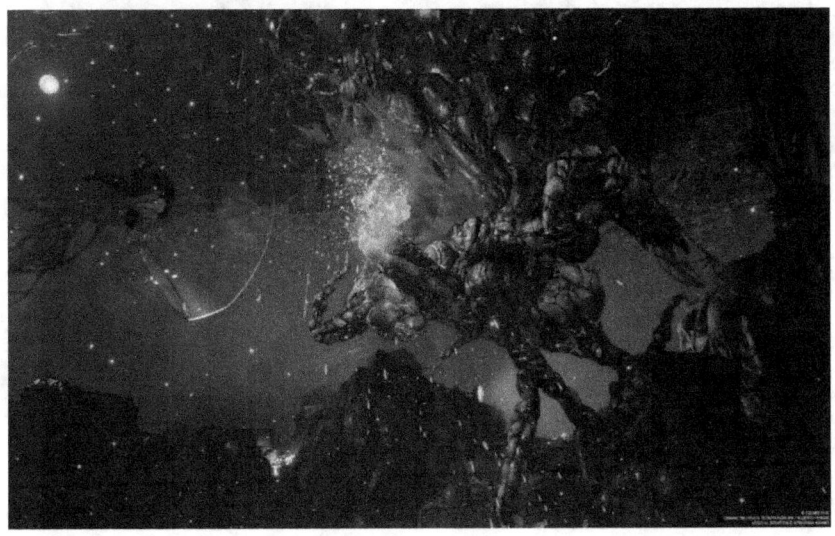

The first thing to watch out for when facing Jenova Emergent is its Pestilence attack. This creates a small purple cloud that moves towards the wall. Another move to dodge is Vengeance, where it shoots a narrow beam of energy in one direction. Blocking won't work against these attacks, so make sure to dodge them. Jenova Emergent doesn't have any particular weaknesses. Once you've put enough pressure on it, you'll be able to target its head.

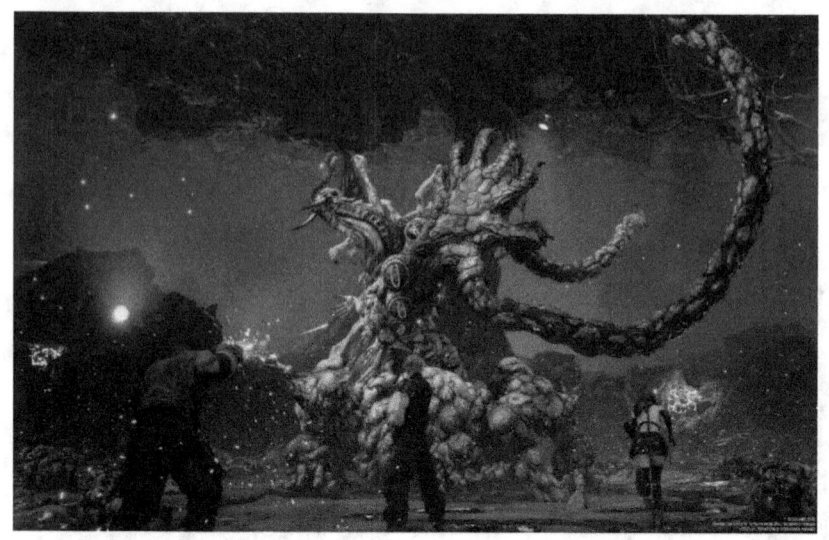

When you destroy the head, you'll stagger Jenova Emergent. This is your chance to deal as much damage as possible before it recovers. After recovering from the stagger, Jenova Emergent will drop to the ground, grow multiple arms, and gain new abilities. One of these abilities is Exaltation, an unblockable attack that shoots five energy beams in different directions. Another move to watch out for is Torment, where the boss grabs one of your party members. As you keep pressuring Jenova Emergent, you'll be able to destroy its arms and eventually its head. This will disable some of its abilities and stagger it again. Once you've dealt enough damage, a series of tentacles will spawn. They're not very strong, so deal with them first before focusing on Jenova Emergent again. Keep pressuring, destroying body parts, and staggering the boss to defeat it. Beating Jenova Emergent marks the end of the fifth chapter, and the next chapter begins as you arrive at Costa del Sol.

CHAPER SIX

FOOL'S PARADISE

Following the adventurous boat journey in the last chapter of Final Fantasy 7 Rebirth, Cloud and the crew finally reach Costa del Sol. This chapter gives them a chance to relax and have some fun. It's like a beach episode, with swimsuits and games everywhere. But don't worry, the story still moves forward. Here's what to expect in Chapter 6: Fool's Paradise.

Exploring Costa del Sol:

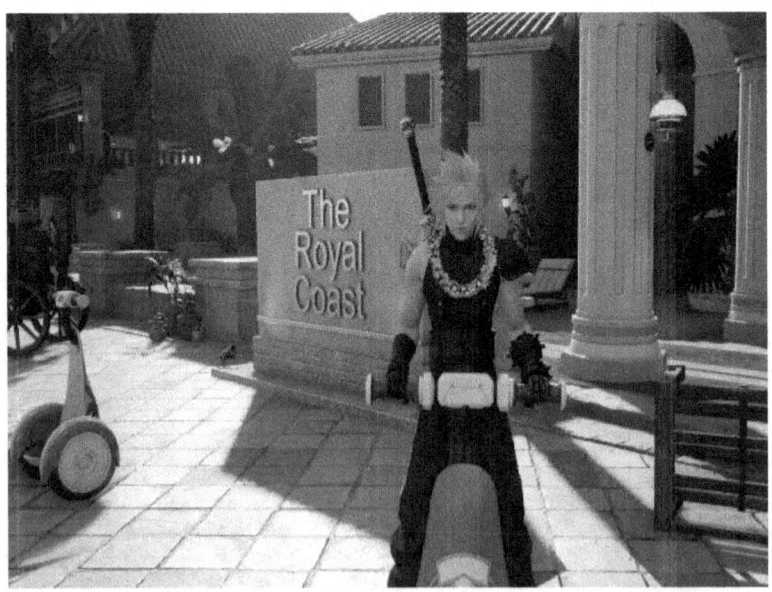

Once the cutscene ends and you're back in control of Cloud, head northwest to leave the dock and enter the town. One of the first things you'll find is a shop selling Celeris. This item gives the drinker a speed boost called Haste in battles. Though it's expensive, Haste can be really helpful.

If you want to get around quickly, you can hop on Wheelies, funny-looking vehicles. Using Wheelies enough can earn you rewards from the tourist information center. Here's what you can get:

Distance Traveled	Prize
200m	Seven Smelling Salts
1,000m	Seven Hi-Potions
2,000m	Headband
4,000m	Pedometer Pin

There are also various shops in town, like a weapons vendor and a bookshop selling Folios. While there are mini-games available, you'll need to progress in the story to unlock them. To move forward, head to The Royal Coast and talk to the person behind the counter.

Unfortunately, there are no available rooms at The Royal Coast, so you'll have to check out the other hotel, Costa del Sol Resort. It's near the weapon shop. They're full too, but when you leave, a cutscene will start. Follow Johnny to his hotel. Once you're at the inn, head upstairs and talk to Johnny.

Get Ready for the Beach:

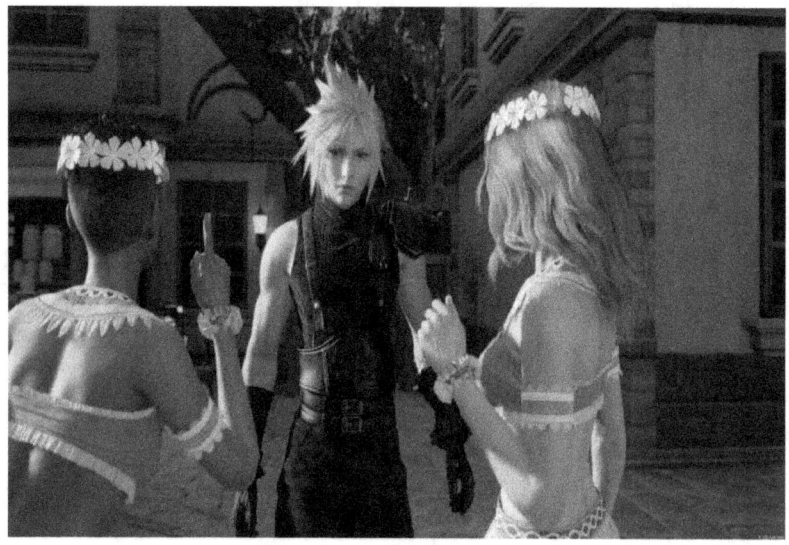

While everyone splits off to do their own thing, you're on your own. Go to Cloud's room and use the stand. Then, head downstairs to leave the hotel. Soon after, there's a cutscene where Cloud feels a bit out of place. You can't progress the story until you find clothes more suited for Costa del Sol. To do that, you'll need companion cards.

To get these cards, you have to join in various events around the area. But first, you need to find someone with the same ticket as you. Go to Pirate's Rampage where you'll find Barret, who has the same ticket as Cloud.

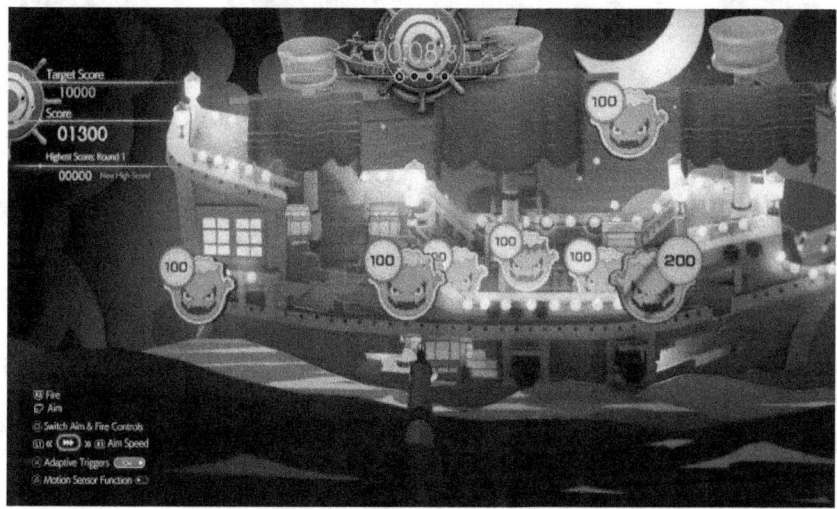

This is your first chance to get companion cards. You need to score 10,000 points or more to earn one. If you can score 15,000 points, you'll get Time Materia as a prize.

Aerith & Tifa:

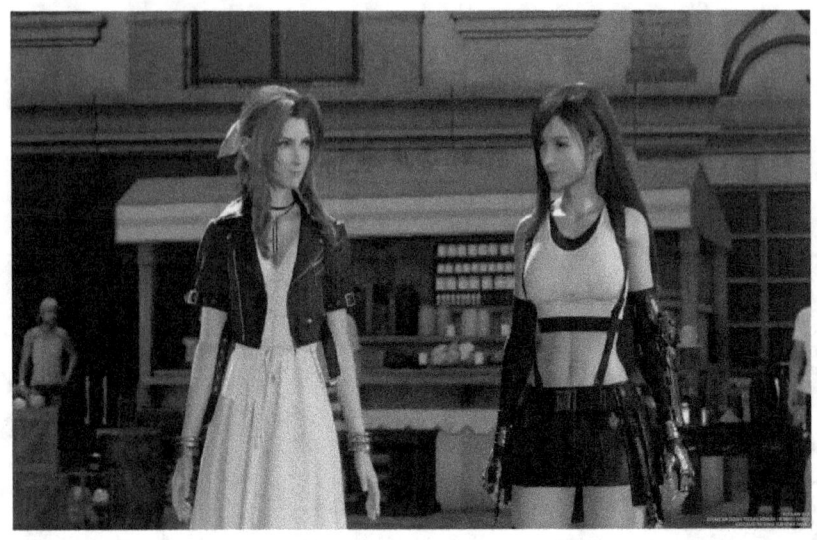

To move the story forward, you only need to get one companion card, which covers the cost of the beach attire. Once you have the outfit, head left towards the changing booths to put it on. Then, head down to the beach to start a cutscene, and you'll take control of Aerith. Leave the room and go to Tifa's door. She'll join the party, and you can choose who to control for this part of Chapter 6.

Leave the hotel and approach the same girls Cloud talked to earlier. Just like with Cloud, you'll need companion cards to get beach attire for Aerith and Tifa. This time, though, you have more games to choose from. You'll need a card for Aerith and one for Tifa. Once you've chosen outfits for both, head down to the beach to continue the story.

After the cutscene, follow Hojo and talk to him when he sits down. This triggers another cutscene, and then you'll have to fight more of the creatures from the previous chapter. Once you've picked a team, deal with the enemies. After another cutscene, you'll face a large mechanical enemy called Grasptropod.

How to Defeat Grasptropod:

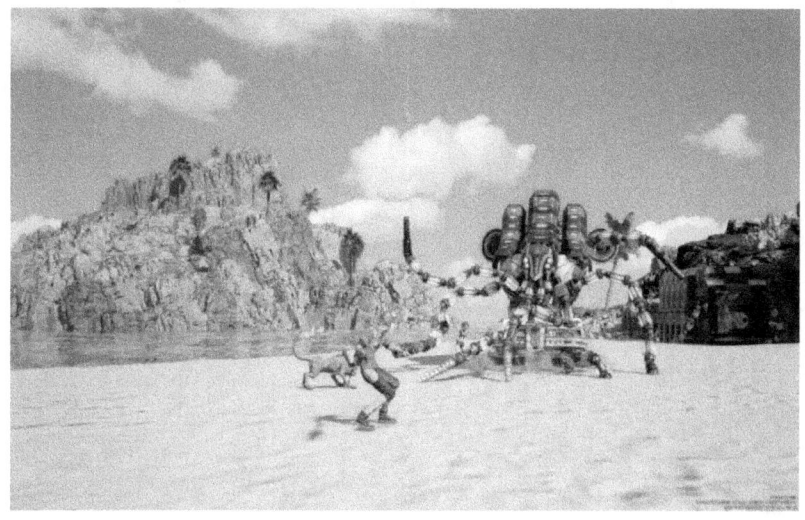

One of its main attacks is an unavoidable move where Grasptropod releases poison clouds around itself. It also regularly shoots out a spray that silences anyone hit by it.

Grasptropod is vulnerable to lightning damage. As the fight progresses, it'll capture a party member, which you can't prevent. It'll happen again shortly after, leaving you with just one party member. When Cloud gets grabbed too, it might seem like winning is impossible, but fortunately, that's not true. Yuffie appears to assist, and the fight continues as usual. Keep attacking the boss while Yuffie comes up with a plan. When the boss begins to spin, stay clear until it overheats. While it's disabled, destroy the cylinders, then resume attacking. Dodge its attacks while maintaining your offensive, and Grasptropod will soon be defeated.

Beach Time:

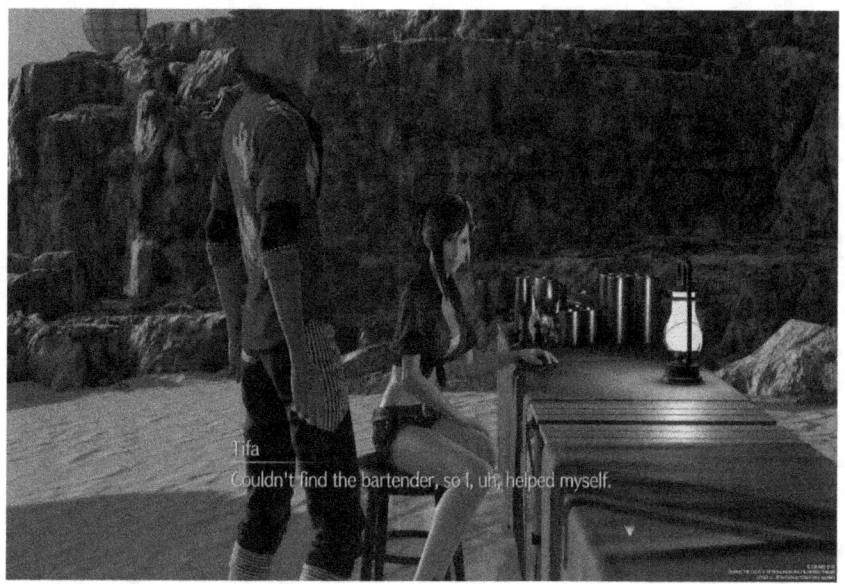

Once the cutscene ends, have a chat with everyone on the beach. Choosing the right responses can strengthen your bond with your companions. It's best to be supportive and not dismiss their concerns. Ignoring them won't improve your relationship with them. After chatting with everyone, you can return to the hotel. Go upstairs and inform Barret that you're ready to leave.

Yuffie Strikes Again:

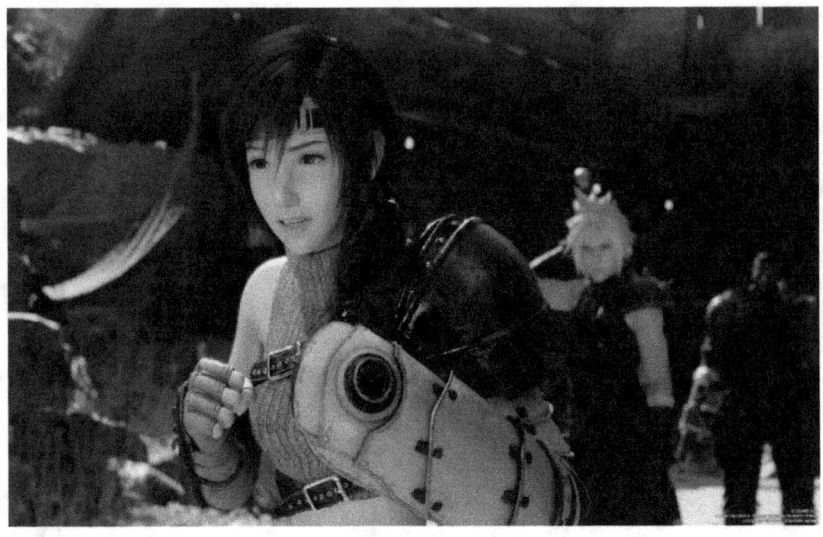

After the cutscenes, you'll encounter Yuffie. You can choose to agree to fight her or tell her to leave. The decision doesn't really matter because you won't actually fight her. Whatever you choose, she'll join the party as Chapter 6 ends, and Chapter 7 begins immediately.

CHAPTER SEVEN

THOSE LEFT BEHIND

After the relaxed beach time in the last chapter, the journey in Final Fantasy 7 Rebirth continues in Chapter 7: Those Left Behind. Now, you can finally venture beyond Costa del Sol, and there's plenty to explore. Being the third region you'll visit, there are lots of side quests and distractions to enjoy, which might tempt you away from the main storyline.

Onward to Mt. Corel:

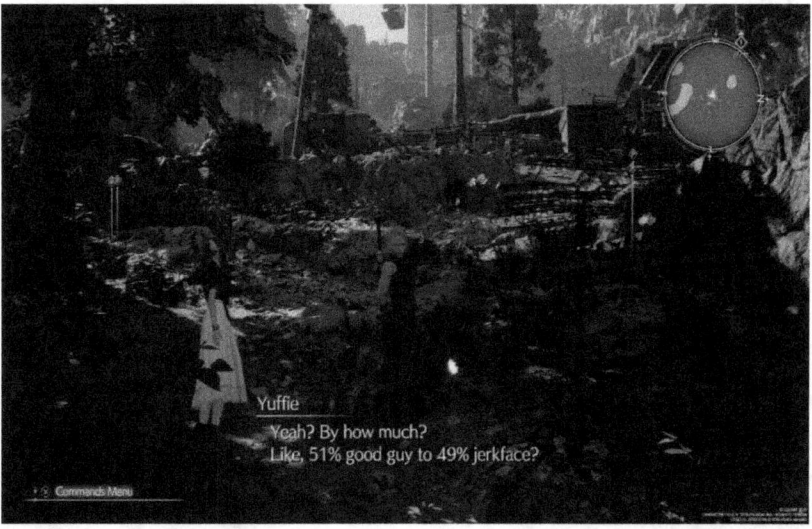

Although your main goal is to head to Mt. Corel, there are several optional tasks to complete along the way. At this point, you'll gain the ability to fast-travel back to the Junon region. Plus, there are a couple of side quests waiting for you. As always, make sure to activate towers and scan lifesprings to learn more about the area.

When you're ready, head towards the location marked with the blue diamond. As you start on the hiking trail, a cutscene will unfold. Proceed along the trail, where eventually everyone except Aerith, Cloud, and Red XIII will move ahead. At the rest station with vending machines, go left to find a chest containing a weapon for Aerith. Nearby, you'll also discover an Enervation Materia.

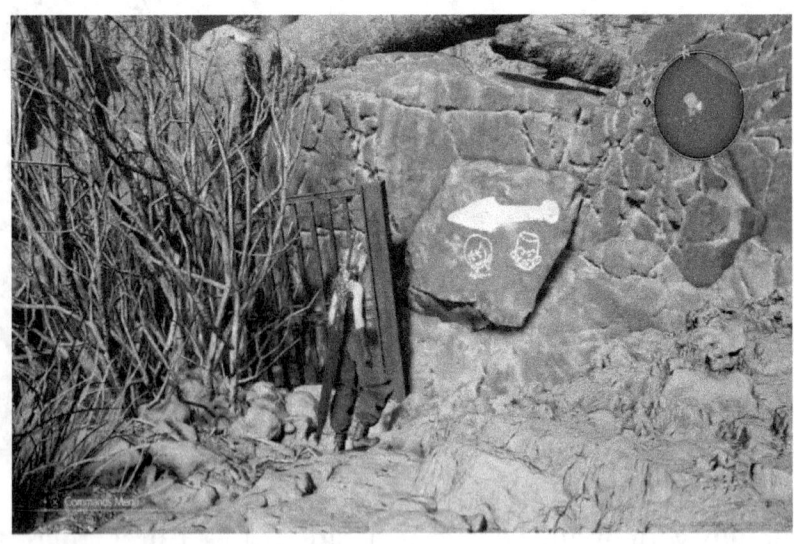

Ready to continue? Proceed further up the trail. When you encounter a flight of stairs, ascend them, as the path to the left leads to a dead end. At the top, turn right and follow the path marked "Trail." Eventually, you'll come across a crude drawing of Yuffie and Barret, with an arrow pointing left. Follow this arrow to get back on track with the trail.

Further along the trail, you'll see another drawing of Yuffie and Barret, this time pointing upwards. Climb up the wall and head to the right. Near a climbable metal wall, you'll find another rough drawing of Yuffie and Barret. Climb up the metal wall and follow the trail sign. Take the stairs next to the drawing and cross the bridge, continuing up the trail.

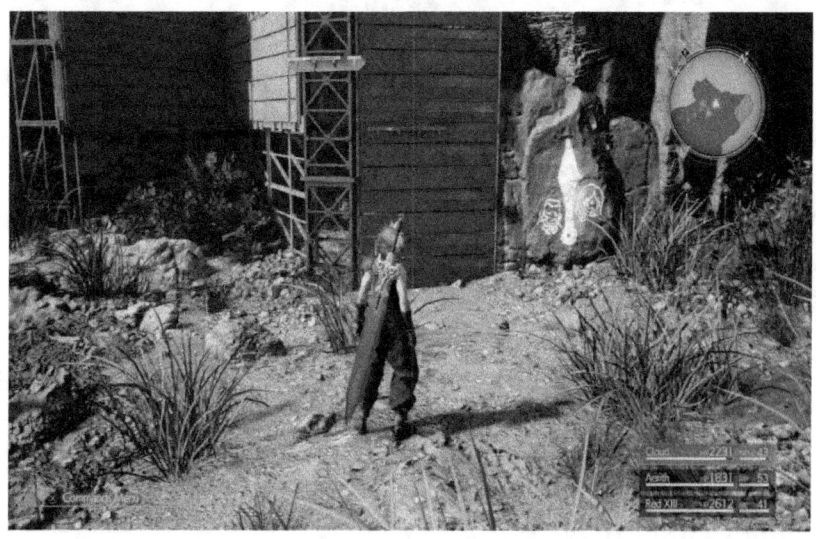

Upon reaching the gate with the Shinra logo, pass through it and enter the tunnel, where you'll find yet another drawing left by Yuffie. At the top of the rock wall, there's a rest station for any needed breaks. It's a good idea to heal up and save your progress here. When you reach the helicopter pad, get ready for a fight.

How to Defeat Custom Valkyrie:

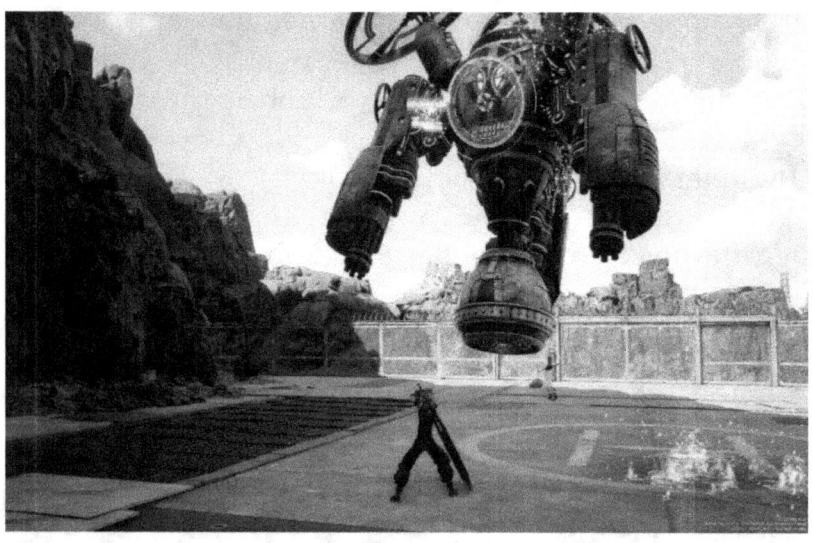

Instead of facing Elena and Rude as in the third chapter, you'll confront a large flying robot, the Custom Valkyrie. It's weak against lightning and wind attacks, so use these to pressure it. After using too much fire, the Custom Valkyrie will need to cool down. Use this opportunity to deal as much damage as possible, as it'll be easier to pressure.

Watch out for the anti-personnel gas the Custom Valkyrie periodically releases, as it applies debuffs to anyone hit. When the boss reaches 50% health, an in-battle cinematic will play, trapping the party in a ring of fire. The boss gains a new weapon, a giant laser cannon, targeting specific party members. Time your dodges carefully. Keep building pressure, staggering the boss, and seize the opportunity to finish it off.

After a couple of cutscenes, the scene changes, and you'll control Zack. Answer the door and follow Elmyra upstairs to where Aerith is resting. After another cutscene, you'll play as Cloud back at Mt. Corel. Use the control panel on the left side of the gate to open it and access the stairs beyond the helicopter pad. Continue up the stairs to rejoin the rest of the party.

Corel Mako Reactor:

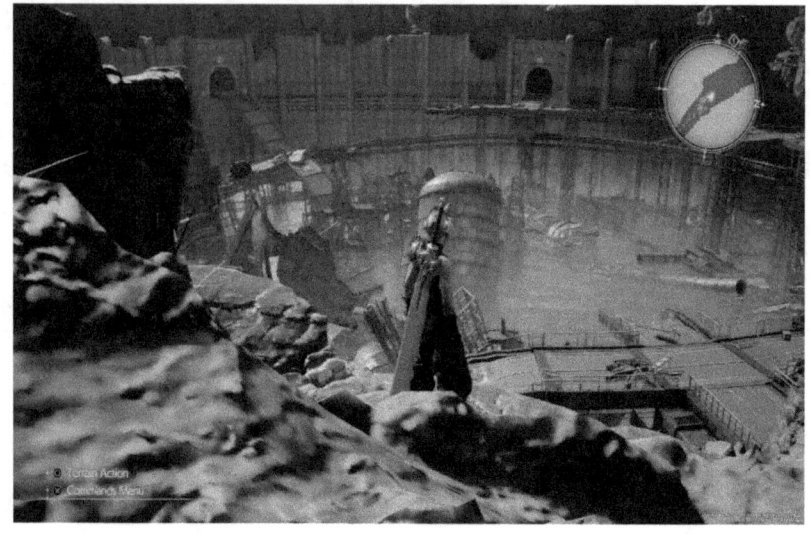

Follow the path ahead to reach the remains of the Corel Mako Reactor. After the cutscene, walk past the cloaked figures and follow Yuffie. After another cutscene, this time follow Barret. At the end of the walkway, you'll find an elevator.

In the next area, you'll have access to fast travel again. Go through the tunnel and turn left to find a chest with 1,700 Gil. Then, turn around and go up the stairs. After a cutscene, Cloud will be out of action for a bit. Meanwhile, you'll play as Yuffie, joining Barret and Tifa as they head through the mines to reach the control room.

Through the Mines:

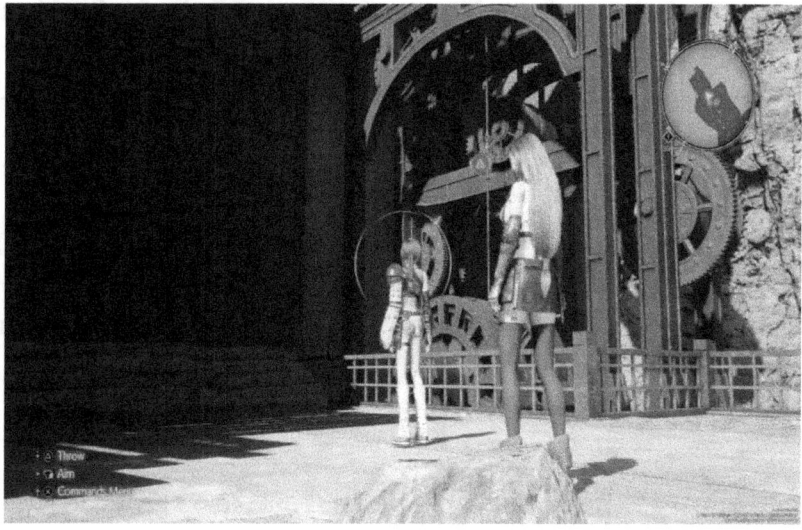

Like Barret in the third chapter, Yuffie can use her weapon to break boxes and obstacles blocking the path. For example, there's a rope in the image above that Yuffie can destroy, opening a door into the mines.

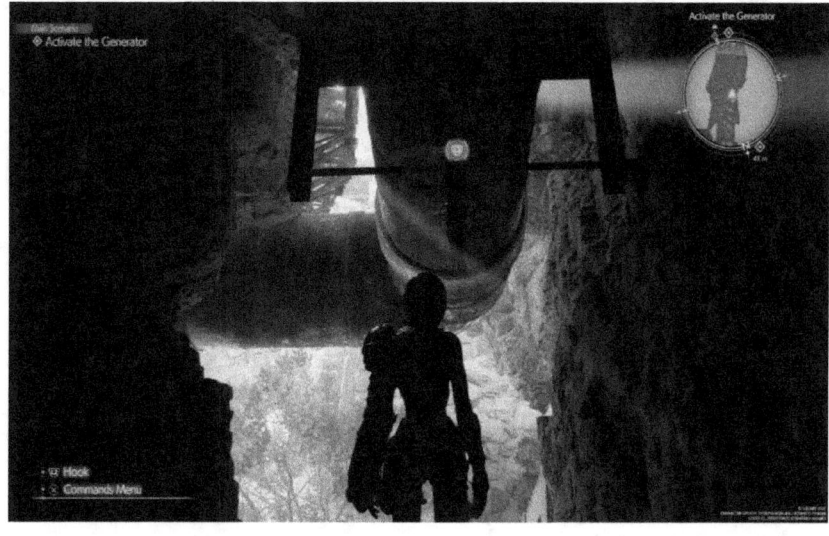

Unfortunately, the lift further up is out of power. But when you approach, Barret points out a grappling hook for Yuffie to use. When you spot a suitable spot, like the one above, you can use the grappling hook to cross. Once in range of a landing spot, press the Circle button. Next to the generator is a chest with a weapon for Yuffie. Activate the generator, then use the grappling hook to return to the others.

Head towards the conveyor belt and use it to reach the next floor. There's an elevator that would go up further, but it can't be used right now. To the left of the elevator is another grappling hook spot. Jump across and turn around. Look up to see another grappling hook point that's currently unusable.

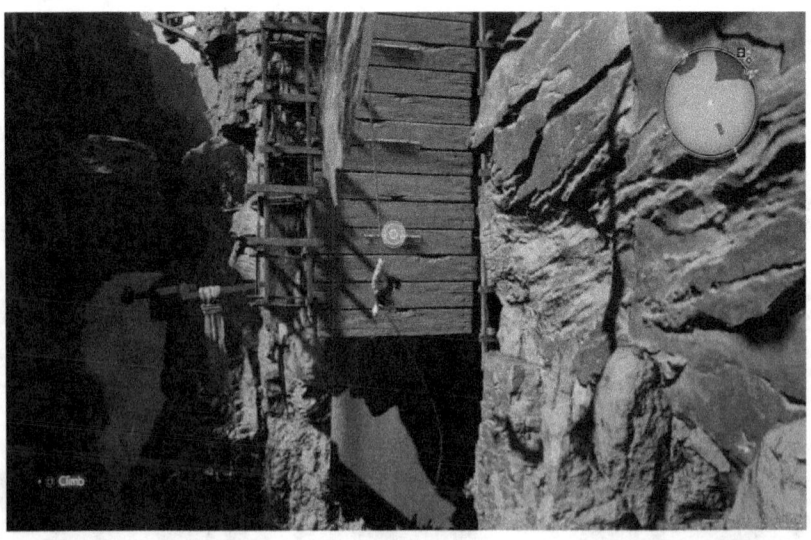

To fix this, move around until you see the Triangle button appear. Yuffie will throw her weapon at the pole, shifting it so the grappling hook can be used. While swinging, you can press L2 to launch towards another spot. Use this to land by the chest, then turn around to spot a spot to climb up the wall.

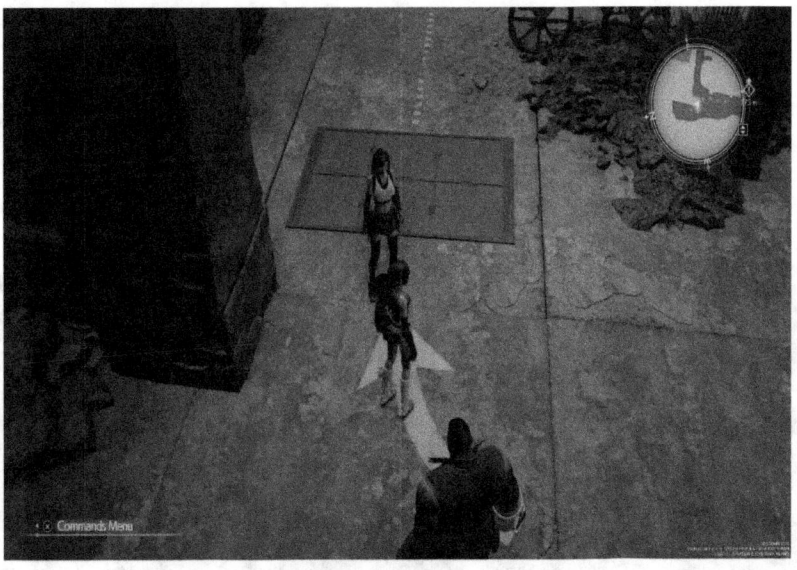

Use the grappling hook to reach this point and then climb to the top. Here, you'll encounter an enemy and the control panel that activates the elevator. Once your party rejoins you, follow the arrow on the ground. Enter the large room with a group of enemies and ascend the stairs. When you exit the mine, head towards the tower directly ahead. Climb the wall and use Yuffie's weapon to drop a bunch of boxes onto the ground. Descend and break them to find a variety of useful items.

After that, turn left and ascend the ramp. Zip down to the next area. Before proceeding, use the ladder to descend and collect the chest, then return to the tunnel entrance. Defeat the enemies in this area and continue through the tunnel towards a rest station and vending machines. When ready, head right from the rest station and defeat the cockatrice in the area.

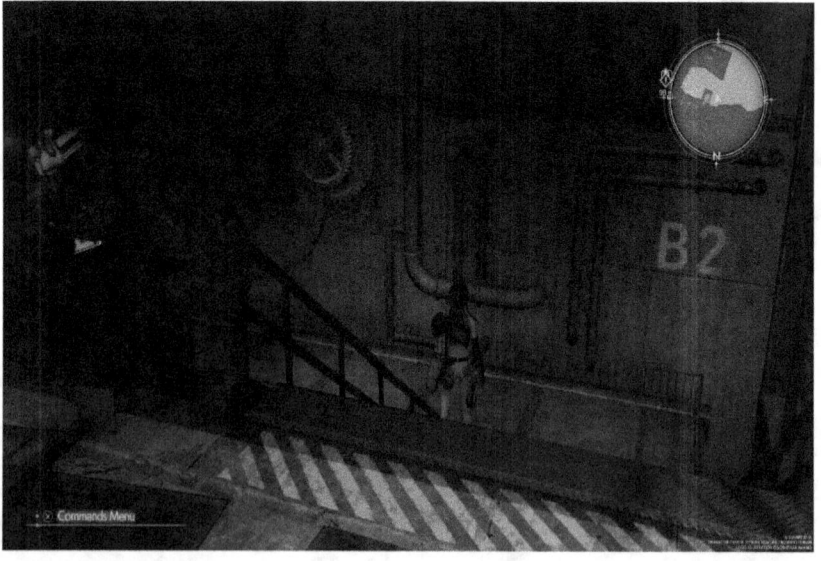

Next, climb the wall and reach the end of the platform. Use Yuffie's weapon to unlock a ladder. Descend and use that ladder to access an area with four consecutive grappling hook spots.

Use them to move closer to another set of grappling hook points, then drop down to reach the chest. Return and use the stairs near the wall labeled "B2." In the next area, there are more inactive conveyors. The generator is on the other side of a water pool, but that's no problem for Yuffie. Look up and use your weapon to dislodge a grappling hook point. Turn left and jump to the next grappling hook point. From there, you'll see several more points you can use to reach the generator.

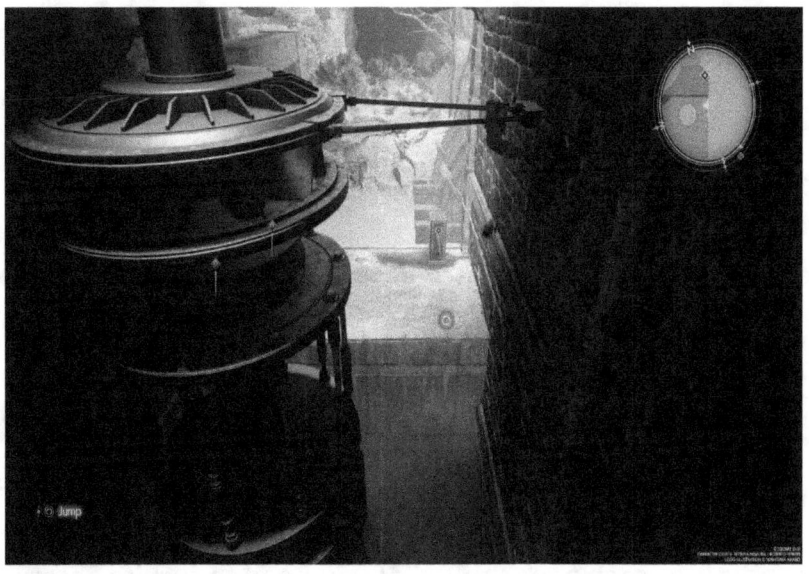

Once you're on the giant metal column, gently push the analog stick forward to move the column closer until you can safely jump down to the generator. When you're ready to return, walk along the broken dock and leap into the water. Swim back to where the rest of the party is waiting, then head towards the conveyor to proceed to the next floor. This will take you back to the rest point you encountered earlier. From there, head towards the other conveyor and ascend it.

At the top of this conveyor, you'll encounter a group of enemies that you'll need to deal with first. Afterward, go outside and follow the narrow path until you come across another elevator that's not working, which Yuffie will complain about. Keep going past the elevator and press Triangle to hit the machinery. This will bring down a grappling hook point temporarily, so be quick to grab onto it. From there, traverse a series of grappling hook points, drop down, and then hit another machine with Yuffie's weapon. Use the grappling hook on this point and swing onto the next one, which will start moving shortly after. Utilize this point to reach a machine that you need to turn to access the switch. However, this time you must keep swinging until Yuffie kicks the switch and activates the generator. This action brings down another grappling hook point. Grab onto it and use it to enter the small room with the bomb. Defeat the bomb and then activate the terminal to restore power to the elevator. There's also a rest station here, so be sure to use it if needed.

How to Defeat Gigatrice:

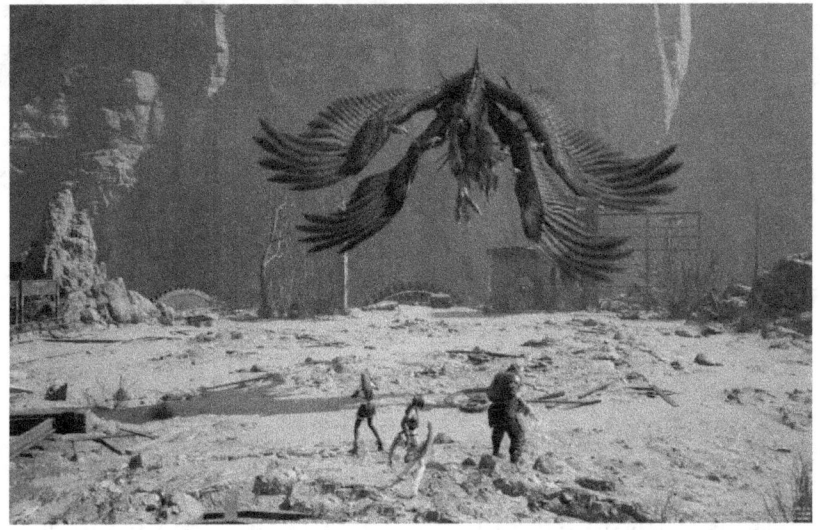

Outside awaits a formidable foe, Gigatrice, a large creature with four wings. Gigatrice is vulnerable to fire damage, so prioritize abilities and spells of that element. Be cautious of its breath attack, which can petrify a target. Utilize Yuffie's Fire Ninjutsu to imbue her attacks with fire, making it easier and quicker to pressure and stagger Gigatrice.

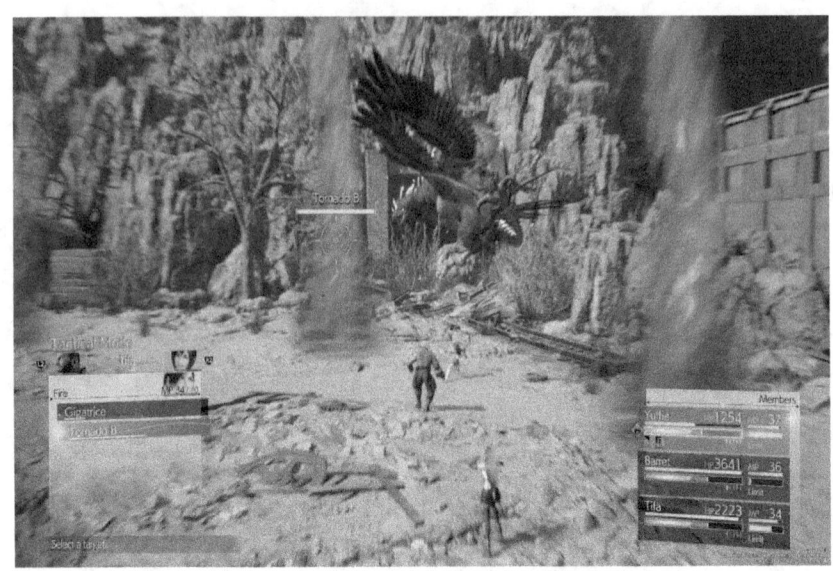

As Gigatrice's health diminishes, it will summon tornadoes periodically. These tornadoes can eventually combine into a larger one that petrifies anyone caught within. Occasionally, a targetable tornado will appear. Use Fire (or Fira) on it to create a fire tornado, knocking Gigatrice out of the sky. Continuously hit it with fire attacks to defeat this airborne behemoth.

Setting Their Path:

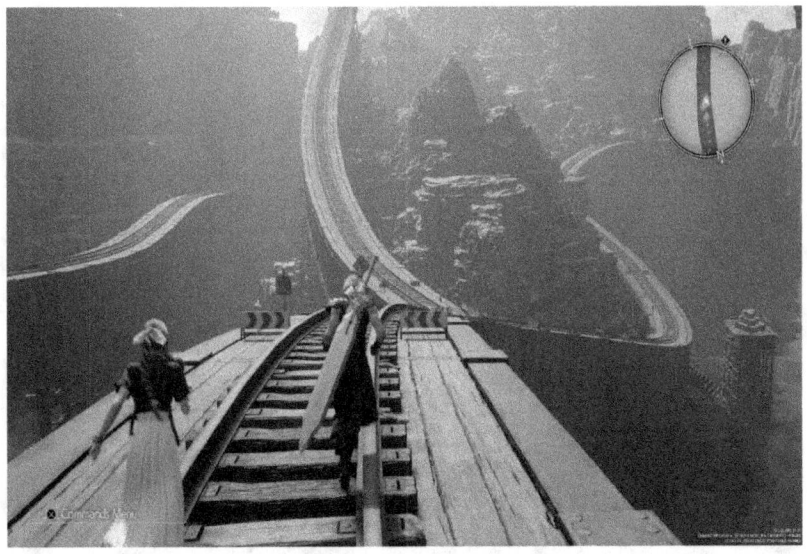

After the cutscene, head towards the control panel. Once the path is clear, switch back to the other half of the party as they traverse the tracks. Encounter a few enemies along the way, but they pose no significant challenge. While walking along the tracks, you'll have the opportunity to adjust Barret and Yuffie's route. Changing the course will increase Yuffie's favor, while leaving it unchanged will please Barret. Regardless of your choice, continue along the tracks to advance the story. Reach the end of the track and use the phone in the metal shack. Interact with the mine cart to start a mini-game. Destroy as many boxes as possible, as some contain useful consumables and materials.

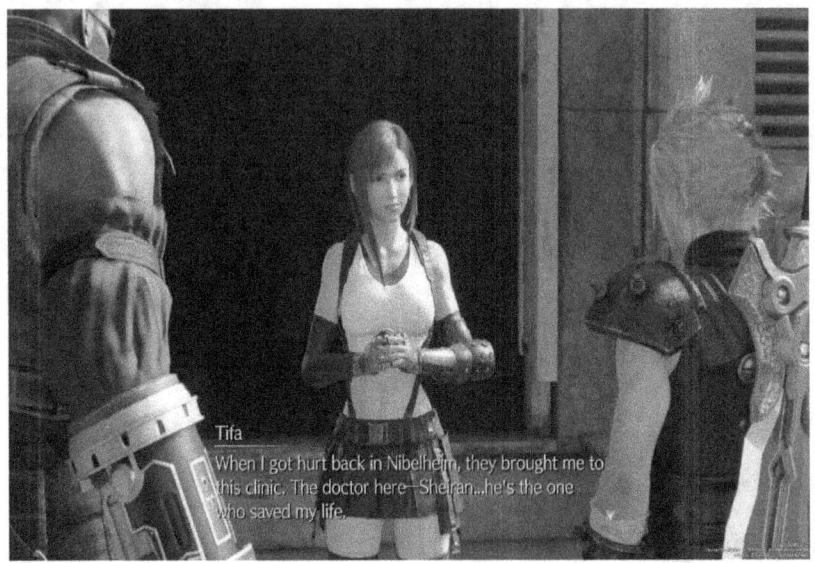

Once the party regroups, proceed along the remaining tracks and cross the bridge. After a less-than-warm reception for Barret, delve further into the town. Eventually, Tifa will pause and express a desire to enter one of the buildings. Accompany her inside to trigger a cutscene, then exit the building. At this point, several side quests will unlock. When ready, ascend the stairs towards the ropeway. Once you ascend to the Gold Saucer, you won't be able to return for a while, so ensure you're prepared before proceeding. Following a lengthy cutscene, Chapter 8 will commence. Top of Form

CHAPTER EIGHT

ALL THAT GLITTERS

In the revamped trilogy of Final Fantasy 7, fans eagerly anticipate revisiting iconic locations, and one standout is the Gold Saucer. Known for its catchy tunes and variety of mini-games, Chapter 8 of Final Fantasy 7 Rebirth promises all this and more. Yet, amidst the fun, Barret faces his past in this chapter. Here's what lies ahead in Chapter 8: All That Glitters.

Welcome to the Gold Saucer:

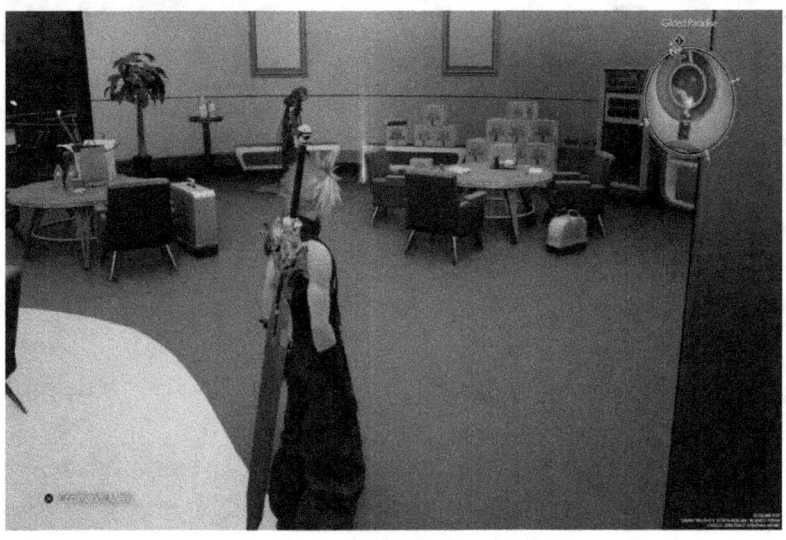

As you arrive, head up the stairs, pass through the hallway, and enter the small round room straight ahead. There, beside the robed figure, you'll discover a healing materia. Exiting the room and descending the stairs triggers a cutscene. Following its conclusion, proceed toward the entrance for another scene before diving into a mini-game.

Retro Boxing:

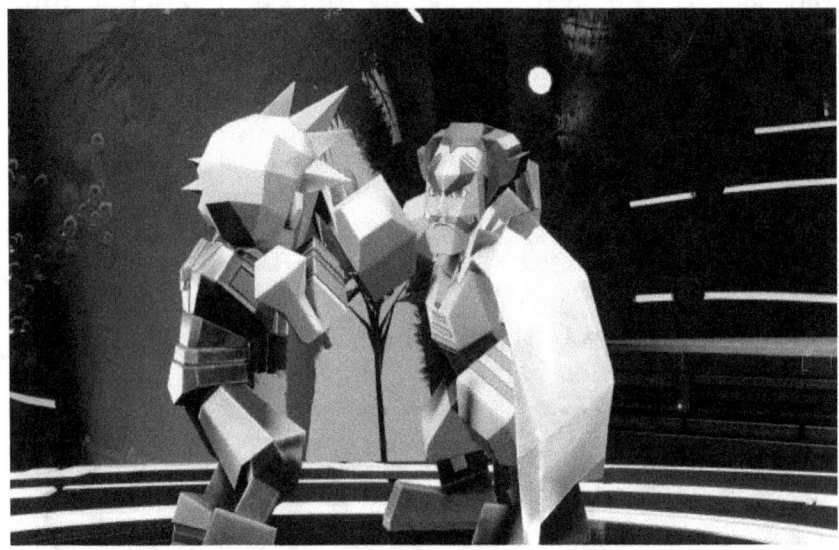

Initially, you'll undergo a tutorial where you're tasked with hitting Dio twice and evading two of his attacks. When Dio readies his right arm, press the right stick to the right, and for his left arm, press the left stick to the left. The challenge lies in landing two consecutive hits, though it's not possible to hit simultaneously despite the instructions. To pass the third part of the tutorial, strike Dio, dodge his attack, and then hit him as directed.

Once the tutorial wraps up, it's onto the actual match. Your goal is to fill your Limit Break bar before Dio does, then press and hold L2 and R2 to deliver the final blow. After the mini-game, continue exploring the Gold Saucer.

Get Some Rooms:

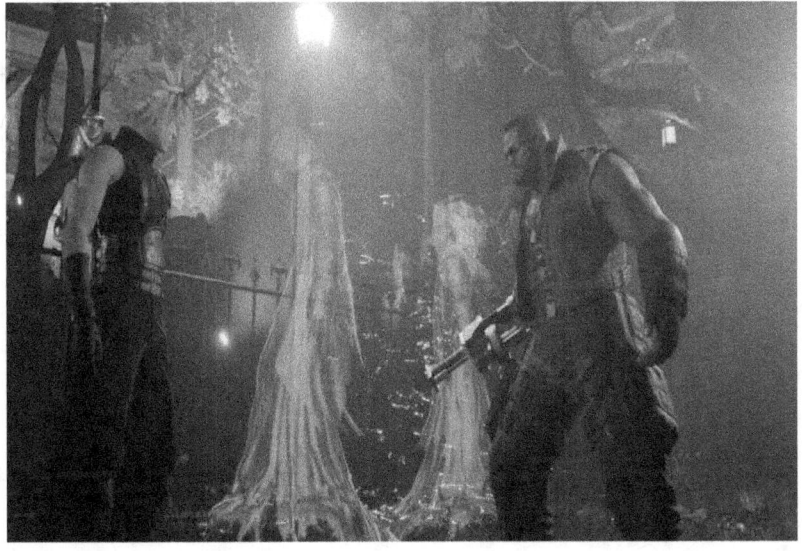

While Tifa, Aerith, Yuffie, and Red XIII head off to enjoy themselves, Cloud and Barret focus on finding rooms for everyone to rest. Follow Barret as he heads toward what seems to be a haunted attraction. Upon meeting Cait Sith, proceed up the stairs toward the Haunted Hotel. Enter and head to the reception desk. After the conversation, go upstairs and approach the elevator.

Upon reaching the fourth floor, proceed to the end of the hallway and enter the door on the left. There's a chest in this room, but it holds nothing useful. When ready, use the bed and rest. The scene shifts back to Zack, observed from an unusual camera angle that seems to be Cloud's perspective. Use the left stick to move Zack toward Aerith and press Triangle to interact with her. Then approach the white materia on the table and interact with it. Finally, inspect the bookshelf and exit through the door. In the hallway, descend the stairs to trigger a cutscene. Shortly after, resume playing as Cloud.

Explore the Gold Saucer:

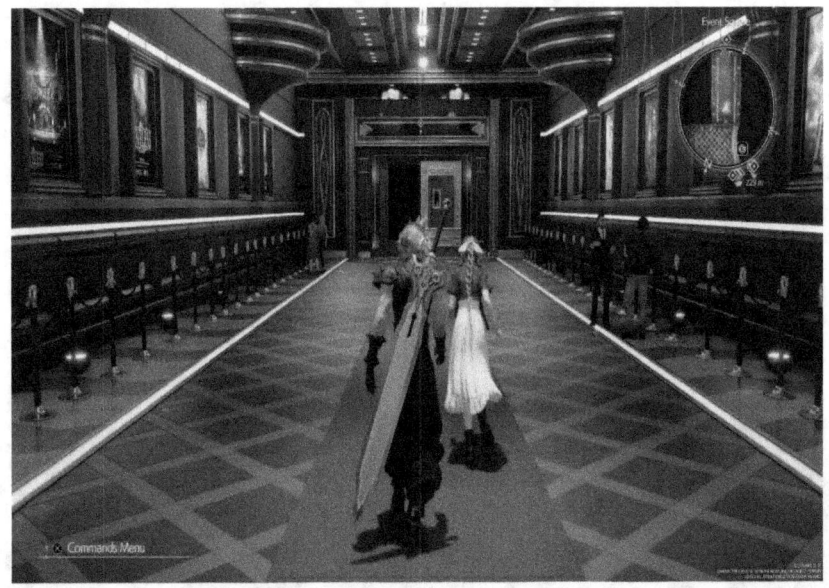

Trigger a cutscene by opening the door and then use the elevator. Upon leaving the Haunted Hotel, you'll receive a tutorial about Guide Moogles and how they facilitate fast travel around the Gold Saucer. To progress, explore every area of the Gold Saucer and participate in mini-games.

NOTE:

- Completing mini-games earns credit toward the objective; winning is optional, but various prizes are available.

When visiting the Gold Theater, head down to the stage area and look right to find an HP Up materia. Once you've explored all the Gold Saucer offers, head to Skywheel Square. Previously closed, it's conveniently open now. Head there to trigger a cutscene.

Find the Culprit:

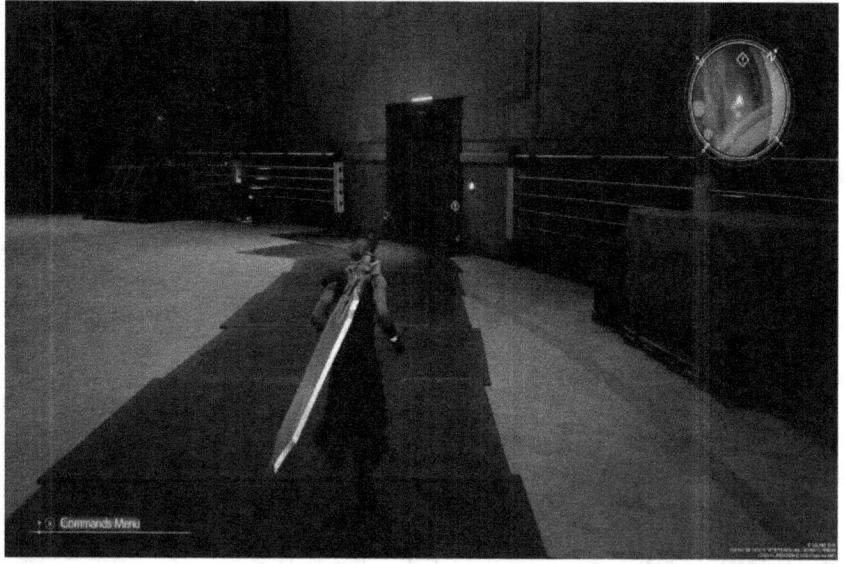

Travel quickly to the Battle Square and enter. Proceed through the right hallway and approach the taped-off area with bodies. Once the cutscene concludes, follow Cait Sith to the elevator. Use the elevator to descend to the Dustbowl. Walk along the empty street until you reach an open area, clearly intended for an ambush, which indeed occurs. After a cutscene, descend the stairs and loot the chest to obtain a new weapon for Cloud. Continue following Garth down to where the chocobo is.

Feeding Piko:

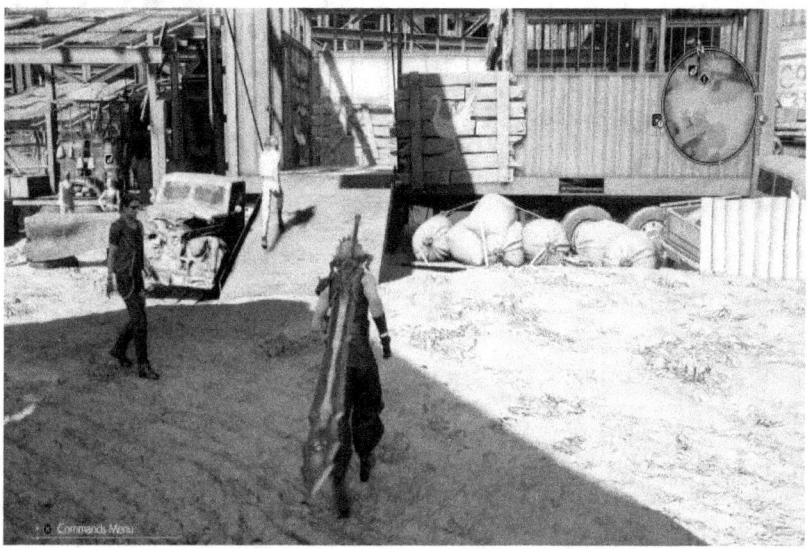

To move forward, you must find food for Piko. Go to Desert Rush and gather at least 15,000 points to get the Sylkis Greens, which Piko needs. In this mini-game, destroy boxes while looking for ones with large yellow electricity symbols, which allow you to break the gear boxes.

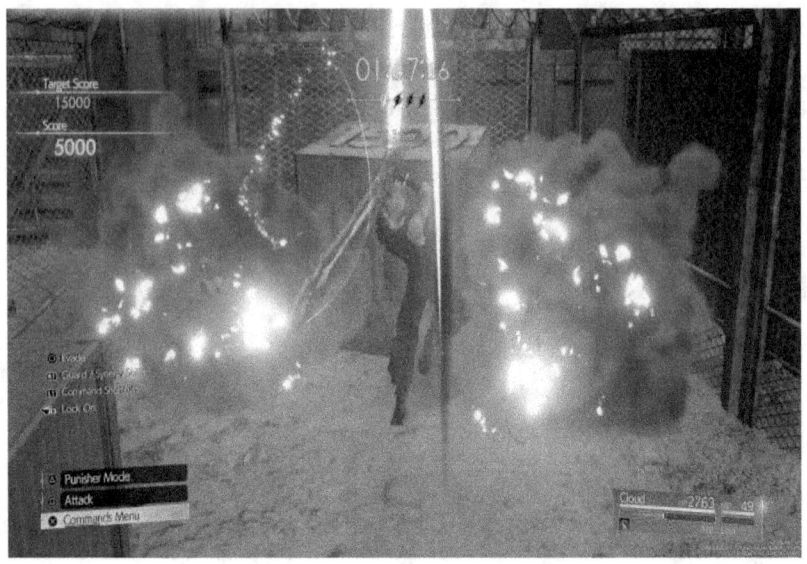

The number of lightning symbols on the gear boxes shows how many electric boxes you need to find and destroy. Use regular attacks on smaller boxes and Braver on larger ones to break them faster. You don't have to complete the activity; you just need to score 15,000 points before time runs out to get the Sylkis Greens.

Get another Sylkis Green by visiting the Bail Jumper. Get a key from the bartender and go to the nearby mine entrance. Climb the ladder to proceed, where you'll encounter a small group of enemies. Climb another ladder to find a Cactaur running off with the Sylkis Greens. Use the grappling hook to cross to the other side and climb the rock wall.

In the open area, face a Cyclone Drake, which is ironically vulnerable to wind damage. After defeating it, go through the tunnel ahead. Eventually, you'll reach a dead end. Use the grappling hook to move across platforms until you find a spot to descend to a rock wall. Climb down and go through the left tunnel. On the other side, face a couple of Death Claws.

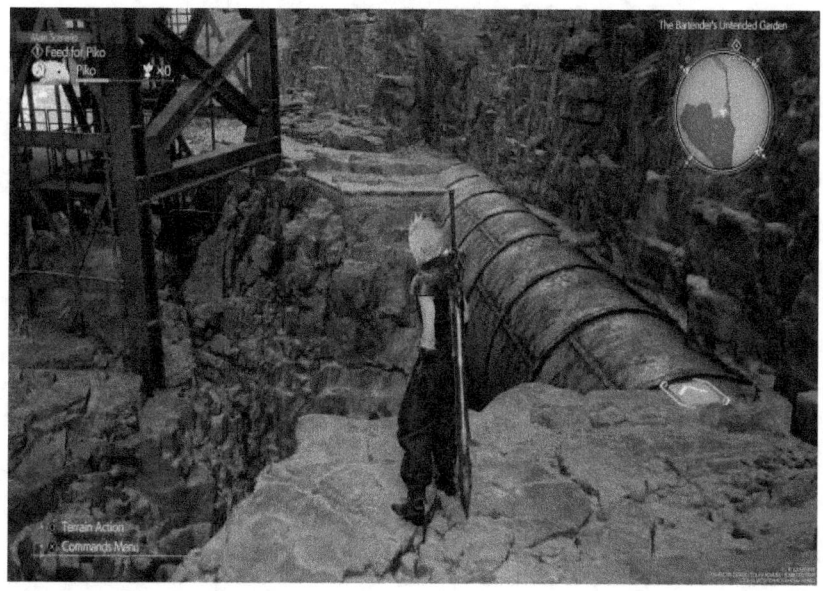

When the path splits, go left and cross the narrow pipe along the wall to chase the Cactaur. Before crossing the pipe, drop to the bottom to find an HP Up materia and a chest. On the other side, you'll find an open area with several Cactuars. Be careful during the fight, as Cactuars can deal significant damage with their Needle attacks.

After defeating the Cactuars, retrieve the Sylkis Green and use the zipline to descend. Return the Sylkis Green to Piko. To find the third and final Sylkis Green, talk to the three individuals across from the Community Noticeboard. They'll start following you. Head east, loot the chest in the corner for 1500 Gil, and go through the narrow gap in the wall. They'll try to "teach you a lesson." Although not very challenging, they're easy to stagger. Defeat them to get the last Sylkis Green and give it to Piko.

Joining the Race:

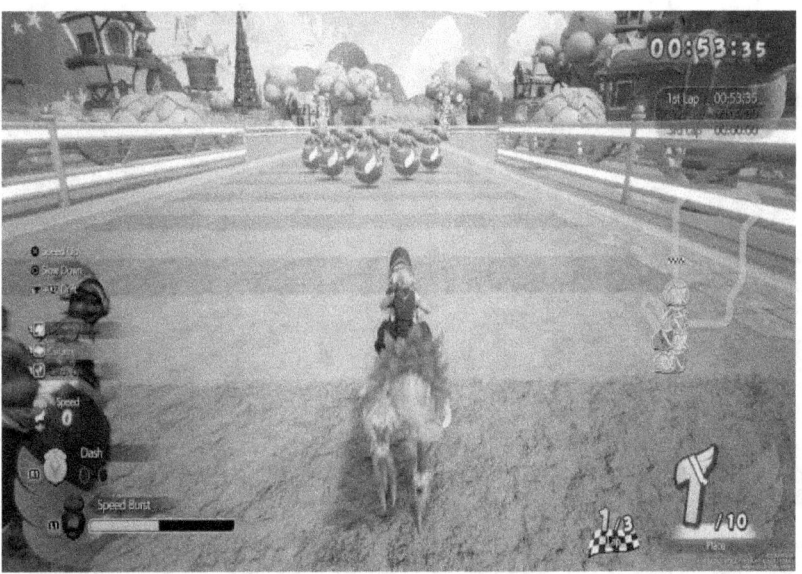

Talk to Garth to sign up for the race. Follow Esther to the elevator. Once you reach your destination, go with Esther to the waiting room. Practice using the chocobo saddle there before the race begins. When an announcement tells all jockeys to go to the paddock, talk to Esther and confirm you're ready.

To win the race, wait for a chance to get ahead and use the Speed Burst to keep your lead. Equipping your chocobo with an outfit will boost its stats, so make sure you've filled all the slots.

Back on the Trail:

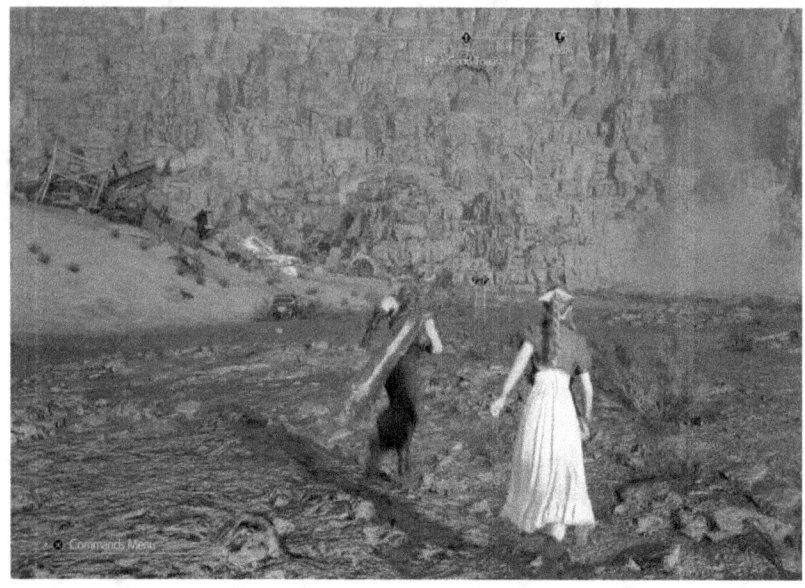

After the cutscene, climb down the ladder. There might be some monsters in the tunnel below, but they shouldn't be too tough. At the end of the tunnel, you'll see a big bird sitting on a tree. Follow the bird, dealing with any enemies you come across. Eventually, you'll come across a large tornado, which triggers another cutscene.

When you meet up with Barret again, head to the marked spot on the map. Open the chest on the right to get a weapon for Barret. Take out the enemies in the area and then head to the rest station. Take a break and gather any supplies you need because Barret will go alone through the hole in the fence. Approach the shack in the middle of the area and interact with the door.

How to Beat Dyne:

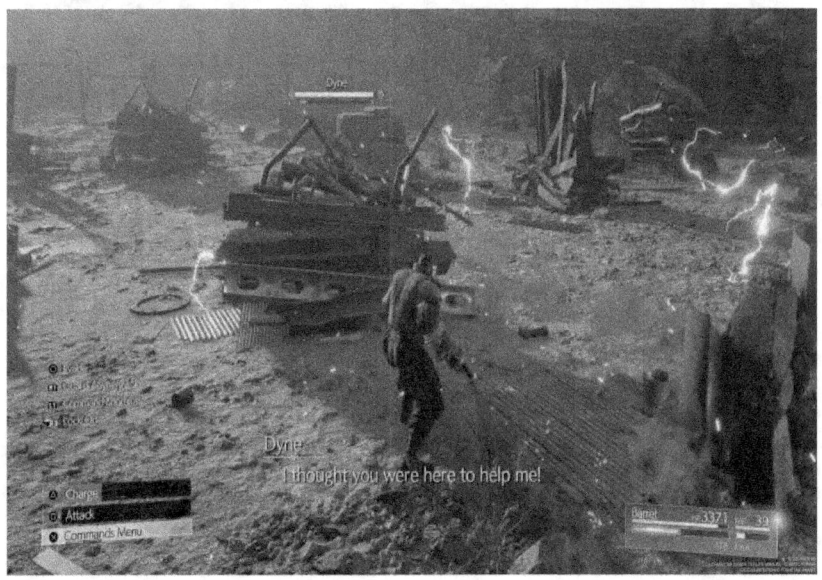

After the cutscene, Barret has to face Dyne one-on-one. When Dyne uses Paralyzing Shot, move away from the lines on the ground. You can use the piles of junk around as cover to shield yourself from many of Dyne's attacks. As Dyne's health drops below 90%, he'll drop mines onto the ground. Avoid getting too close to them.

Dyne will occasionally use Repentance, an attack that destroys cover and can't be blocked. Move away to avoid getting hit. He'll also use Point Blank, charging in to fire a shot directly at Barret. It's tough to dodge, but it's possible.

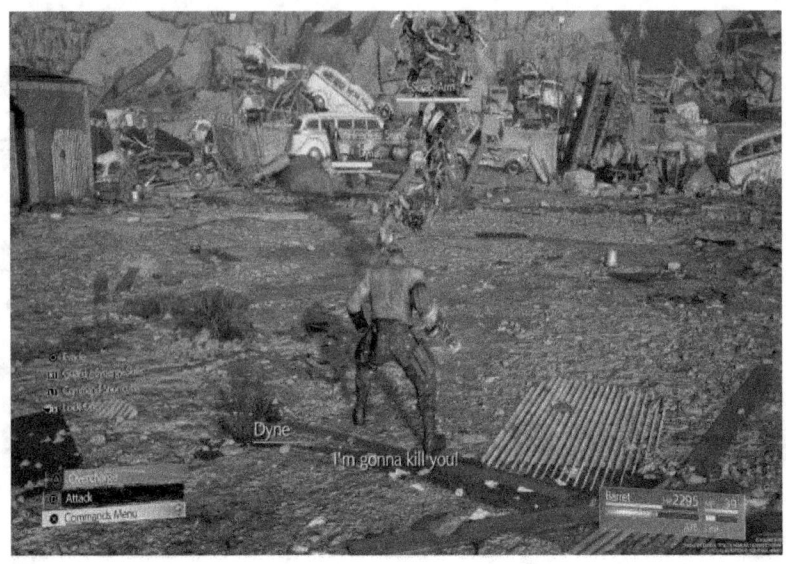

When Dyne's health gets to 50%, scrap around the arena will gather to form a large arm. The arm might break off and attack from underground or shoot lasers. Focus on destroying these parts quickly to make Dyne easier to deal with. Paralyzing Shot changes into Paralyzing Wave, leaving a bullet pattern on the ground.

Even after you destroy the scrap arm or scrap whips, they might come back. Shift your focus to them, destroy them, and keep attacking Dyne until he's defeated.

How to Beat Anuran Suppressor:

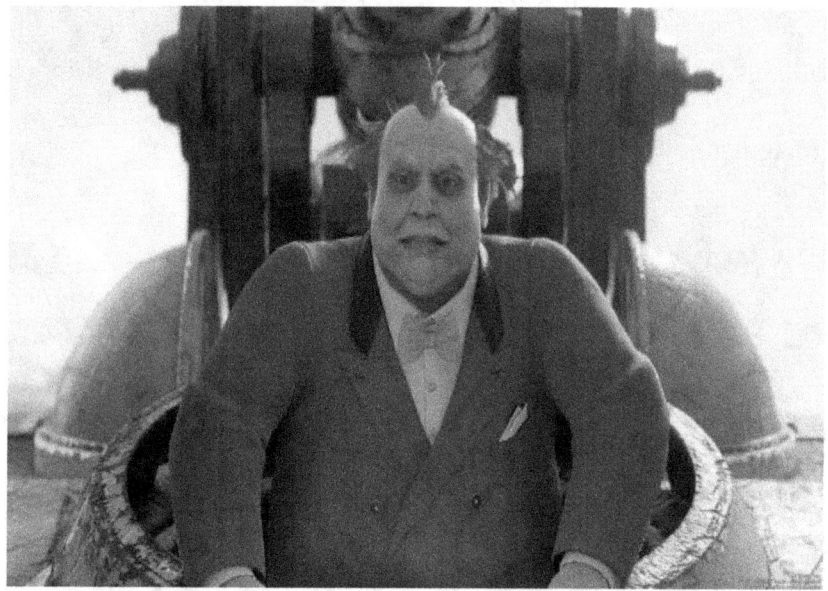

After beating Dyne, your mission isn't done yet. Once the scene ends, you'll control the rest of the party again. Follow the path ahead until you reach an open area. Shinra unleashes a giant mech piloted by Palmer. Despite its electric attacks, the Anuran Suppressor is weak against lightning damage.

When Palmer shows up and starts boasting, focus your attacks on him to put extra pressure. When the Anuran Suppressor's health drops to 50%, automated systems take over for Palmer, making it more dangerous. Now, you can also target its legs. Destroying them adds significant pressure, and taking out both legs staggers the Anuran Suppressor. Use this chance to deal as much damage as possible with Limit Breaks and Synergy Abilities. After defeating it, a cutscene follows, leading to a mini-game.

How to Escape From Shinra:

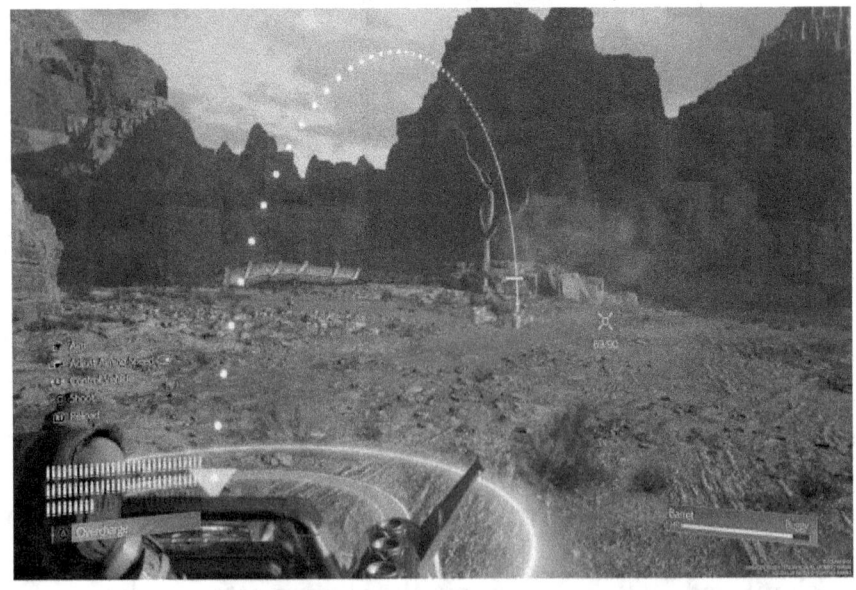

In this part, you'll control Barret on a buggy. Use his gun arm to take down the enemy forces chasing you. After dealing with the motorcycles, a helicopter joins the fray. When it attacks, use

Overload to deal heavy damage and finish it off with regular bullets.

In the next wave, you'll face motorcycles and a helicopter. Avoid the circles that appear; with good timing, you can dodge them easily. In the following wave, the Anuran Suppressor will chase you. Dodge its attacks and aim for the glowing gun underneath it. Once you defeat the Anuran Suppressor (again), you'll be safe.

Find Biggs:

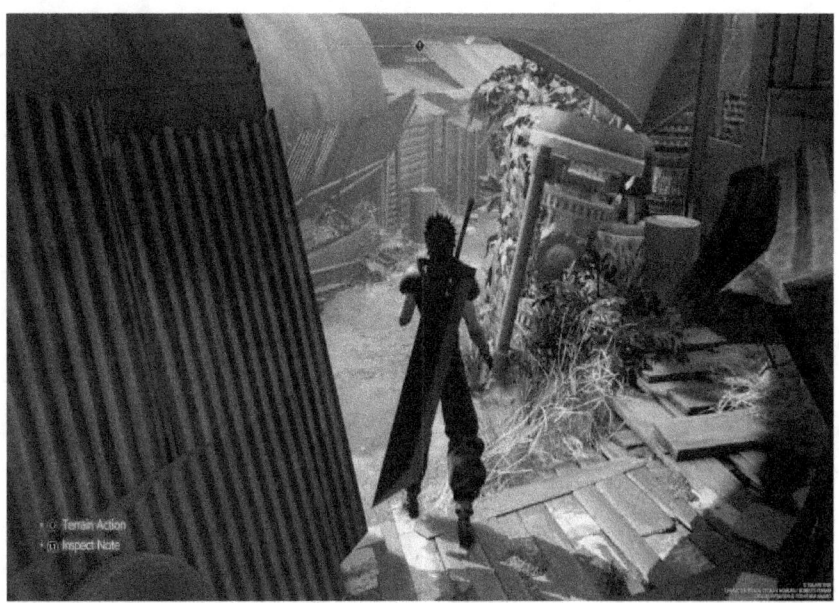

After the scene, you'll switch back to Zack's perspective. Go through the narrow alley straight ahead. As you explore, ask people about Biggs. Keep searching until an explosion happens. Follow the blue icon until you trigger a scene, ending the current chapter.

CHAPTER NINE

THE PLANET STIRS

After the thrilling events at the Gold Saucer, get ready for more adventure in the next part of Final Fantasy 7 Rebirth. Chapter 9, named "The Planet Stirs," ties up loose ends in Corel and introduces Gongaga, a new area to explore. This chapter is packed with things to do, from side quests to exploring the vast open world.

Getting to the Reactor:

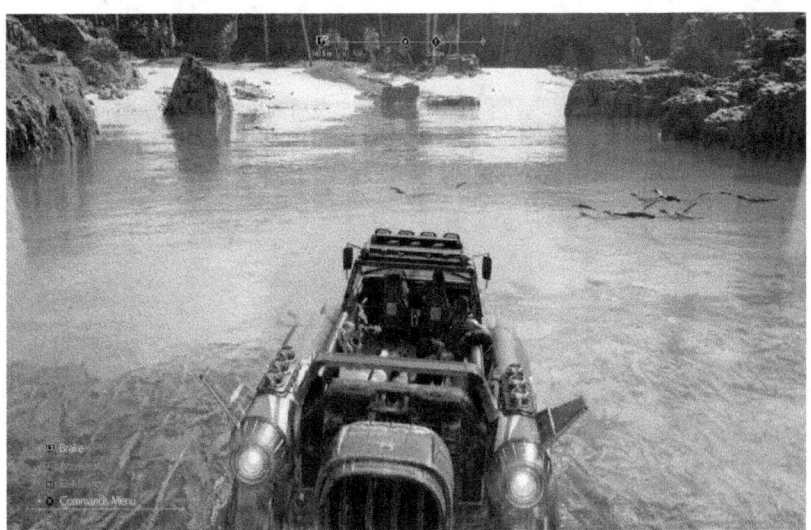

As the chapter begins, you'll find yourself riding in the Buggy, just enjoying the journey with no control over it. Sit tight, enjoy the scenery, and listen to the conversations. Soon enough, you'll take the reins of the Buggy and learn how to drive it. In this area, there are towers to activate and a Lifespring to discover. While there aren't any new side quests yet, you can revisit any old ones if you like.

NOTE:

- Remember, you'll need to use the grappling hook to activate the towers here.

When you feel prepared, head south toward the reactor. Once you arrive at the designated spot on the map, you'll enter the lush jungle of Gongaga. Explore this new terrain and activate towers to gather information. Follow the blue waypoint to reach the village mentioned by Cait Sith, located far to the south.

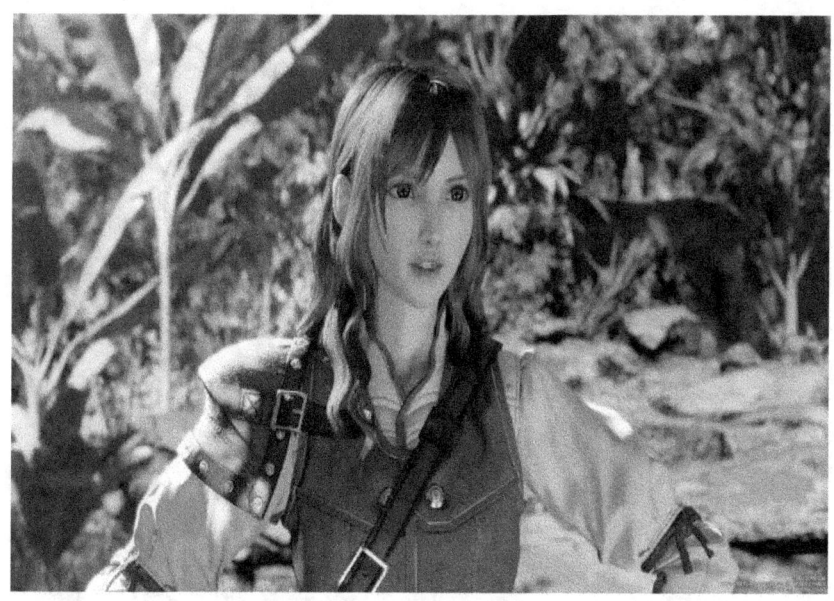

Upon reaching the village, you'll encounter a familiar face from Crisis Core, Cissnei, which triggers a cutscene. After that, follow Cissnei into the village. Inside a house with a rest station, you'll discover a chest containing a weapon for Yuffie. To advance the story, go to the house where Aerith enters, as shown in the image. Watch the cutscene and then talk to Aerith outside. During your conversation, you'll have the chance to comfort Aerith regarding Zack's parents. Afterward, head to Cissnei's house to rest. Approach the bed and select "Until it's time to leave" to move the story forward.

Investigating the Reactor:

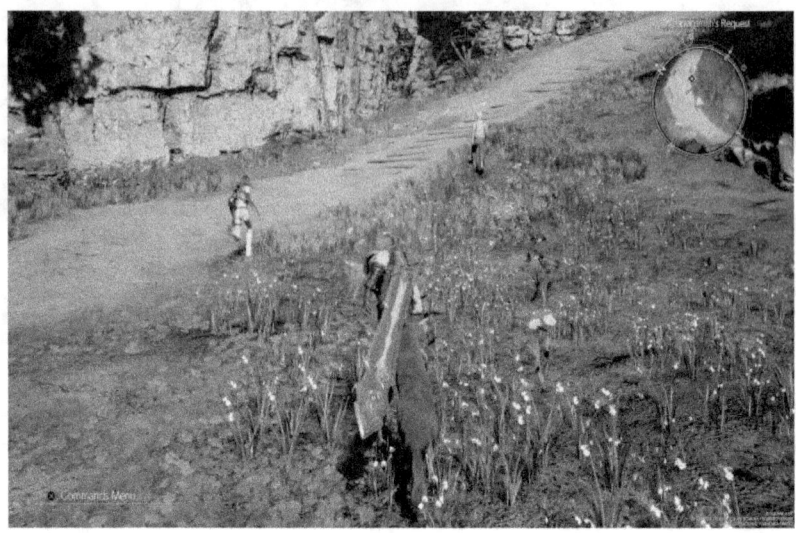

The calm moments are short-lived as Yuffie rushes in, alerting Cloud to an issue at the reactor. After the cutscene, head south toward the remains of the reactor. As you near the southern exit of the village, the guard allows you to pass.

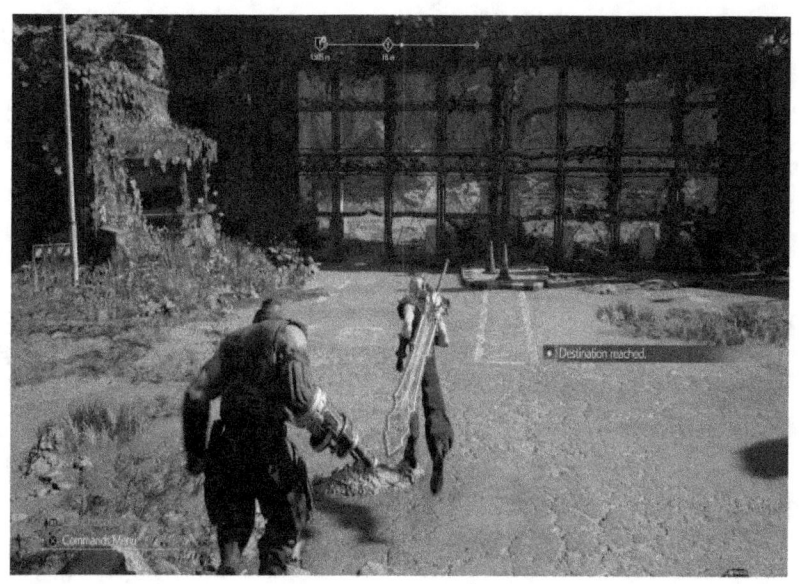

The reactor may seem close, but it's a bit of a journey. Along the way, you'll come across a tower that can be activated. Though it's optional, activating it rewards you with more Party EXP and provides valuable information for Chadley. Plus, it becomes a handy fast travel point later on. Upon reaching the reactor, slip under the hole in the gate on the left. After the cutscene, approach the vending machines.

To your right, you'll see stairs leading down into the facility. Descend and go through a long hallway that opens into a larger room with a small group of enemies. In the next room, check the right side to find a chest containing a weapon for Cloud.

After grabbing the loot, backtrack to the previous room and enter the partially open door. While exploring this area, you'll notice a Whisper flying down the hall to your left. Before chasing it, explore the right into a side room occupied by enemies. Look to your right to find a hole in the wall leading to another room with a chest. There's also a hole that allows you to drop back down into the hallway.

Restoring Power to the Door:

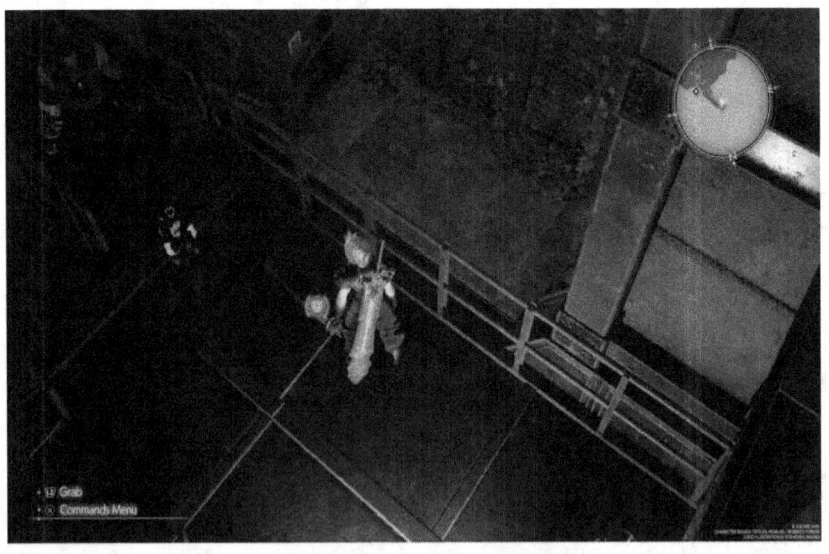

While on your path, keep an eye out to your right for some stairs leading downward. Go down them and cross the small water area that Barret and Cait Sith mentioned. About halfway, be prepared for a surprise attack from a group of small enemies. At the end of this passage, you'll see a terminal, but unfortunately, it's out of power.

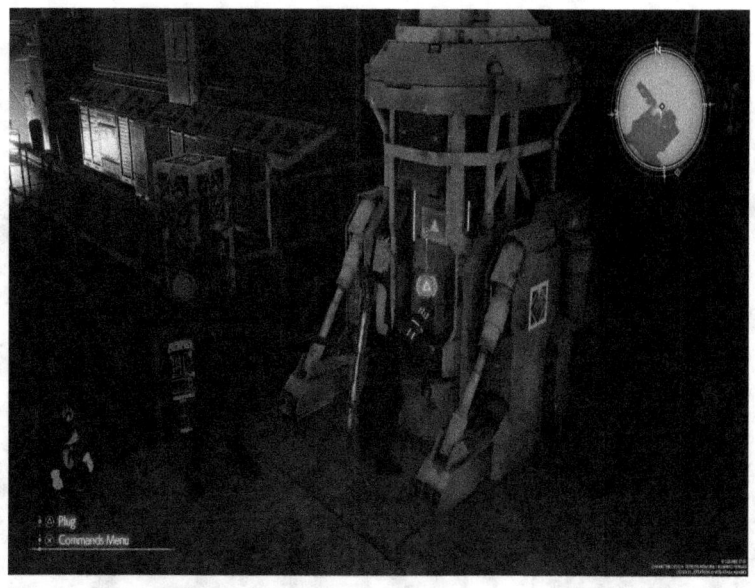

To fix this, head left up the platform and grab the cable lying on the ground. Hold down L2 to pick it up (keep holding L2 or you'll drop the cable) and carry it to the terminal. Press the Triangle button to insert the cable, and the door will unlock. On the other side, you'll see three Whispers flying away. Go through the left door to get past the barricade.

Once past the barricade, go straight down the hallway ahead. In the next room, you'll face a couple of Grandhorns on a raised platform. Beat them and cross the broken walkway where more Whispers might appear.

Raising the Water Level:

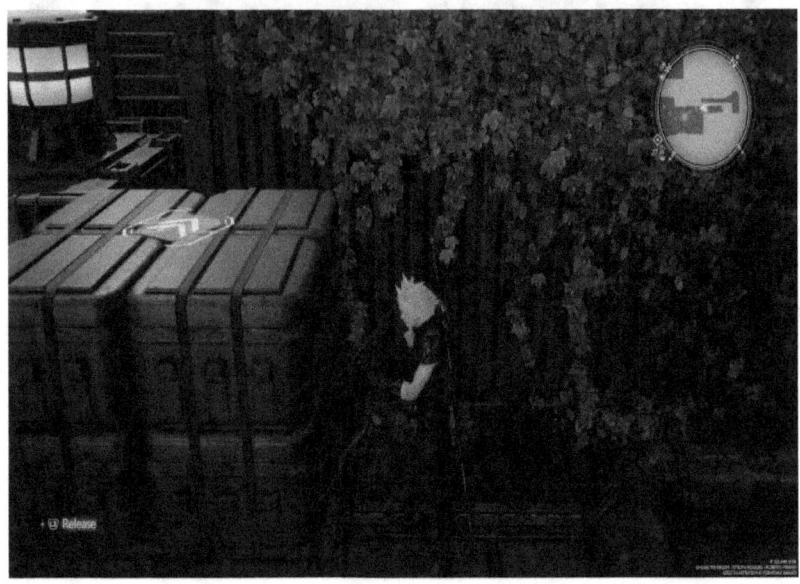

Descend the ladder and swim left toward another ladder. Climb it and then go up a set of stairs to find a partially open door. This door leads to the control room with another powerless terminal. You'll see a cable on the left, hidden behind a box. Go to the box and hold down L2 to move it.

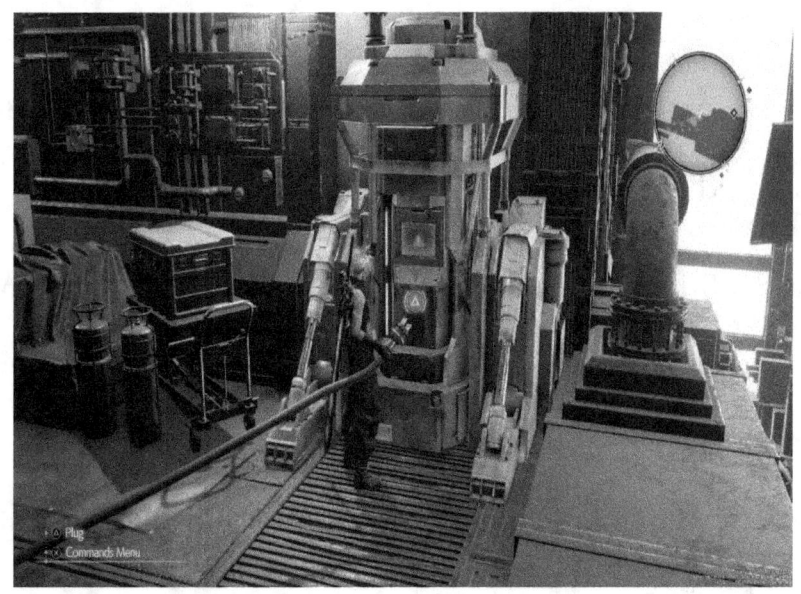

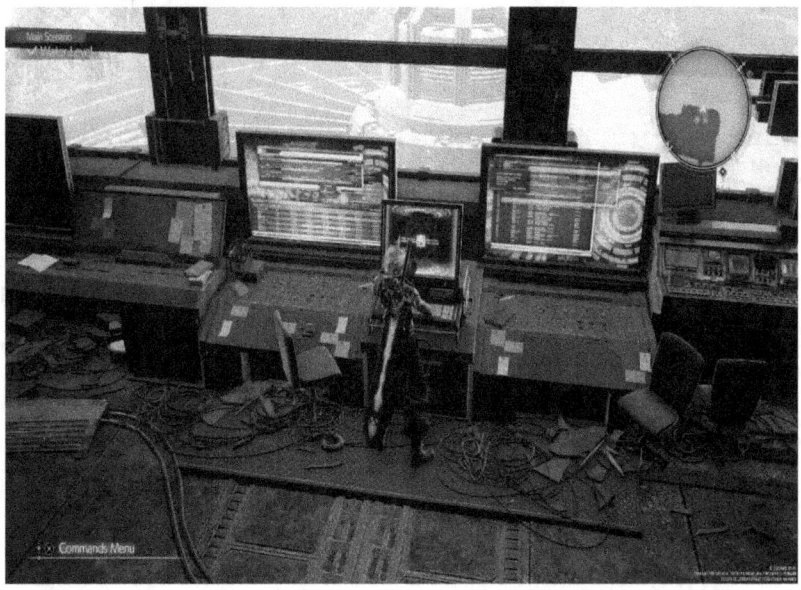

This lets you grab the cable and connect it to the generator nearby. Return to the box and climb it to access a small side area with a chest containing a Golden Collar for Red XIII. Go back to the control room and activate the console next to the large window. Descend back down, allowing you to swim to where you saw the Whispers earlier.

This path leads to a rest station and some vending machines. Take a break here and make use of the amenities, and don't forget to pick up the green materia in the corner. When you're ready, continue down the other part of the hallway leading outside.

Right after the cutscene, you'll face a couple of Amalgams. Despite their frightening appearance, they're not too tough, and they're weak against fire. When they release spores, step back and wait for the cloud around them to disappear. After defeating them, jump across to the next platform where three more Amalgams will attack you. Once you defeat them, get ready for a real challenge.

Defeating Specimen H1024:

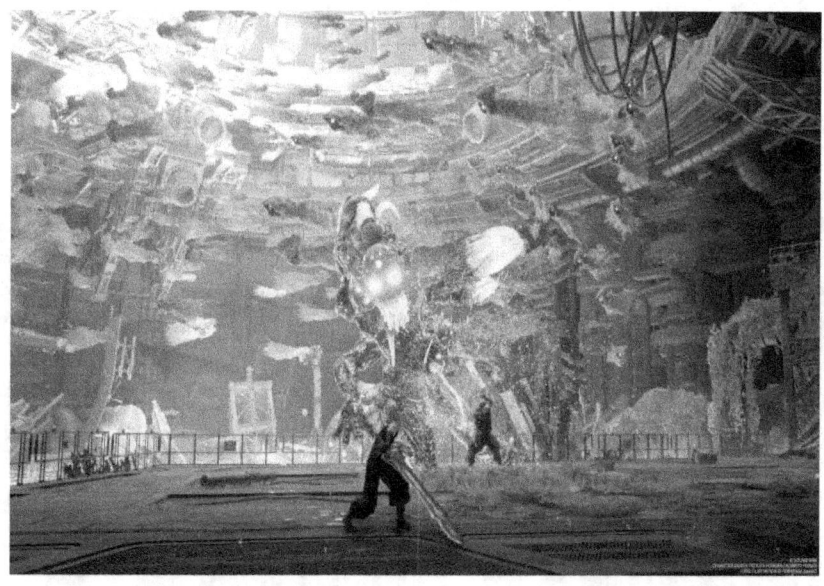

Hojo always creates terrifying monsters to stop you, and Specimen H1024 is no exception. This beast is weak against ice damage. When the boss triggers Mako Expulsion, move away to avoid the blast. Keep hitting it with ice attacks to pressure and stagger it. Then, when staggered, use any active Limit Breaks and Synergy Abilities.

When the boss's health drops to 50%, there will be a cinematic, and the fight will resume. The boss doesn't introduce any new tactics in this phase, but it seems more vulnerable to pressure.

As its health goes down, it gets more aggressive. Make sure you save some ATB actions for healing as the battle comes to an end.

Fast Travel with Chocobos:

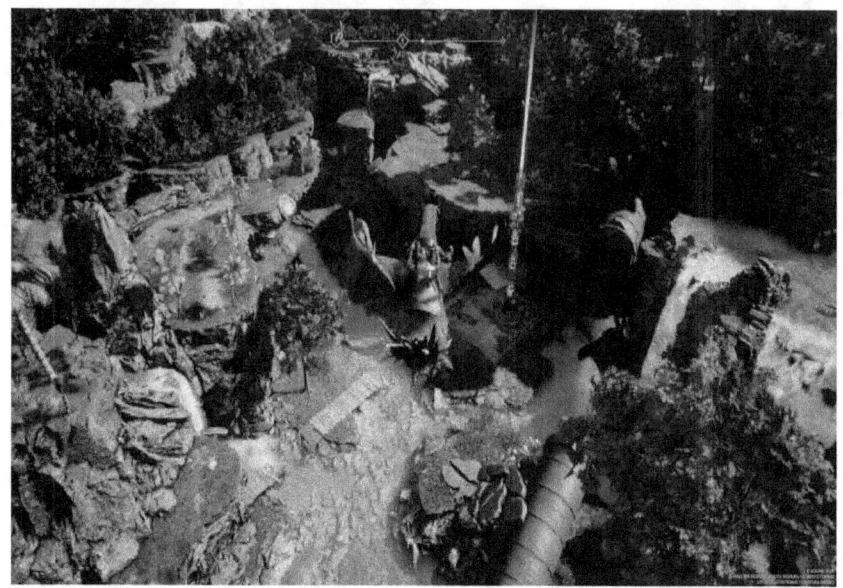

After the battle, control switches to Tifa and the others. Follow Cissnei to where the chocobos are. Thanks to their ability to jump on mushrooms, you'll get to the reactor much faster than the other group did. When you arrive, take care of the Shinra forces guarding the entrance.

Equipped with grappling guns from Cissnei, you'll easily overcome obstacles. Go down into the reactor using the stairs past the vending machines, just like Cloud and the others did.

Continue until you reach the water-filled hallway. Swim to the next platform, then turn back and use the grappling gun to go up to the next floor.

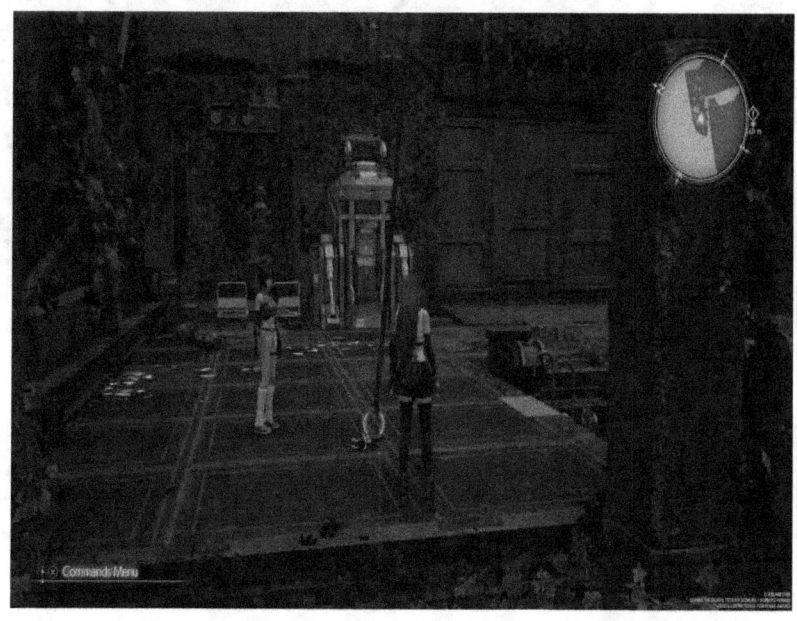

Look for chances to go up further. Eventually, you'll get to a big room with enemies and another powerless generator. The cable can't reach the generator in its current position, so look to the right and use the grappling gun to reach the next floor. Beat the enemies ahead, then go back to find another grappling gun spot leading up another level. On this walkway, use the grappling gun to reach a platform connected to the power source by a cable.

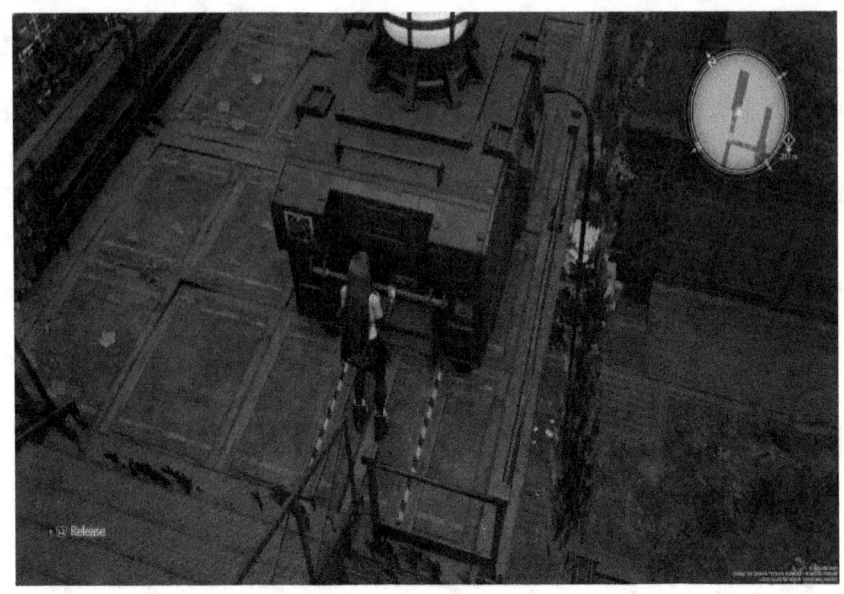

Push the power source along the track, then use the nearby rope to go down. Pick up the cable and insert it into the generator to open the door. Use the grappling gun to go up to the next area, where a big group of Shinra forces is waiting. Focus on taking out the Riot Troopers first, as they'll protect other soldiers from your attacks.

After dealing with Shinra, go left through the overgrown ruins and use the grappling gun to get to the top of a rusty platform. Drop down onto the circular platform and defeat the robot enemies patrolling it. The path forward is clear from here, using the grappling gun as needed. When you reach the rest station area, defeat the robots and use the vending machines if needed. When you're ready to move on, use the grappling gun to go up to the next area quickly, as Shinra helicopters will be shooting at you.

How to Beat Crimson Mare Mk. II:

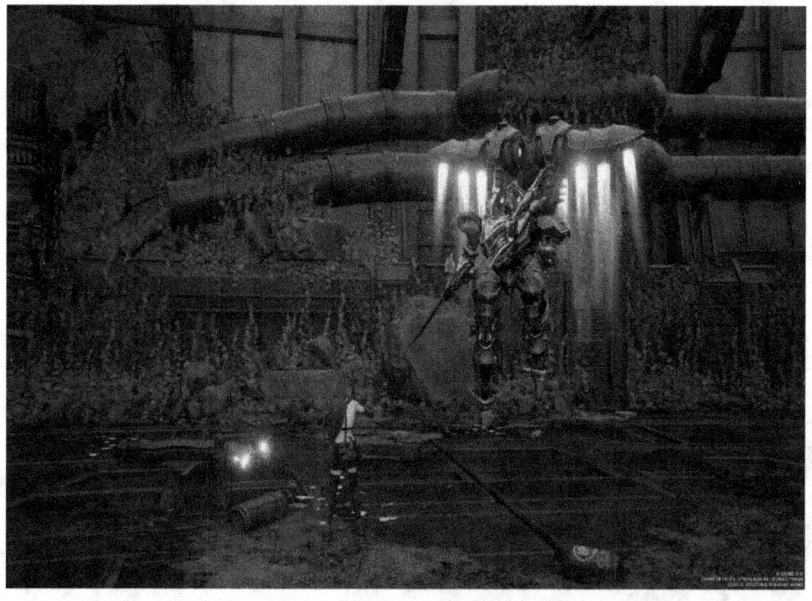

Right from the start, focus your attacks on the hand sabers of Crimson Mare Mk. II. This boss is weak against electricity, so use Thunder or Thundara spells whenever you can. As the battle goes on, the boss will start using makocannons instead of sabers. Make sure to destroy these too, as it will put more pressure on the boss. Once you've taken out enough arms, staggering the boss becomes much easier.

After Crimson Mare Mk. II recovers from being staggered, it'll gain two new arms. These gauntlets detach occasionally and fly around the arena. Concentrate on dodging their attacks because even if you manage to hit them, they can still hurt you up close. Destroy the arms and focus on defeating the boss. After the boss battle, Tifa will be alone. Quickly climb the platform and use the grappling gun to reach her. Then, a cutscene will follow.

Remembering the Past:

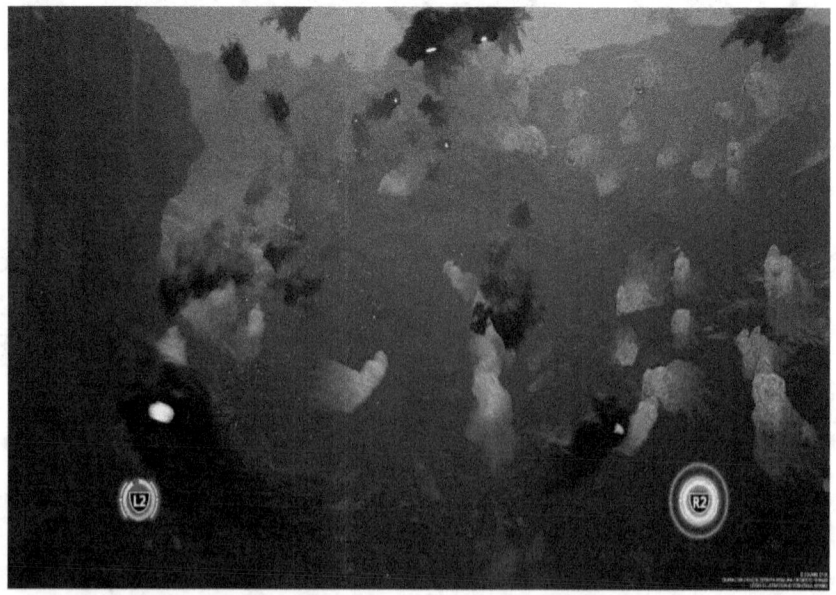

Despite the captivating visuals and light show during the following cutscene, stay focused. When two types of Whispers appear, hold down L2 and R2 together. Shortly after, floating buildings will appear. Focus on them and hold down the Triangle button to see memories unfold. Keep repeating this until you move to the next area. Follow the instructions to hold down L2 and R2 when needed. After that, you'll go back to Cloud's perspective.

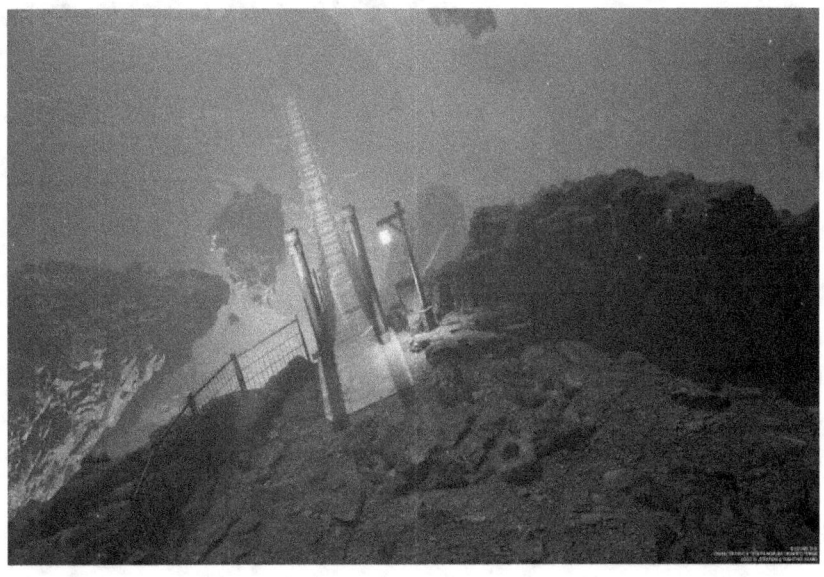

Approach the Weapon slowly. After another cutscene, Cloud and the others find themselves back in Gongaga village. Leave the room and regroup with the others. After the next cutscene, you can head south to exit the village and continue the story. Or, if you want, you can spend some time on side quests.

Taking Flight:

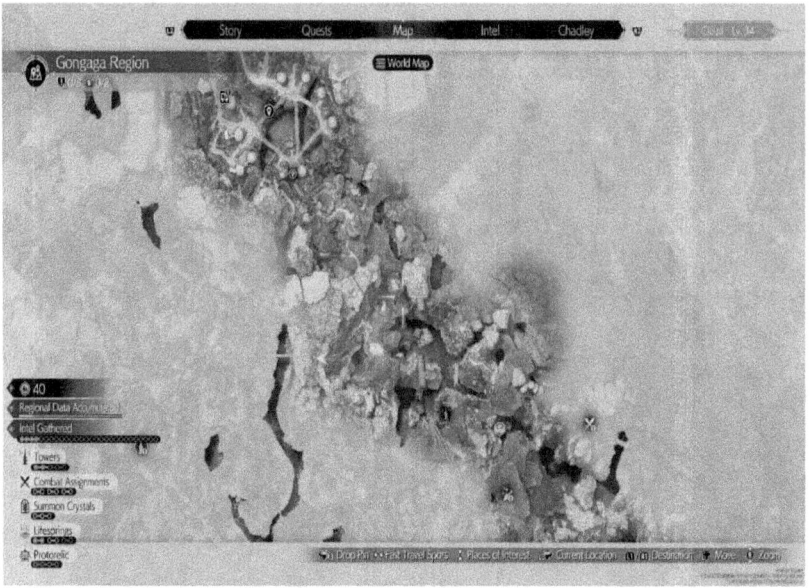

When you're ready to leave, go through the gate on the south side of the village toward the freeflier pilot. Follow the path shown in the image above. It will take you across a bridge and along a trail until you reach a mushroom where your chocobo can bounce off. Continue to the Verdant Plateau Tower, heading northwest until you reach your destination.

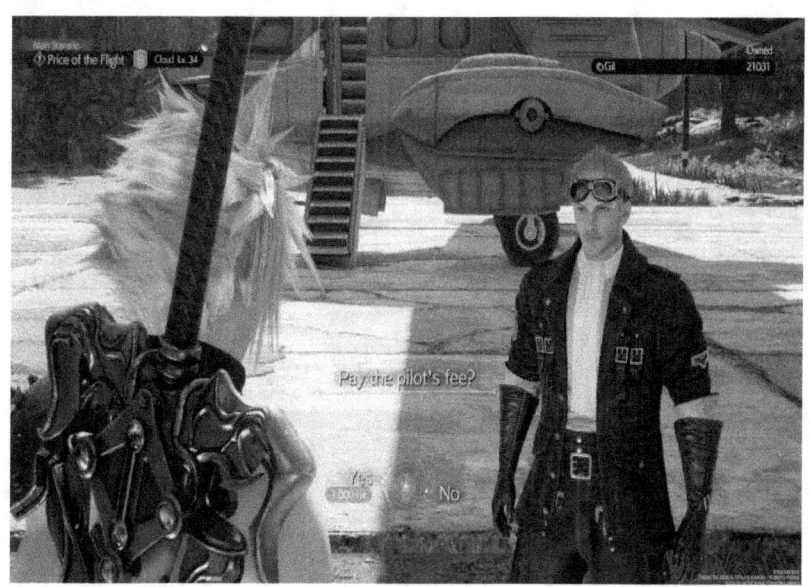

Once you reach the airstrip, approach the random phone booth in the middle of the area. Use it to start a cutscene. Pay the pilot, Cid, 1,000 gil, and he'll agree to help the party. After the cutscene, you'll control the airplane using the motion controls of the PS5 controller. You can maneuver the plane, but you don't have complete control over its direction. Once you've landed the plane, the current chapter ends, and the tenth one begins.

CHAPTER TEN

WATCHER OF THE VALE

Every place you visit in Final Fantasy 7 Rebirth is special and full of things to find. After leaving Gongaga behind in the last chapter, your next stop is Cosmo Canyon. Here, you'll discover the famous planetarium and where Red XIII grew up. While there are a few side tasks you can do here, most of them only unlock after you've made some progress in this chapter. Here's what's waiting for you as you start Chapter 10: Watcher of the Vale.

Welcome to Cosmo Canyon:

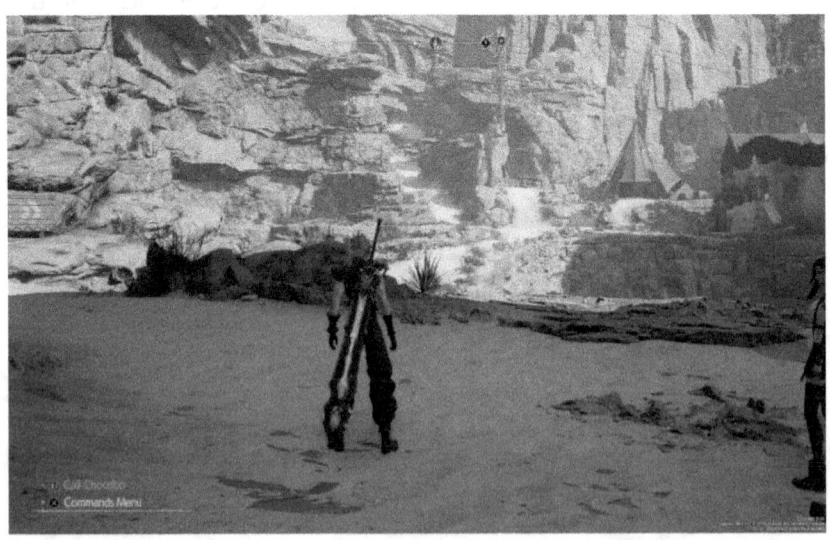

Chapter ten begins as Cid's airship takes off. Your first job is to head towards the tower in the north. Since it's on your way to your main destination, it's smart to activate it. Activating the tower also shows you where to catch the Cosmo Canyon chocobo. Follow the signs pointing you to Cosmo Canyon to move the story forward. Before long, you'll see Cosmo Canyon on the horizon. Go down the path and cross the bridge to start a cutscene. At this point, you can't fast travel, and Red XIII leaves the party for a while. Explore the village, climb the stairs, and check out the shops for supplies or gear you might need. Later on, there's another cutscene waiting for you.

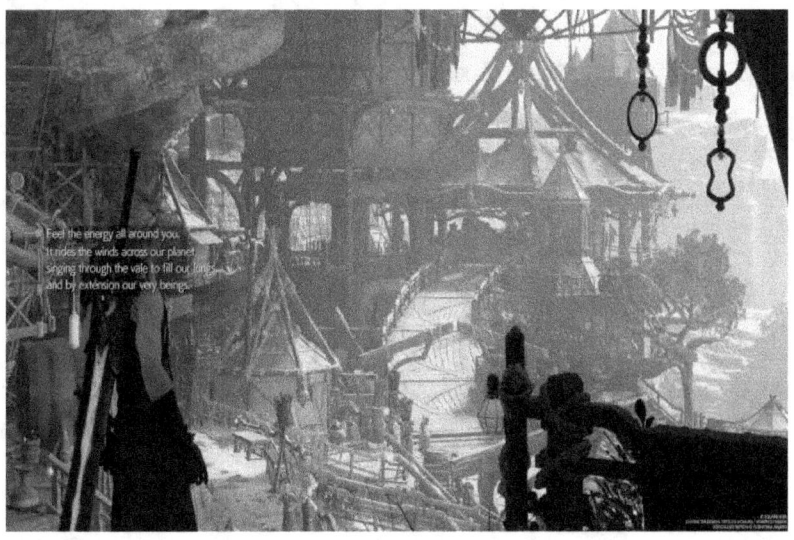

Head towards the planetarium. Use the elevator and hold down the Triangle button to go up. Once you're at the top, follow the walkway until you find Red XIII.

The Planetarium:

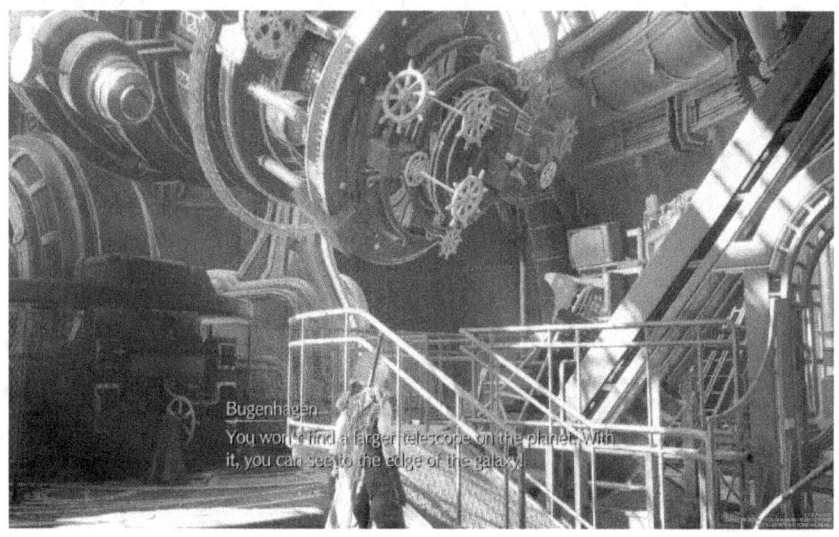

Go into the planetarium and have a look around. Check out the objects scattered around the room. You'll find more things to interact with on the second floor. There are double doors on the second floor that you can't open until you've looked around the planetarium, including the third and fourth floors.

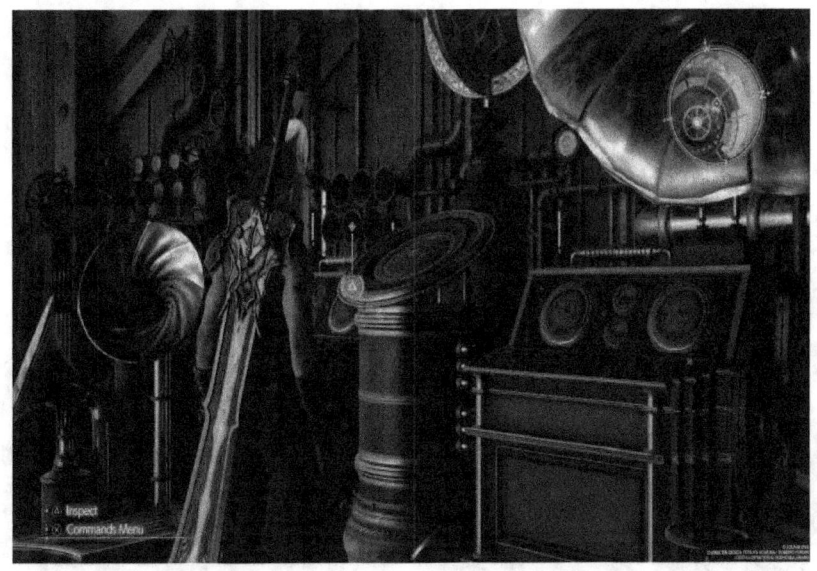

Once you've checked everything out, go downstairs to the second floor and check the device that made a noise. This will unlock the room beyond the double doors. After the cutscene, leave the planetarium and talk to the attendant who lets you into the storeroom. Inside, you'll find valuable items, including a new weapon for Cait Sith.

Go back to the elevator and go down. As you walk along the street after getting off the elevator, an attendant will come up to you and ask you to follow them. Eventually, you'll find a group gathered in a circle. After the cutscene, go down to the plaza where everyone is. To move the story forward, talk to Aerith by the bonfire. You can also talk to your other party members to strengthen your bond with them.

Follow Bugenhagen:

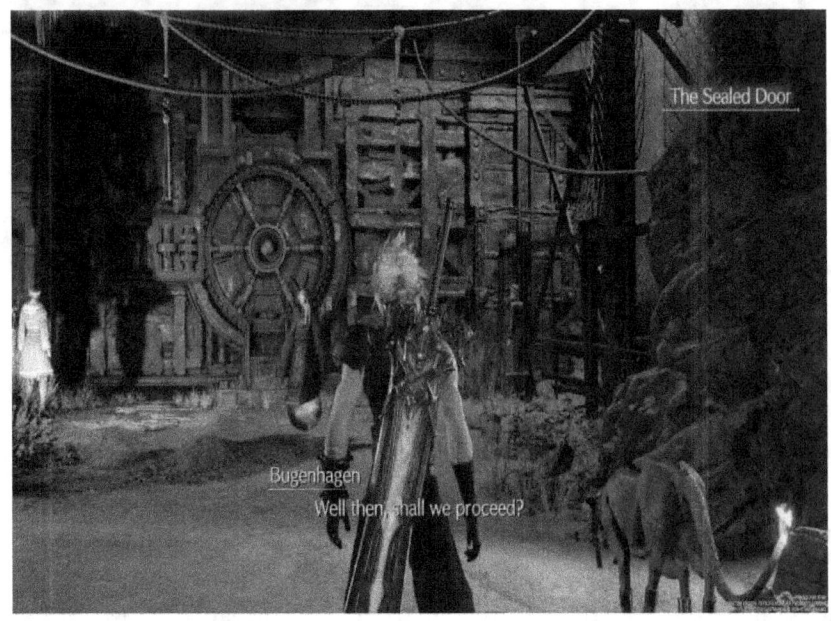

After the cutscene, follow Bugenhagen to a section that's been sealed off. Let Bugenhagen know when you're ready to go on, and he'll open the door. Follow him and get on the elevator. After getting off the elevator, your party will change, leaving you with only Barret and Red XIII. If you need to, use the vending machines before going deeper into the cave.

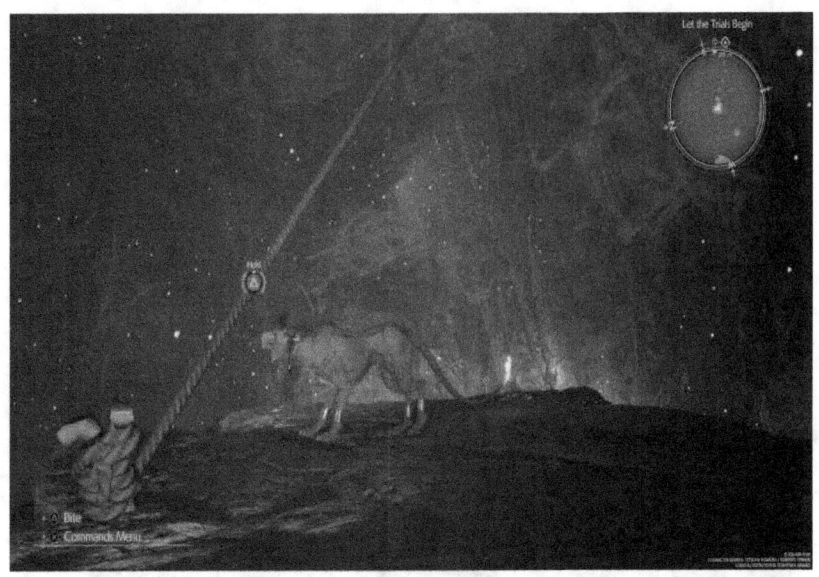

After defeating a group of enemies, you'll learn how to climb glowing walls as Red XIII. Look to the west and climb up the wall. This lets you get past the rocks and go further into the tunnel. Keep going south until you find a big stone door tied with rope. To open it, climb the nearby pillar and hold down the Triangle button to cut the rope holding the door shut.

The Trial Begins:

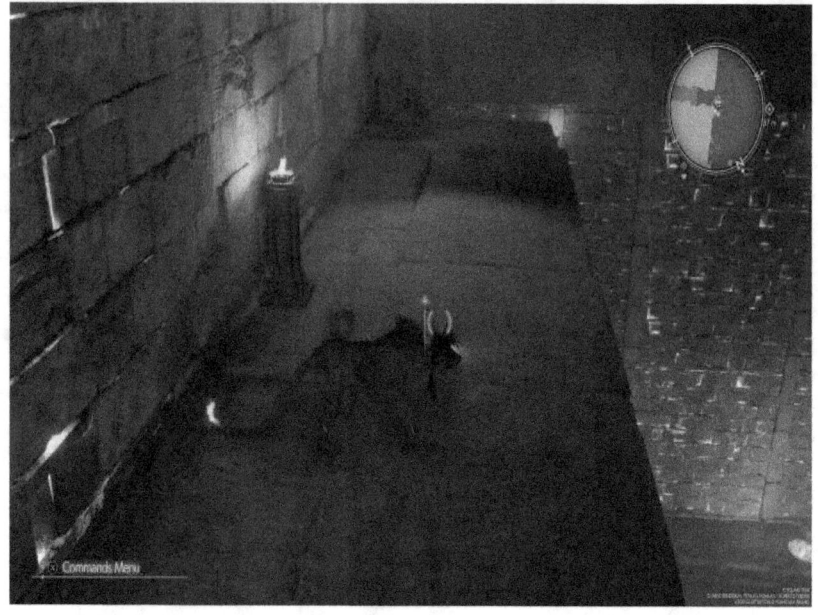

Enter the next area through the door. In front of you, there's a long flight of stairs going down. Go down all the way and pass through the doorway. Approach the statue to start a cutscene. To progress, you'll need to find artifacts and bring them back to Bugenhagen. Once you're in the circle, place the artifact. If it's not the right one, keep searching.

On the right wall is an artifact that, when found, turns into healing materia. The correct artifact is on a ledge directly behind the statue. After bringing it to Bugenhagen, a cutscene and battle will happen. When the battle ends, pick up the statue and take it into the next room. When you reach a ramp leading to a chamber with four podiums, take the artifact down there.

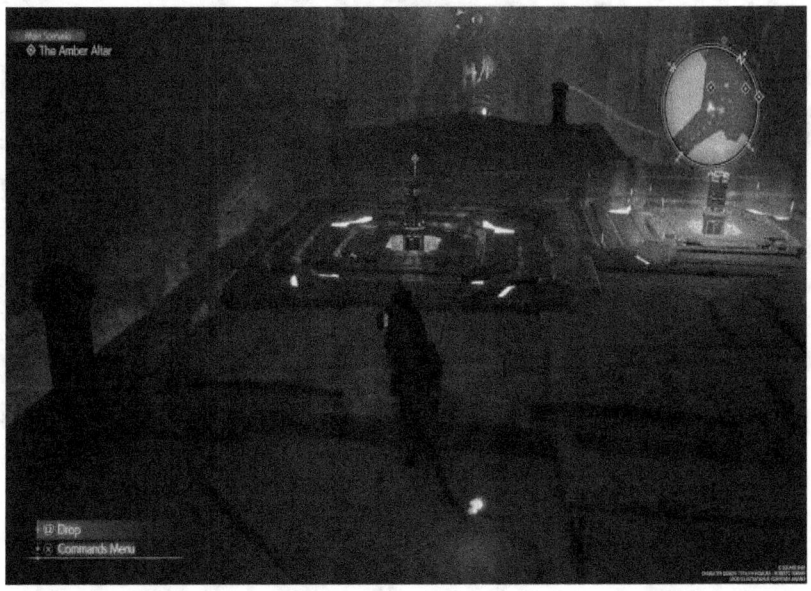

Put the statue on the leftmost podium and press Triangle to position it. Then, go to the right and get the yellow statue for the yellow podium. After that, go down a path to the right. Use the rock wall to get to another passage, remembering that Red XIII must go alone. Approach the altar and get the last statue. As you leave, one of the statues will come to life. Beat it and continue carrying the statue back to the last podium.

Once all four statues are in place, the door will open. This was just the first trial; more are waiting beyond.

Pass the Gates:

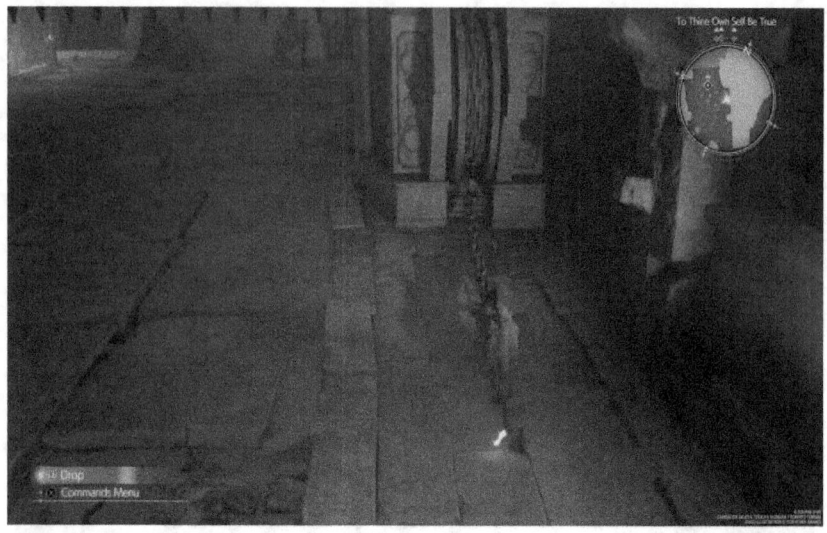

In this new area, go down multiple sets of stairs, defeating any enemies you encounter. Eventually, you'll reach the first gate. To open it, go to the right and lift the chain by holding L2. Once the gate is fully raised, it will stay open. Go forward and face the reanimated Gi statues.

Go down the left stairs and approach the chain. Pull it all the way to create a bridge across to the other side. Follow the path up and climb the wall after grabbing the chest containing three Gold Needles. Soon, you'll reach the second gate, which opens like the first.

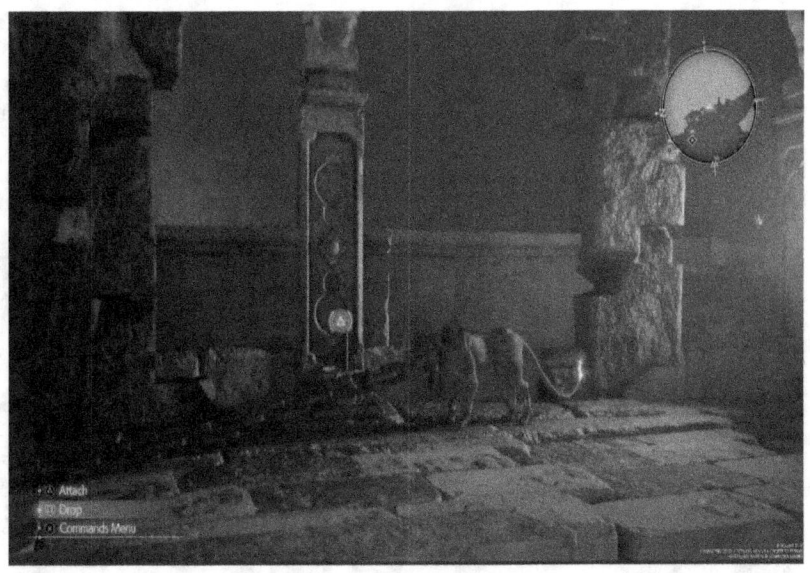

The gate's locking mechanism is broken, so pull the chain back and then press Triangle to fasten it to a nearby metal pole. Go through the open gate and defeat the awaiting Gi. Keep moving forward and climb the wall or walk up the ramp to start a cutscene.

Pull the chain all the way and cross the extended platform. Climb the wall and pull another chain. This will unlock another platform below, leading to the next gate. Climb the wall on the left and break open the boxes for some easy items.

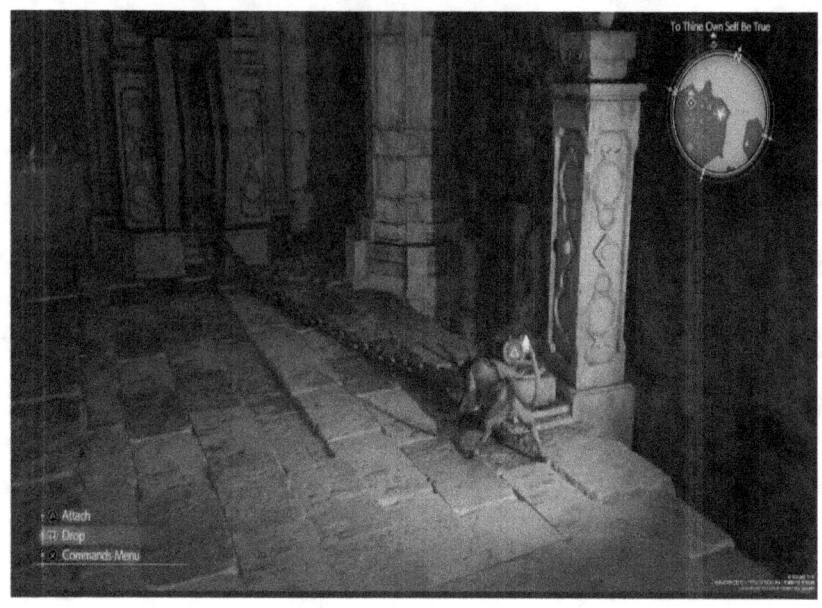

For the next gate, the metal pole needed to attach the chain is missing. Find it on the left side of the gate. Insert the hook, grab the chain, and attach it to the hook to open the gate. Once through, you'll find a rest station and vending machines. Take this chance to prepare, as a tough challenge lies ahead.

Defeating Gi Nattak:

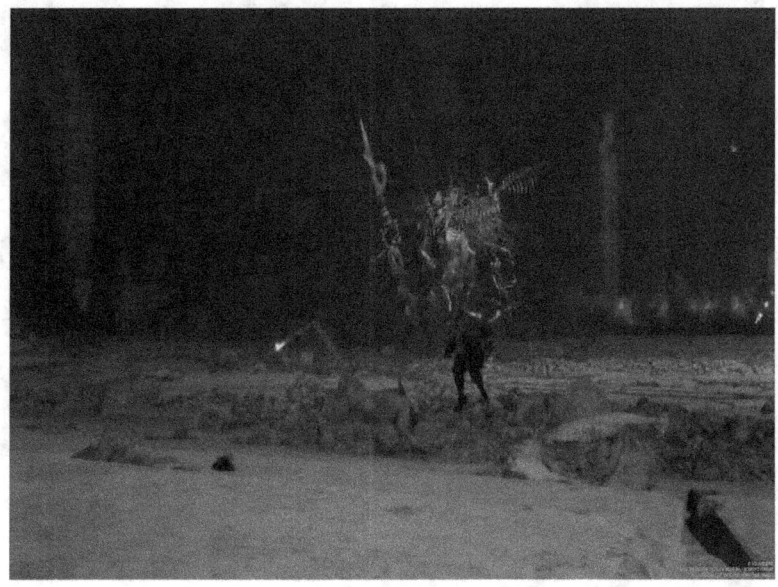

Gi Nattak is a tricky opponent, constantly teleporting around, which makes it hard to land hits. Unfortunately, there are no specific weaknesses to exploit. It's best to control Barret during this battle because Red XIII struggles to hit this boss effectively. When Gi Nattak uses Phantasmal Scourge, it sends homing energy bolts into the air. Try to dodge them as best you can and avoid trying to block them.

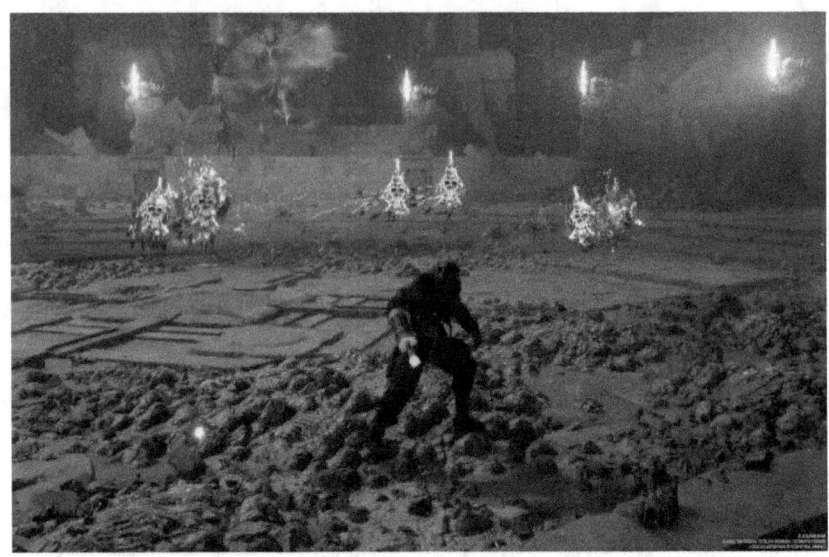

As the battle goes on, Gi Nattak will summon Soul Flames that cast Fira. It's crucial to eliminate them quickly to minimize the damage they inflict. Additionally, Gi Nattak will possess one of these Soul Flames, cursing a party member with effects like Halve HP, Halve MP, Deplete ATB, or shrinking the battlefield.

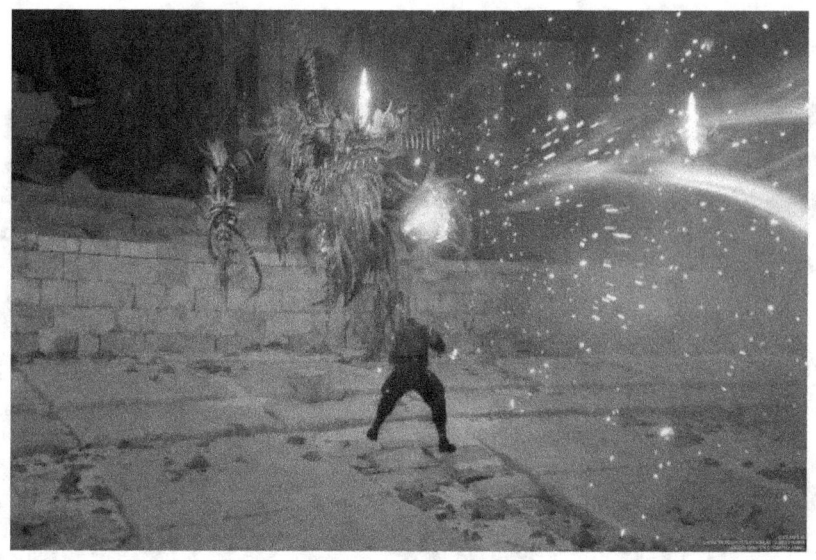

When Gi Nattak's health drops below 20%, it casts Doom on the entire party, giving you limited time to defeat it before succumbing to the doom counter.

NOTE:

- The Doom timer continues ticking down while you're selecting commands. If you need to strategize, pause the game to buy time.

Unleash all your attacks on the boss. Use Synergy Abilities, Summons—whatever it takes to defeat Gi Nattak swiftly. Time is of the essence in this battle. Once the fight ends, go through the door to proceed.

Following Gi Nattak:

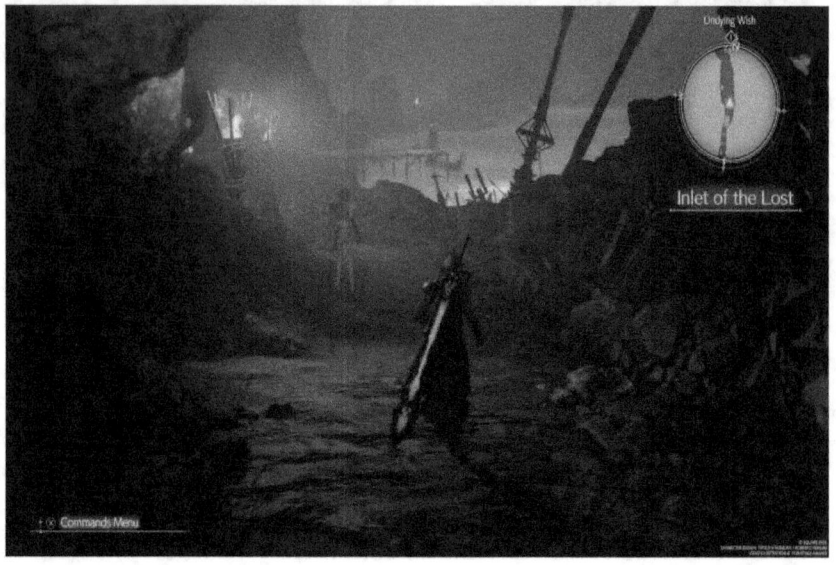

After the cutscene, regroup with the entire party. Head down the tunnel straight ahead to reach a dock where Gi Nattak awaits. While Cloud and the others board the boat, the scene shifts to Zack and Biggs discussing their circumstances. After this scene, follow Biggs outside the house. There's not much to explore during this segment, so focus on following Biggs and enjoying the cutscenes.

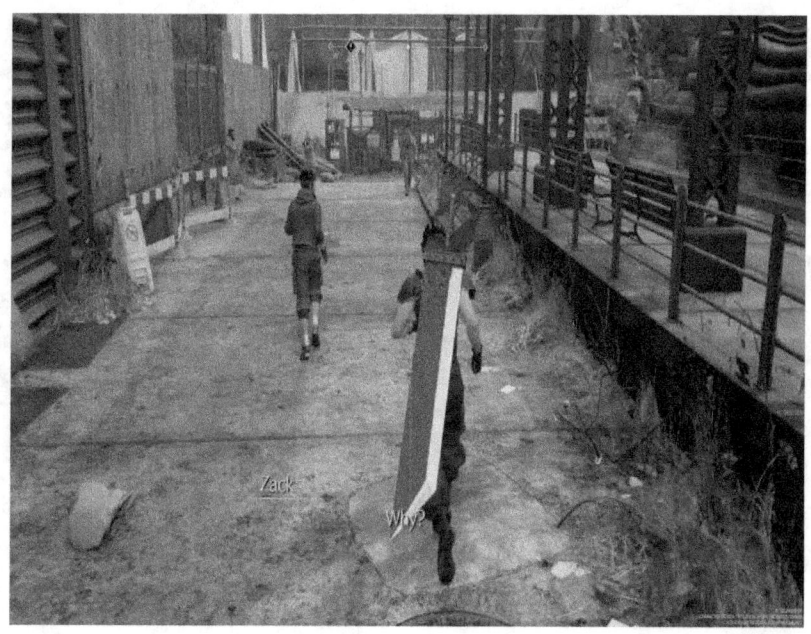

Once Biggs sets off alone, head down the alley directly ahead. Upon reaching Aerith's house, the scene will shift back to Cloud and the rest. To the left of the rest area lies a chest containing a weapon upgrade for Aerith. Use the vending machines if necessary, then proceed towards the statue ahead. Follow Yuffie as she eagerly leads the way.

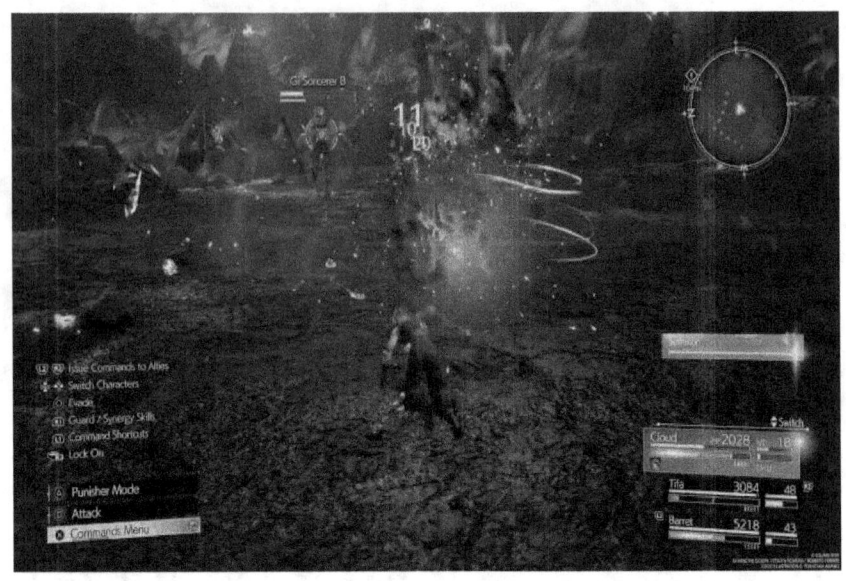

Confront the attacking Gi and continue following Yuffie, who seems to prioritize speed over caution. Defeat another group of Gi and proceed up the path. When facing a group of Gi, including two sorcerers, prioritize eliminating them quickly as they'll continuously revive any fallen Gi. Upon catching up with Gi Nattak, a cutscene ensues, and the party is transported back to where they began.

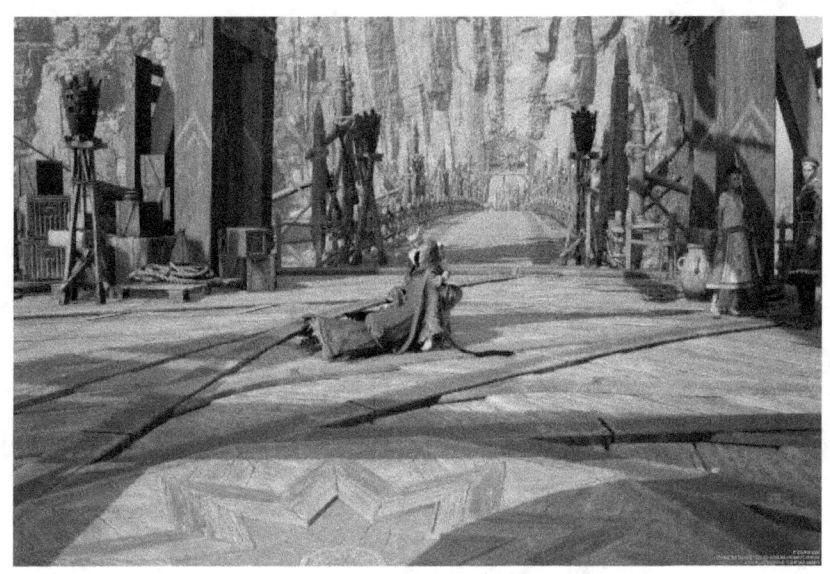

Return and use the elevator to ascend. There, you'll find Bugenhagen. Approach him to trigger a cutscene, then speak to one of the nearby guards for a quick return to the settlement entrance. Following a lead on the black-robed figures from an earlier chapter, one is discovered near the gate. Head to the entrance to trigger a cutscene. At this point, the community board may offer some side quests. Alternatively, to continue the main story, return to the airstrip.

Use the phone to summon Cid. Choose Nibelheim and enjoy the scenery as the Little Bronco transports you to your next destination and the subsequent chapter of Final Fantasy 7 Rebirth.

CHAPTER ELEVEN

THE LONG SHADOW OF SHINRA

After uncovering information about the Black Materia in the previous chapter of Final Fantasy 7 Rebirth, Cloud and the group learned from a mysterious figure in black robes that they must return to Nibelheim. However, upon arriving in Cloud and Tifa's hometown, they discover more than they anticipated. This chapter is longer, filled with numerous challenges, bosses, and unexpected twists. Here's what to anticipate as you embark on Chapter 11: The Long Shadow of Shinra.

Homecoming:

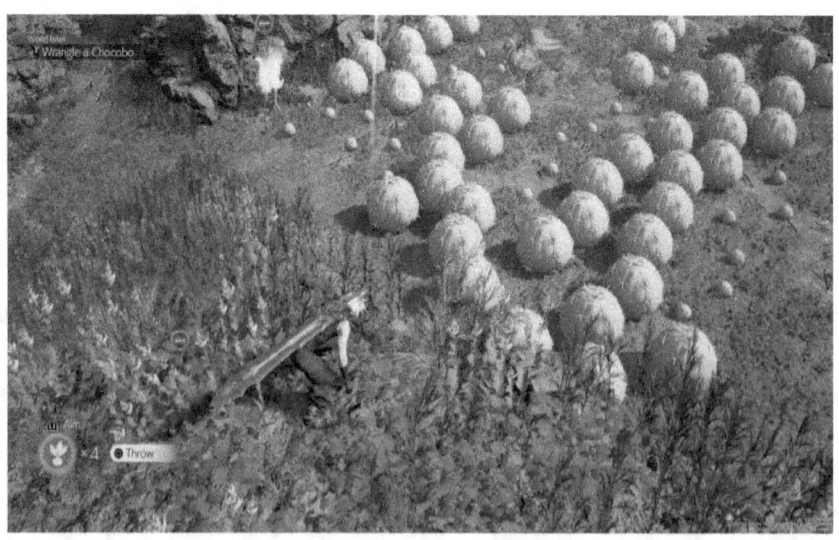

Since you're in a new area, consider taking some time to activate towers, gather information for Chadley, and explore before diving into the main story. As you approach the location marked by the blue waypoint, you'll notice something peculiar. Contrary to Cloud and Tifa's description, Nibelheim isn't just a pile of burnt ruins. Once the cutscene concludes, you'll have the chance to wander around Nibelheim and converse with your companions. To progress the storyline, head to the hotel. Go upstairs and open the door to initiate another cutscene. Keep chatting with your allies and locals until prompted to check in with Cait Sith. Make your way to the town hall and locate Cait Sith on the right, rummaging through the database.

Finding the Inspector:

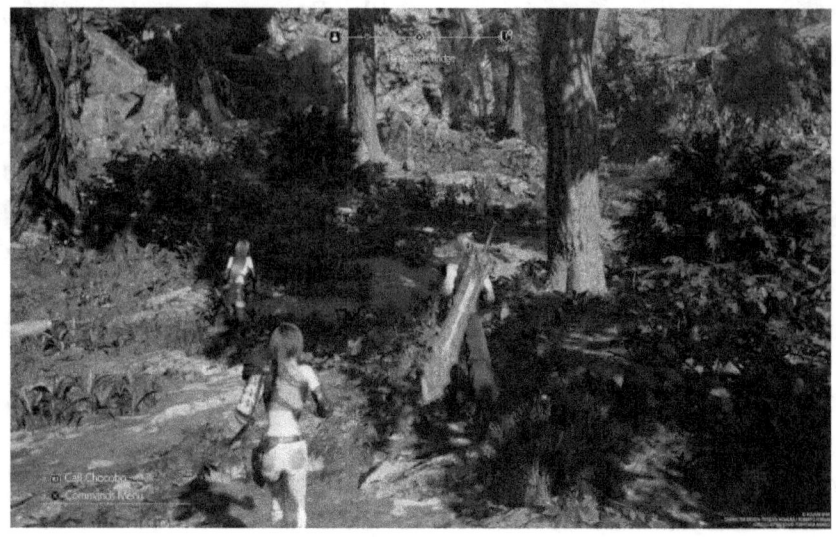

Unfortunately, Cait Sith wasn't able to find the information he needed. The only way to access the full database is by obtaining a keycard from Shinra Manor, but without it, entry is impossible. The person with the keycard is inspecting the reactor, so you'll need to locate him. After the cutscene, Tifa and Yuffie will join you. Follow the blue waypoint to reach a bridge that was previously inaccessible during the opening chapter of Final Fantasy 7 Rebirth. Once you cross the bridge, head left and loot the chest containing a weapon for Tifa. Proceed left across two sets of bridges. A rest area awaits to the left after the two bridges, with enemies to the right.

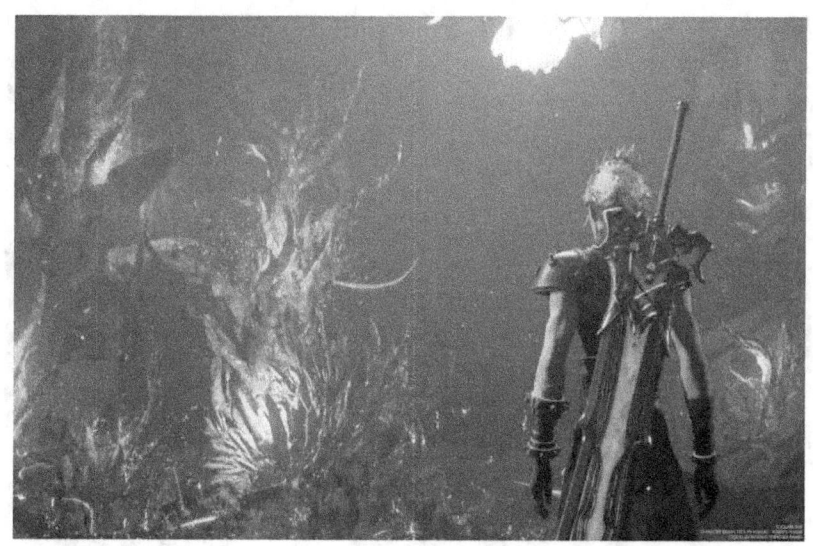

Defeat the enemies and enter the cave. As the cave expands, head southwest to another area. Here, you'll encounter the natural Materia seen during the first chapter. Move north from there. Eventually, you'll reach a climbable rock wall. The narrow path to the reactor is no longer available, but Yuffie uses her grappling hook to create a new route. Ascend the rope and continue up the mountain. Defeat the Zu and follow the path ahead. Soon, you'll reach a wide area guarded by two Screamers. Eliminate them and climb the rock wall. Move right to a platform containing a chest with a weapon for Cloud. After reaching the top of the first rock wall, encounter another one.

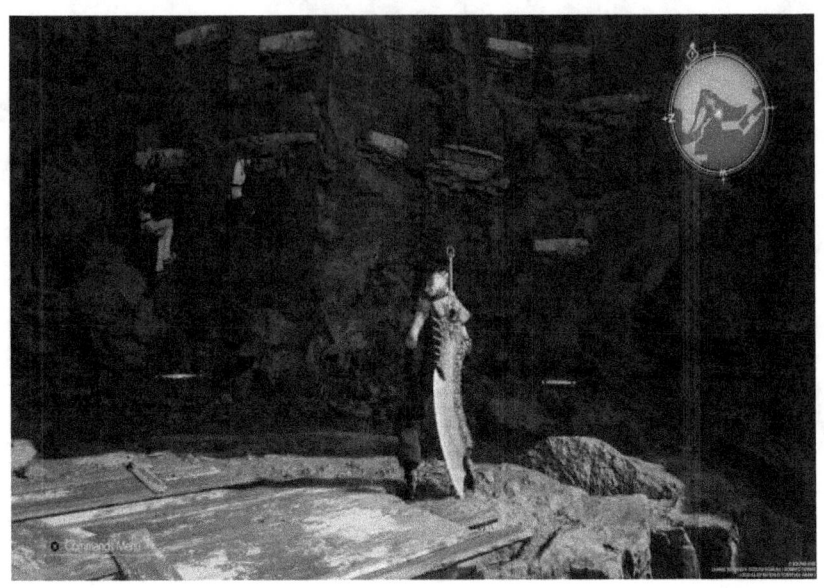

On this rock wall, you have two options. To the left, you'll find some materials to gather. To the right, you'll continue toward the reactor. As you climb, look for a small side path to the left with a chest containing an X-potion. Proceed up the mountain, encountering a Dragon guarding the entrance to a cave. This is more of a mini-boss than a full boss fight. Exploit its weakness to ice damage. After defeating the dragon, enter the cave to find an inoperable elevator and three pipes. Approach the pipes and descend. Although the pipes initially lead to different areas, they converge at another platform with additional pipes to descend.

How to Bypass the Locked Fence:

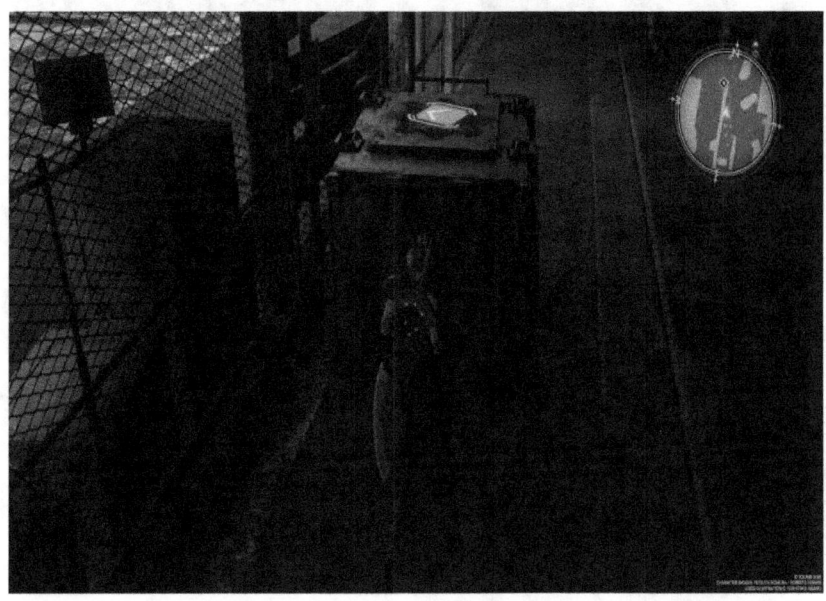

Continue descending until you arrive at an area blocked by a locked fence. To proceed, grab the movable box and push it until the blue symbol appears on top, indicating that it can be climbed. Follow the walkway until you reach an outdoor area. Although there's a terminal here, it's currently unusable since you lack the keycard.

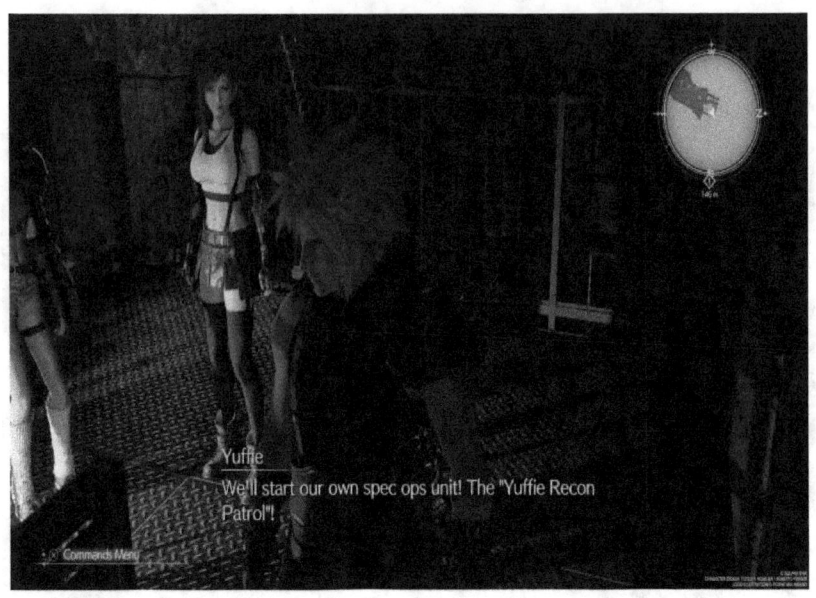

Instead, venture through the cave and head north. Shortly beyond, you'll encounter an elevator where Yuffie engages in lively chatter. Upon reaching the top, you'll arrive at the reactor. Take advantage of the rest area and vending machines before advancing. Enter the reactor and descend further using the elevator, where a boss fight awaits.

How to Defeat Diabolic Variant:

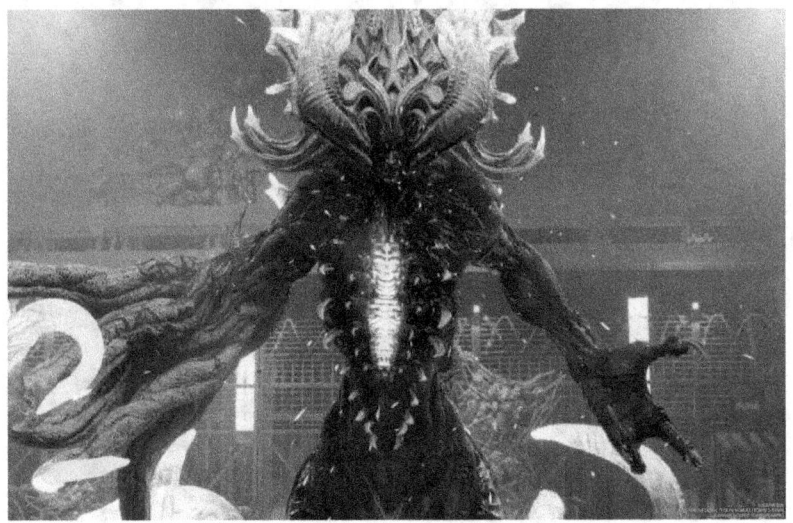

This formidable creature is vulnerable to ice damage. Equip Blizzara or Blizzard for this battle. At the beginning, target Diabolic Variant's tentacle arm to apply pressure. When it unleashes Ensnare, move away, as this attack cannot be blocked. Be prepared for the heavy damage inflicted by Firaga, which Diabolic Variant casts periodically.

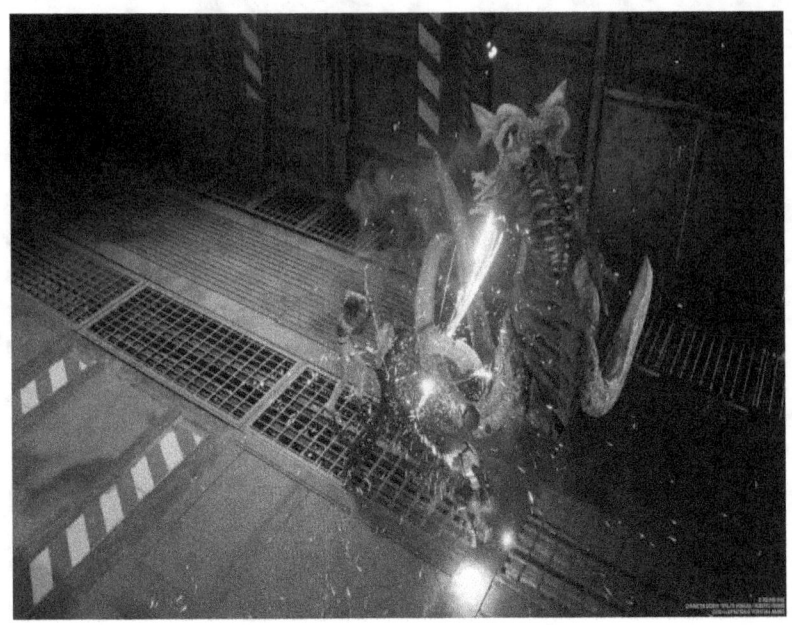

When Diabolic Variant employs Enshadow, the area will be enveloped in a dark, poisonous mist. The boss will then split into two versions. Focus your attacks on the one with either lower arm health or higher pressure. Once one version is staggered, concentrate on damaging it until it's destroyed. Although another copy will spawn, it too becomes staggered when the original does.

Onward and Downward:

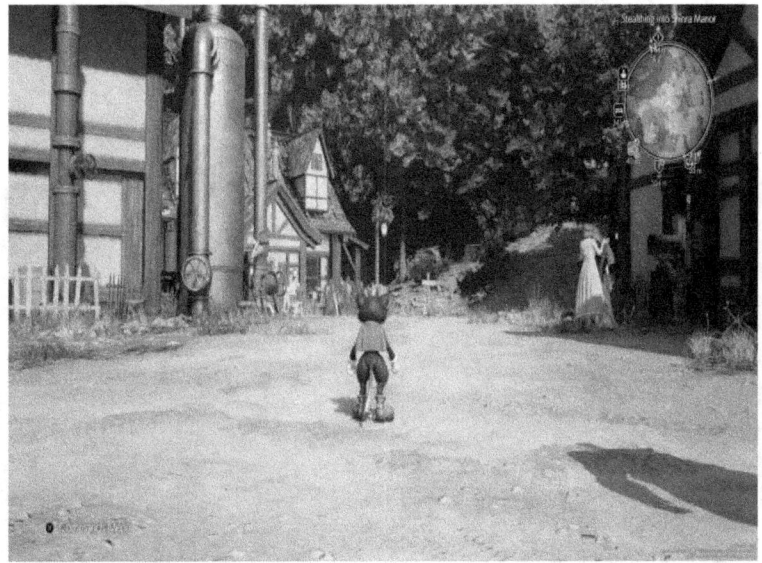

After defeating the boss, proceed through the door and descend the ladder. Before long, you'll reach the room where Sephiroth discovered Jenova. Approach the open doorway to locate the keycard. Following the cutscene, control switches to Cait Sith, Barret, and Aerith.

Head north towards Shinra Manor. Outside the manor's gate, conveniently placed rest stations and vending machines allow for restocking. Once prepared, enter the manor through the gate and turn left to access the room with the elevator. Use the elevator to descend to the basement. However, the plan to locate the terminal quickly goes awry.

Cait Sith to the Rescue:

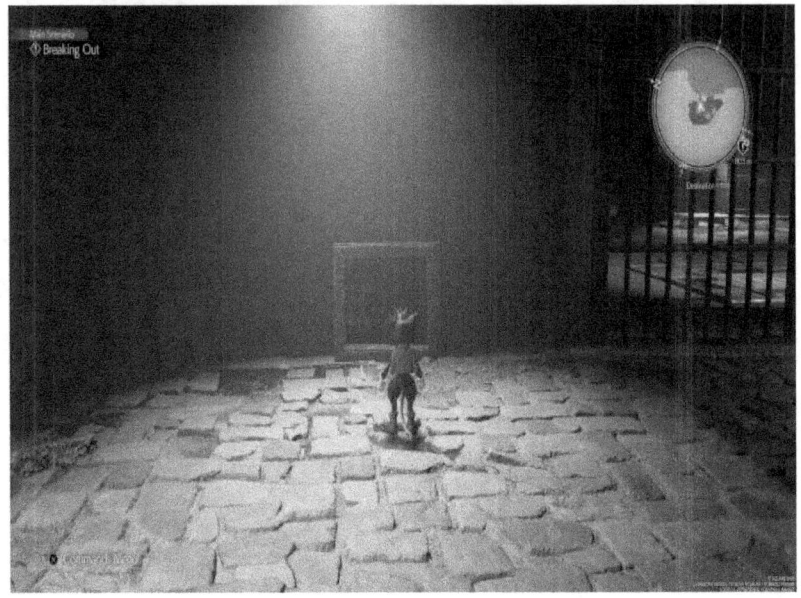

The group finds themselves trapped in a cell, except for Cait Sith, who can navigate through the nearby air duct. Approach the air duct and press R2 to roll through it. Enter the next room and defeat the enemy guarding the prison cell. Following that, receive a tutorial on summoning the moogle to assist with moving boxes and other tasks too challenging for Cait Sith.

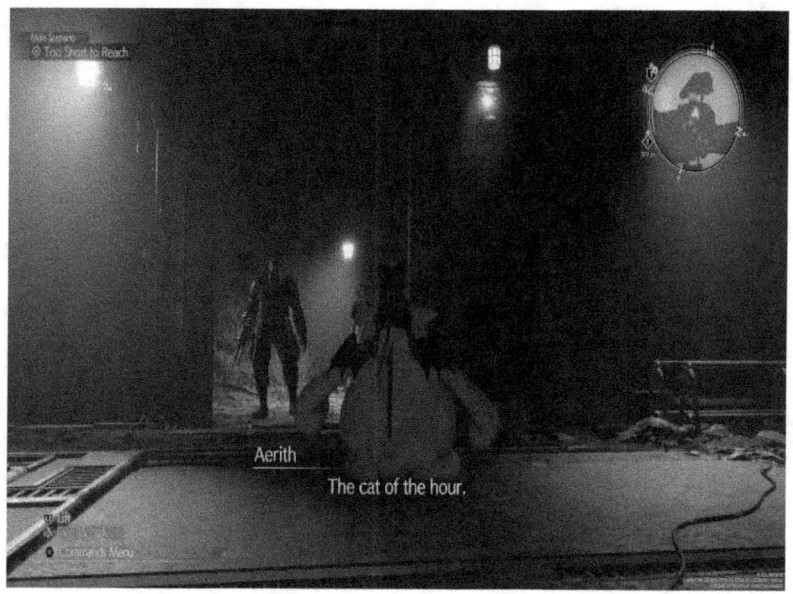

Grab one of the nearby boxes and aim it at the small electric box above the jail cell on the right. If needed, the switch on the floor generates additional boxes if you run out. Once Aerith and Barret are freed, grab another box and throw it at the box on the left side of the room. This action opens a door leading to a chest containing a weapon for Cait Sith.

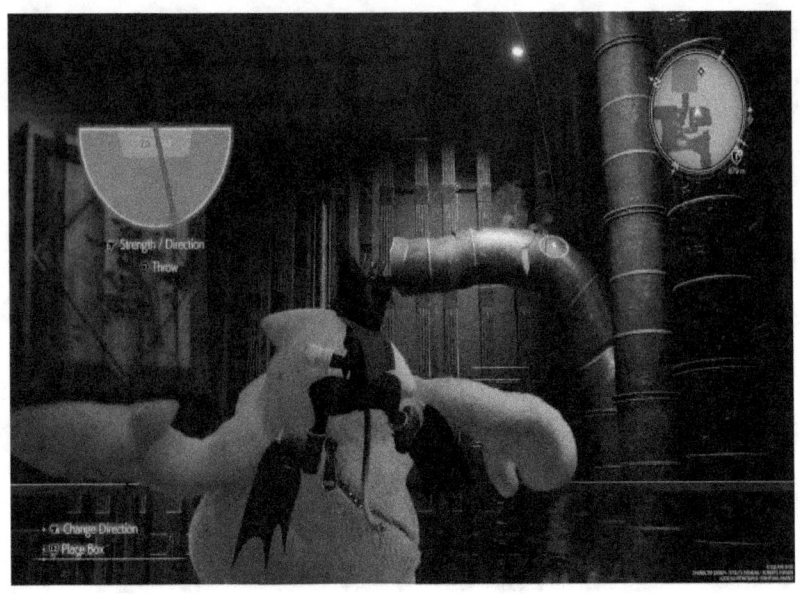

Proceed down the hallway and handle the group of enemies lurking there. Enter the next area where you'll find a console that activates the elevator. However, the elevator gets stuck and won't descend fully. To fix this, grab a nearby box and aim for the broken pipe under the elevator. Once the pipe breaks off, the elevator will be operational. Take the elevator up and proceed to the next area.

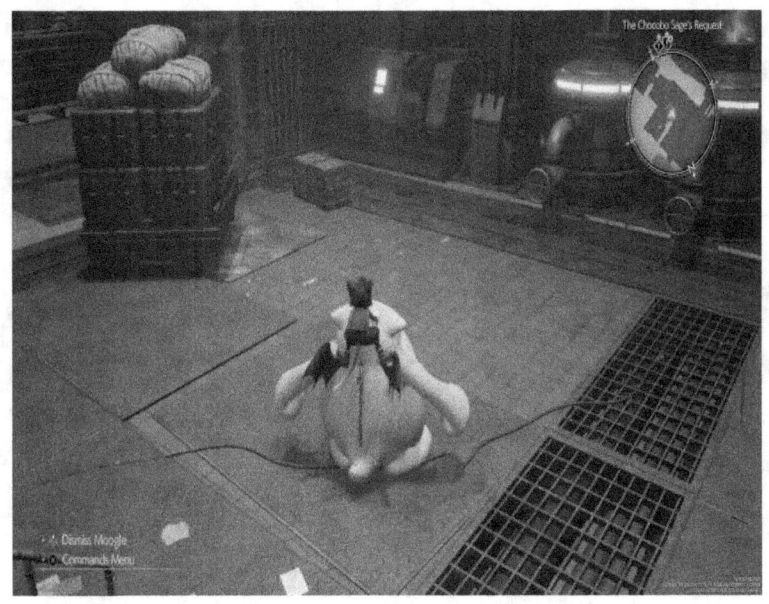

In the following room, deal with a couple of monsters before entering the ground-level air duct. One of the machines on the wall has a glowing red spot on it, but the device that dispenses boxes is too high up, causing them to break upon descent. To resolve this, enter the side room with the chest and pull the crate with bags into the previous room.

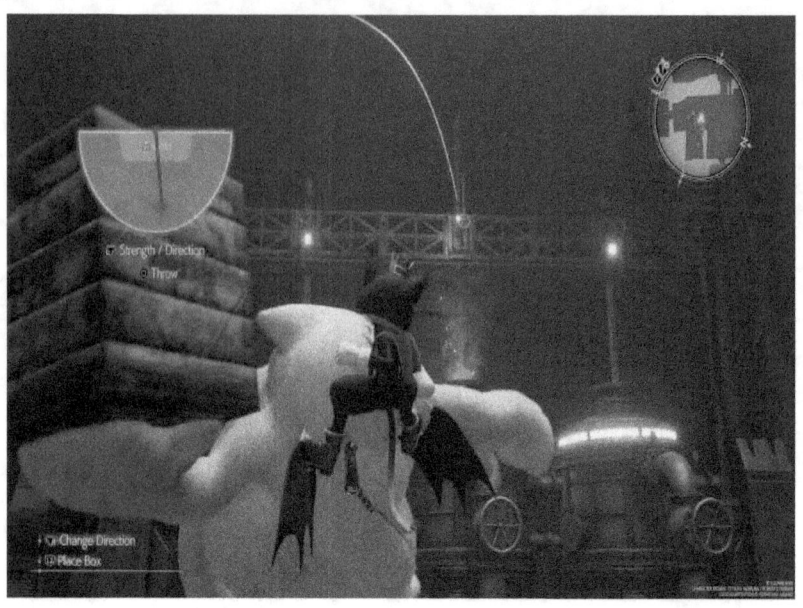

Position it directly below the box chute to prevent them from breaking. Aim a box at the spot and throw it to "fix" the machine, causing the door to open. Move east and enter the next room.

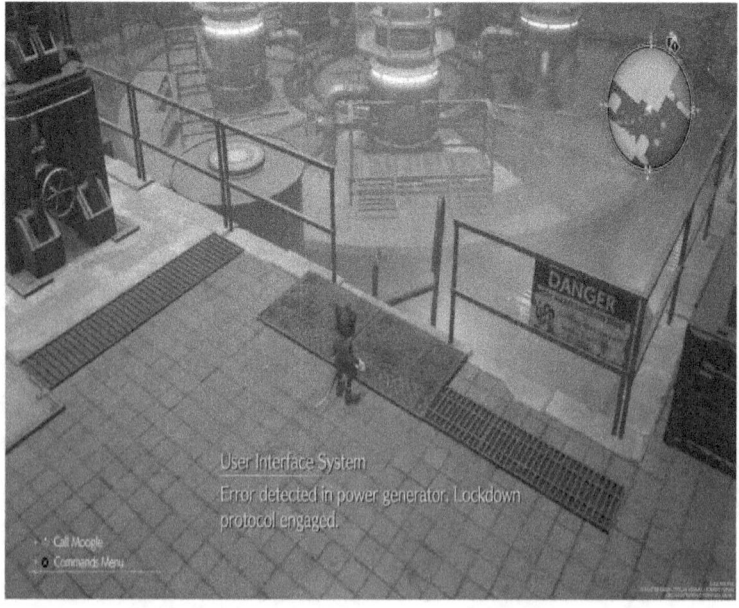

One of the generators has malfunctioned. To repair it, grab one of the blue boxes and throw it into the rotating red cup around the generator. After making this throw twice, the door will open. Beyond this gate is another elevator that will take you up. Yet again, you encounter another obstacle: a generator that is once again out of power.

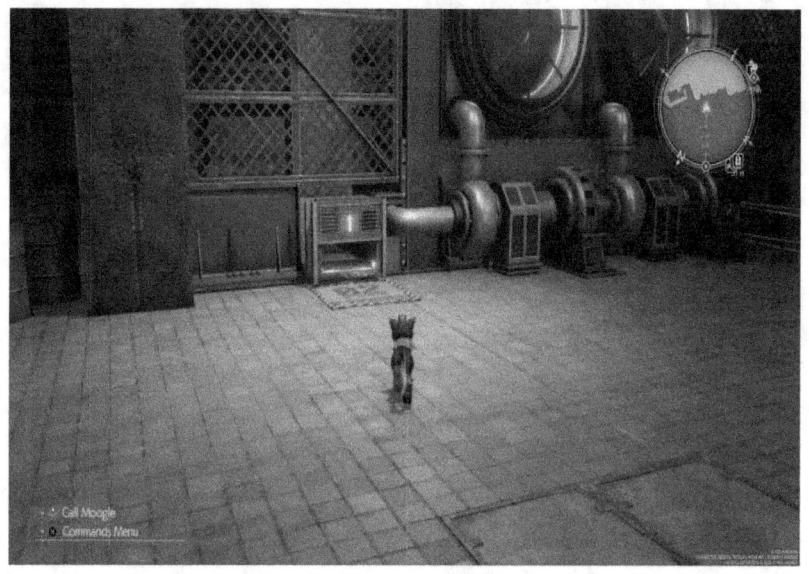

A nearby blue air duct is closed, but you can use the nearby switch to open it. Enter the air duct and on the second floor, you'll encounter some monsters, a chest with dry ether, and a duct leading to the third floor. On the third floor, there are both red and blue ducts, along with a switch visible on the first floor that controls the opening and closing of these ducts.

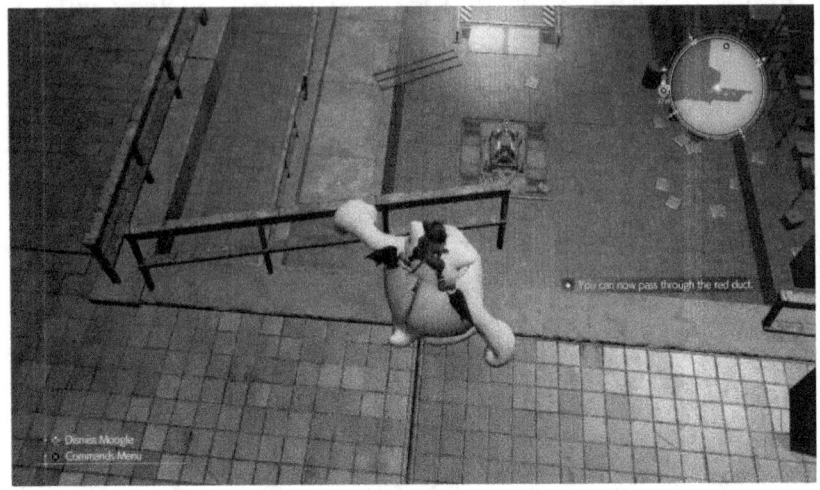

Grab a box and aim it at the switch. Use the red duct to reach the fourth floor. There, you'll encounter two Adjudicators. Defeat them and operate the terminal to activate the elevator. Before the elevator can move, you'll need to place three boxes onto it.

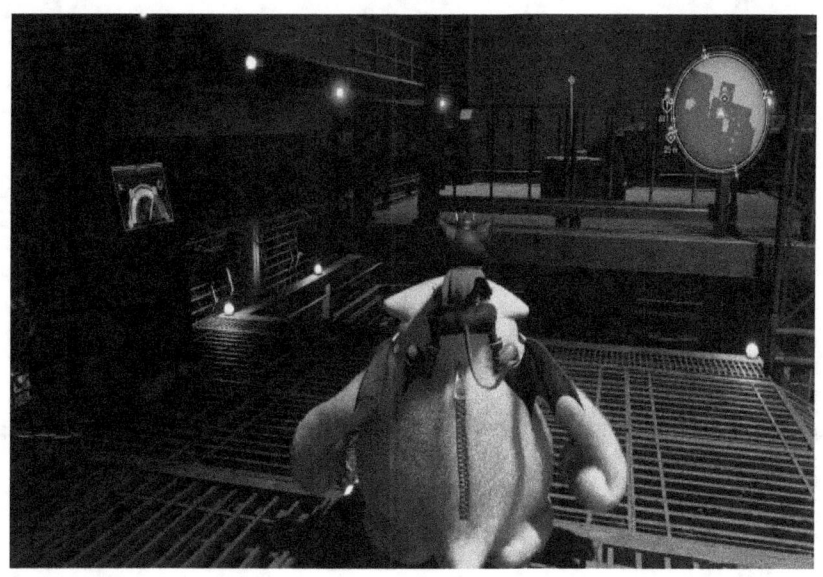

Once you've done that, board the elevator and destroy the boxes. Step off the elevator and operate the nearby terminal.

How to Defeat Yin & Yang:

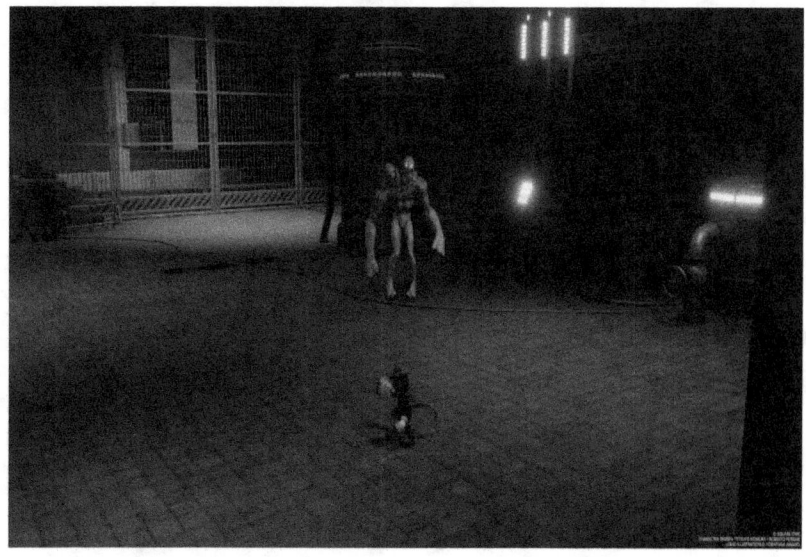

Before you can move forward, you'll have to face a huge monster called Yin & Yang. It's a tough fight, especially since you'll only have one party member. But, there's a trick: Yin & Yang is easier to handle when you put pressure on it and stagger it. Once it's staggered, you can deal some serious damage. Using Moogle Magic to summon Cait Sith's equipped Summon can really help weaken or even defeat Yin & Yang.

After you defeat the boss, go through the doorway and take the elevator. But watch out, because there's a mini-game that interrupts your journey halfway. You'll need to destroy all the boxes on the other side of the elevator shaft within a time limit. Each box you destroy gives you different materials. You don't have to destroy all the boxes to keep going with the story. When the elevator stops, you'll find a hallway with a rest station and vending machines. Activate the terminal when you're ready to continue, and it'll trigger a cutscene.

To unlock the door, you need to find and enter a password that Hojo mentioned is somewhere in the room. Look for carts with bags on top and pull the second and third ones back to reveal the following numbers:

Enter this number into the door keypad to open it. But be careful, because there's another boss fight waiting for you beyond the door.

How to Beat Forgotten Specimen:

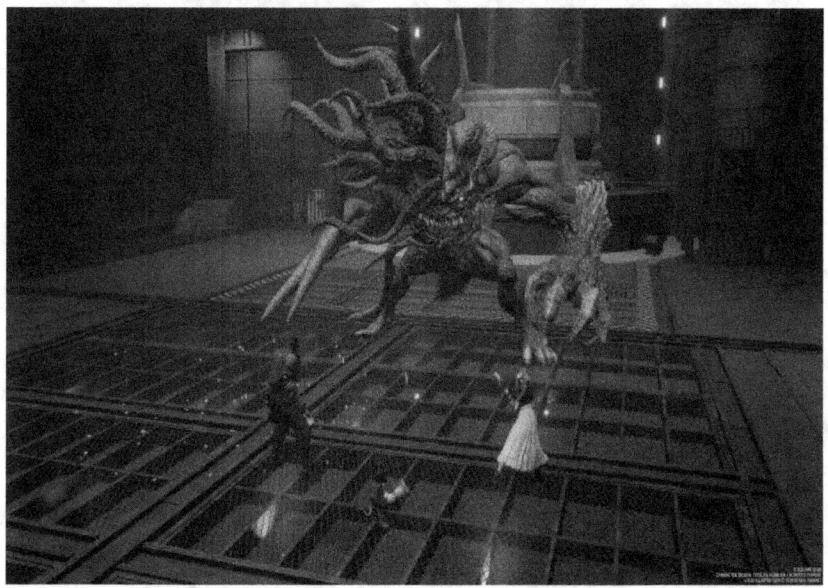

This big monster relies on strong physical attacks and occasionally spits out mako at your party. As the battle goes on, it'll change and start using spells like Biora, which you can't dodge. Make sure you're ready to cure any party members affected by it with an antidote or by casting Poisona. Plus, it might put one of your party members to sleep.

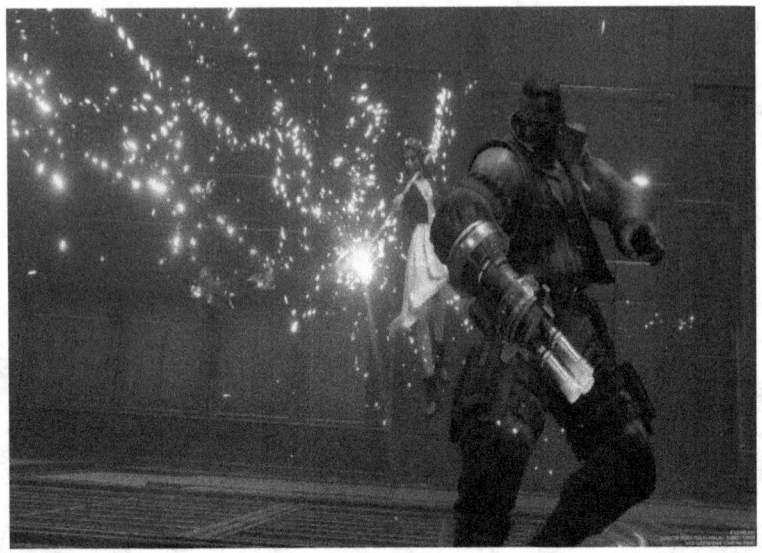

Once it hits 50%, the second phase starts. It'll cast reflect and drop green pools in the arena, so make sure you don't stand in them. It'll keep making more pools as the fight goes on, making the fighting space smaller. In this phase, you can target both its arm and tentacle, with the tentacle weak to physical damage and the arm weak to magic.

Destroy these parts and focus on the boss once it's staggered. If you manage your party's health carefully, you can beat this monstrous experiment.

The Coffin:

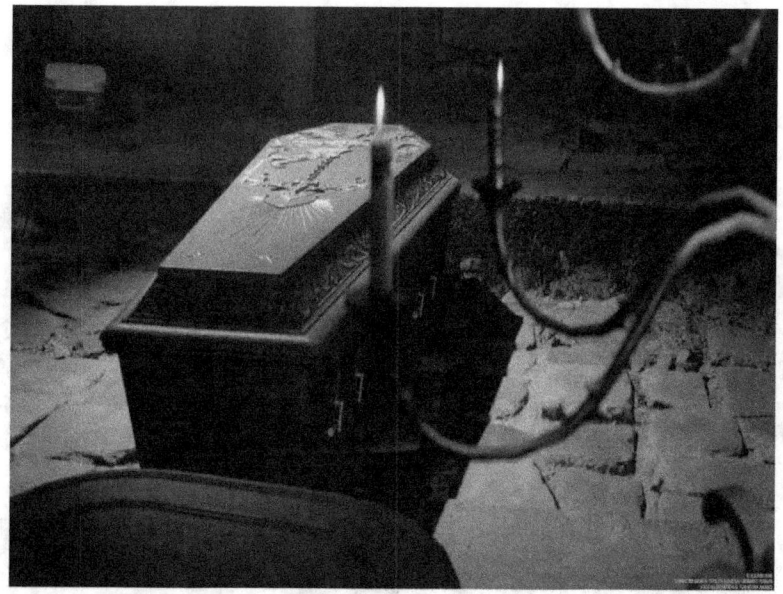

After the cutscene, go through the newly opened door. Use the elevator to go back upstairs and keep searching for the terminal. Soon, the rest of your party will catch up with you. In a room to the left, you'll find double wooden doors leading to a room with a coffin. When Vincent Valentine shows up, confirm that your enemy is Sephiroth as instructed.

After this scene, leave the room and head towards the door with the Shinra logo. While Cait Sith checks the terminal, look for an open door with a glowing pipe on the ground. Go inside and switch to a first-person perspective. Use the left stick to control

Cloud as he moves towards the machines. But be ready for a showdown when Vincent gets upset about your intrusion.

How to Beat Galian Beast:

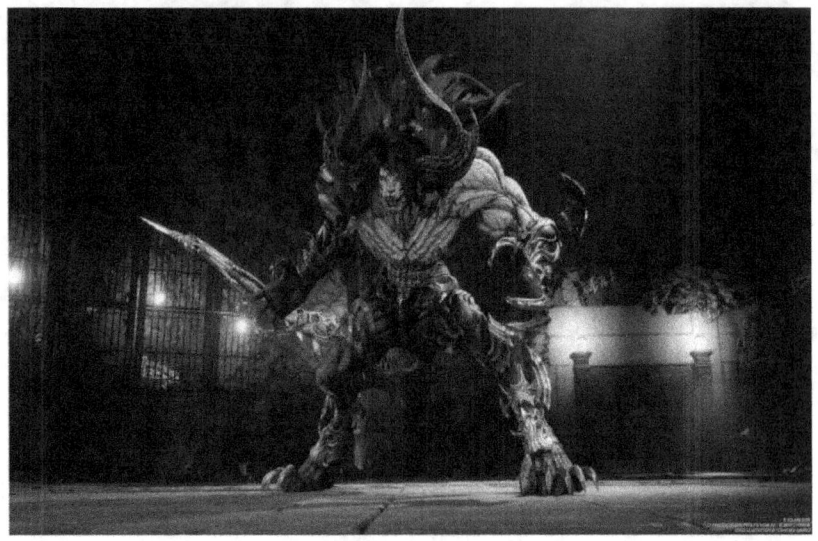

Vincent transforms into the Galian Beast, becoming really powerful. He's weak against fire, so use Fire or Fira spells whenever you can. The Galian Beast might throw random objects around the room, so stay alert. When it pauses, take the chance to attack and build pressure. Once you stagger it, use any Limit Breaks or Synergy Abilities you have.

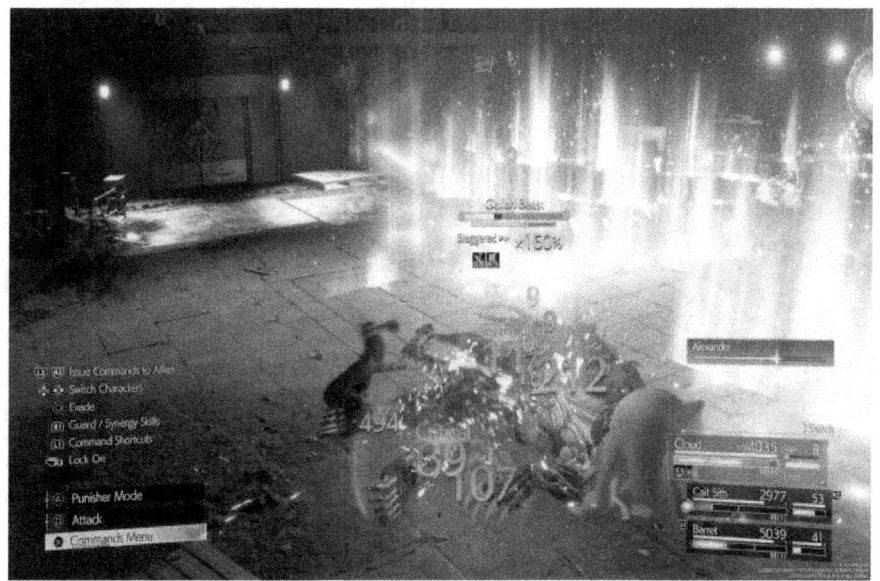

When the Galian Beast's health drops to 50%, it gets faster and deadlier. Block and dodge to minimize damage while keeping up the fire attacks. After you defeat the Galian Beast, use the elevator to go back to the first floor. Leave the manor to trigger a cutscene, then head back to the village. Even though there's a new destination, the chapter isn't finished yet.

How to defeat Roche:

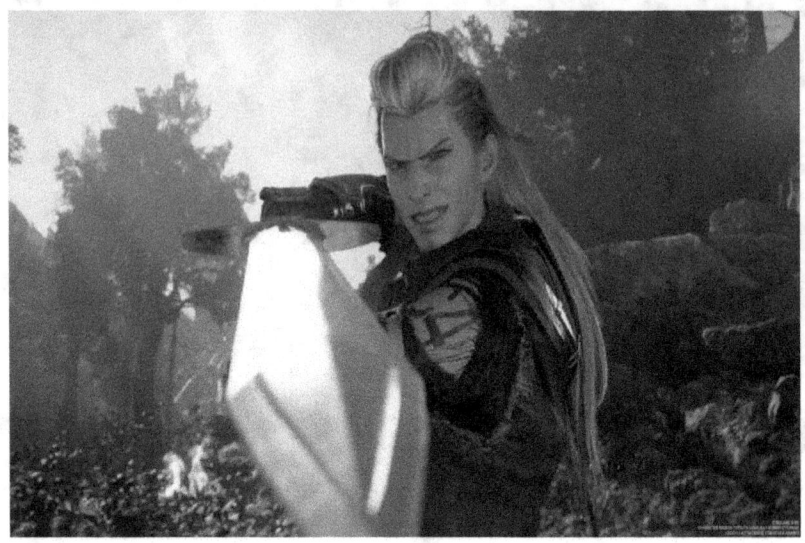

Roche challenges Cloud to a rematch, and this time, he's even tougher than before. In this one-on-one battle, Roche is more resilient, but you can pressure him by striking him after he uses special attacks. Save your most powerful abilities, like Cross-Slash, for when he's staggered, as they deal significant damage. As Roche's health drops to 20%, he remains pressured, making it easier to stagger him and secure victory.

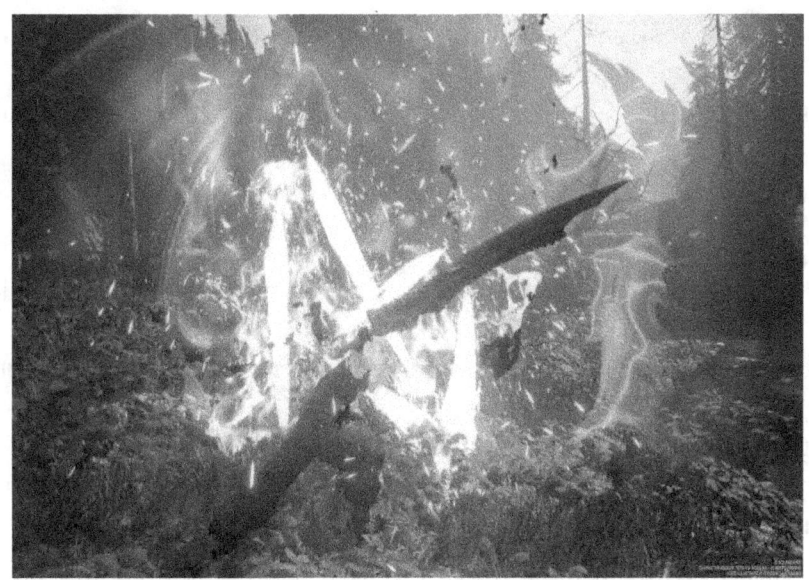

Investigate the Smoke:

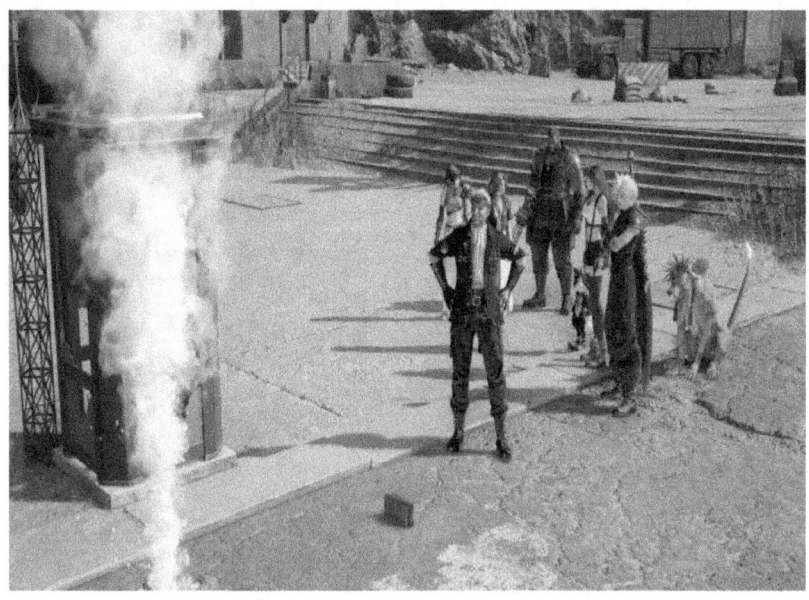

After a series of cutscenes, you find yourself back in Nibelheim.

Your objective is to investigate the smoke at the airstrip, but if you're not ready to proceed to the next chapter, there are other tasks available. Check the community board for the new side quest called "My White-Haired Angel."

When you're prepared, head to the airstrip and speak to Cid. However, things don't go as planned during this flight, and the airplane unexpectedly makes a water landing as the twelfth chapter begins.

CHAPTER TWELVE

A GOLDEN KEY

After a significant event in Nibelheim in the previous part of Final Fantasy 7 Rebirth, Cloud and his friends set out to find the Keystone required to enter the temple. As you enter Chapter 12, the world really opens up. You can now travel quickly to different places and engage in numerous extra activities. However, this chapter is shorter compared to the ones before. Nevertheless, here's what awaits you in Chapter 12: A Golden Key.

When You're Grounded, Take to the Water:

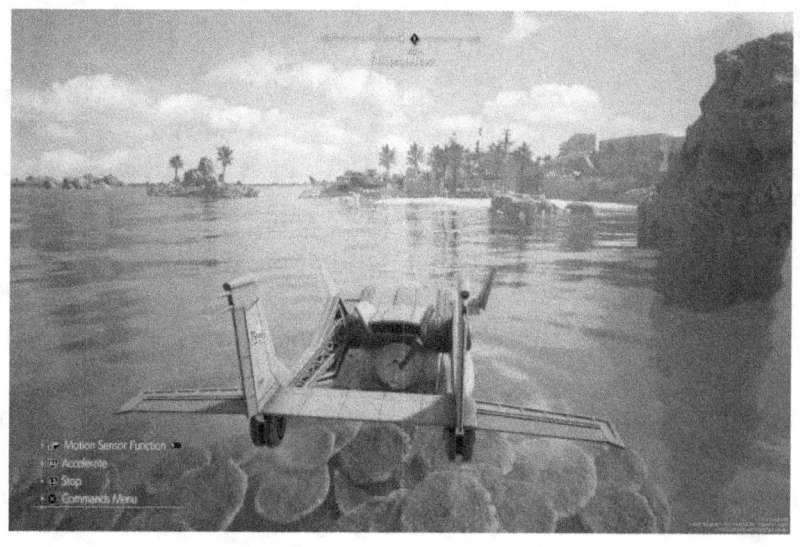

Despite the less-than-perfect landing, Cid manages to convert the plane into a makeshift boat. After the scene concludes, you'll be in control of the plane-boat hybrid. Navigate along the river until you reach Costa del Sol. Along the way, keep an eye out for boxes floating in the water containing items you can collect. To disembark from the plane, head to the dock and hold down the Triangle button.

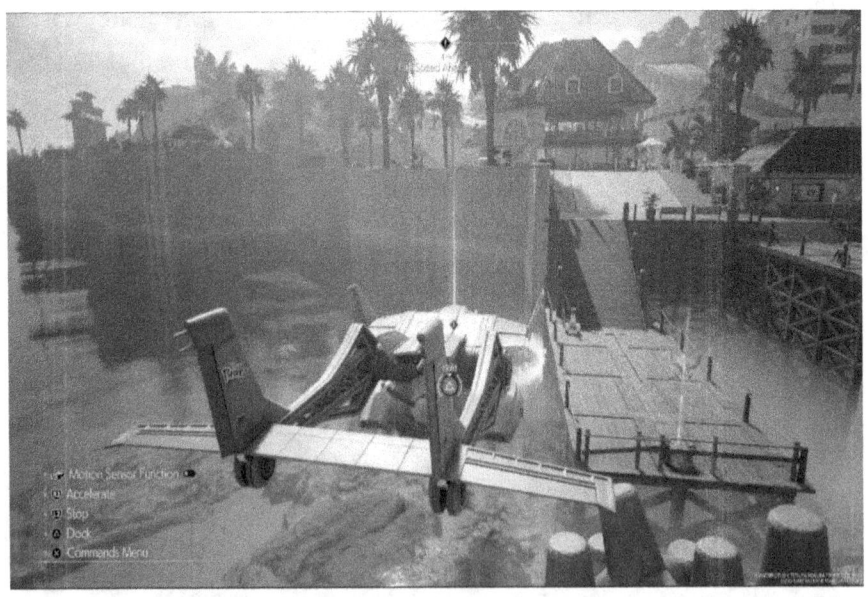

After the scene, you gain the ability to fast travel to various locations. Nearby, there's a chest that allows you to craft a Corsair's Compass (provided you've found all four pirate relics, which are located within the chest). Additionally, there are new side quests available for you to undertake. When you're ready to progress the story, fast travel to the Gold Saucer.

Track Down Dio:

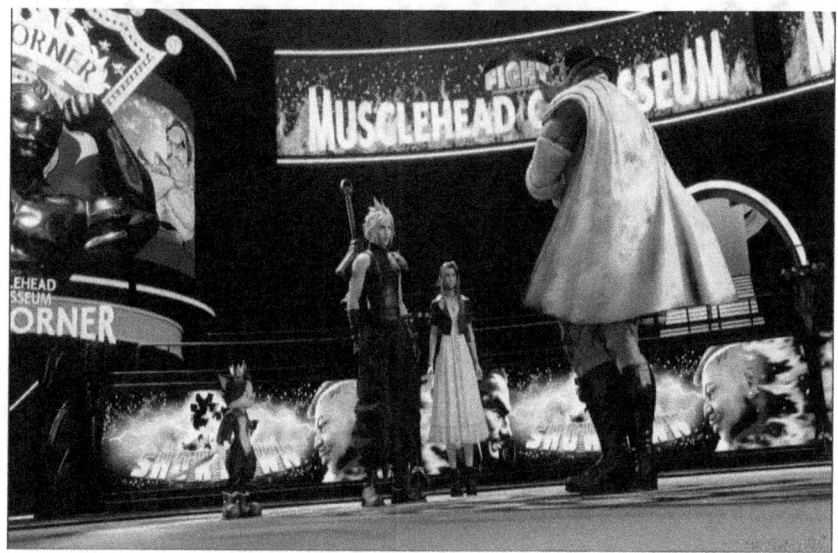

Upon arrival at the Gold Saucer, your initial task is to locate Dio. Make your way to the Battle Square. Speak with Aerith and follow her into the arena. Approach Dio to initiate a scene. However, things take an unexpected turn, and you'll only obtain the keystone if you emerge victorious in the next battle. Before engaging in the fight, head to the haunted hotel to prepare. But before you can proceed further, it's time to witness events from Zack's perspective. Head to the second floor where Cloud is to witness a scene.

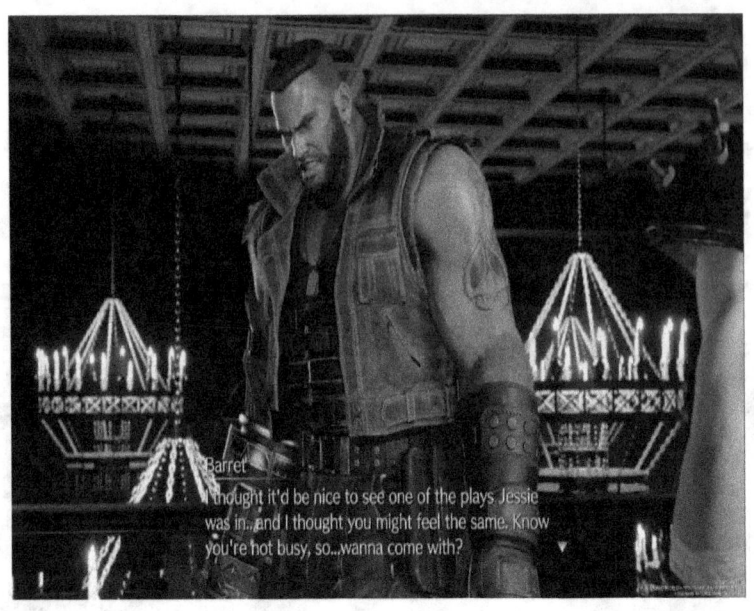

Following the scene, exit the garden and hop on the motorcycle. Interact with it to switch back to Cloud's viewpoint. There will be a knock on your door, and depending on your proximity to certain characters, the person outside will vary. In this playthrough, it's Barret.

Loveless:

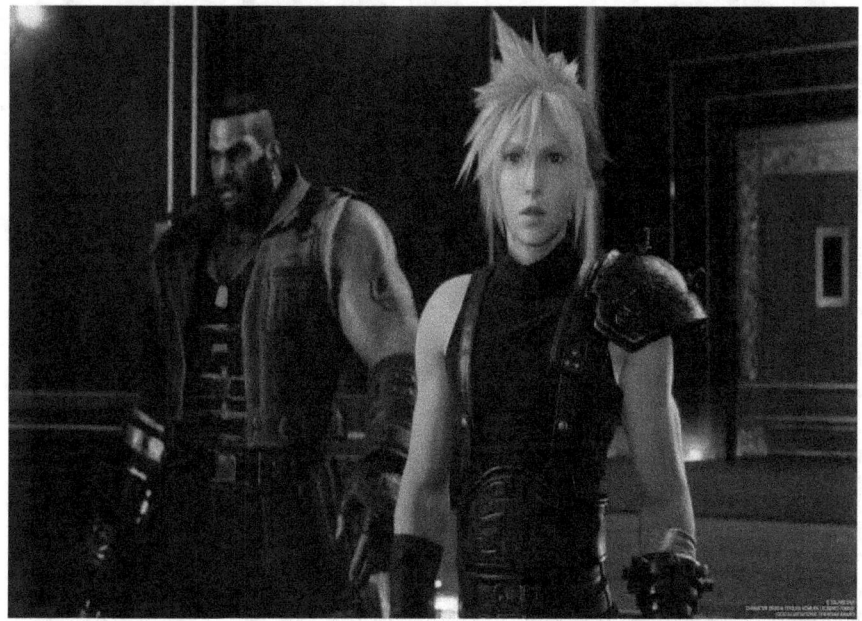

Barret has managed to secure tickets to see Loveless. Fast travel to the Event Square and speak to the Usher at the end of the hall to trigger a scene. After the show, engage in a mini-game where you'll have to make choices. Look to the right and select your weapons for a tutorial or interact with the bars to commence the story.

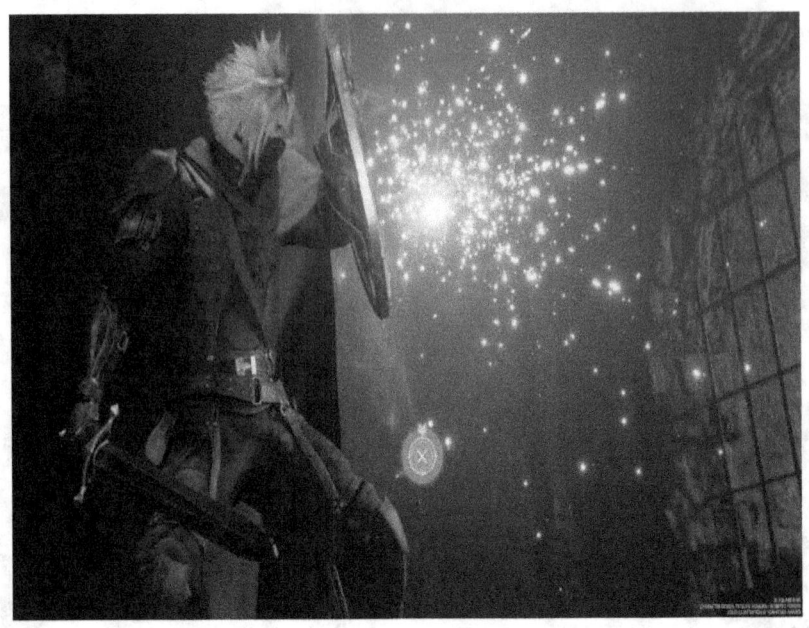

In the mini-game, press the buttons as instructed. As the story unfolds, you'll need to decide whether to fight Varvados (Barret) or Garm (Red XIII). In this playthrough, we chose to explore the future with Rosa. Then, for the final act, you must choose between Garm, Varvados, or Rosa. Rosa was selected. Following the mini-games, another scene ensues. If you performed well, you'll receive a trophy. To proceed, head to the skywheel.

Prepare for the Tournament:

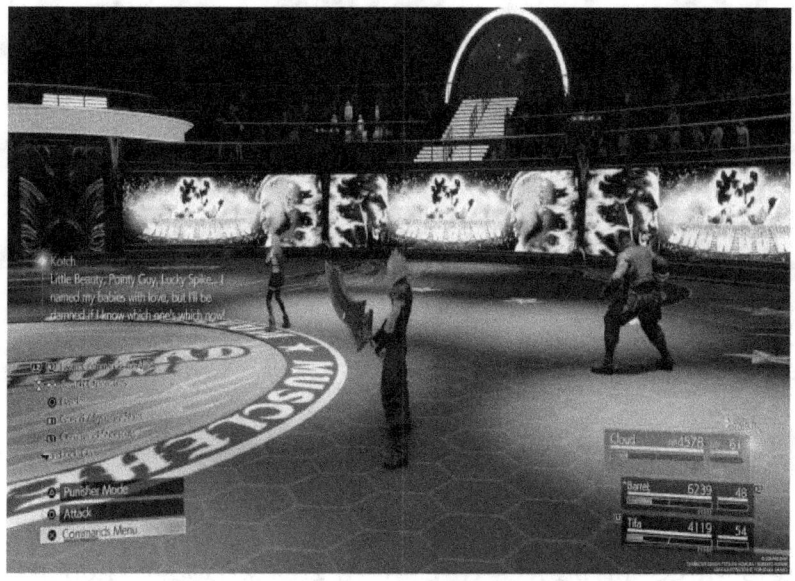

Your team for the tournament consists of Cloud, your earlier companion, and a third member of your choice. Once you're ready, head to the counter to begin. In the first round, you'll take on Don Corneo's henchmen. They're not too difficult, just keep an eye on your health and heal when necessary.

Next, you'll face Cactaurs in round two. These speedy little foes are tricky to hit. Wait for them to pause, then strike with Fira to stun them. Stay quick and aggressive to avoid their powerful 1,000 Needles attack.

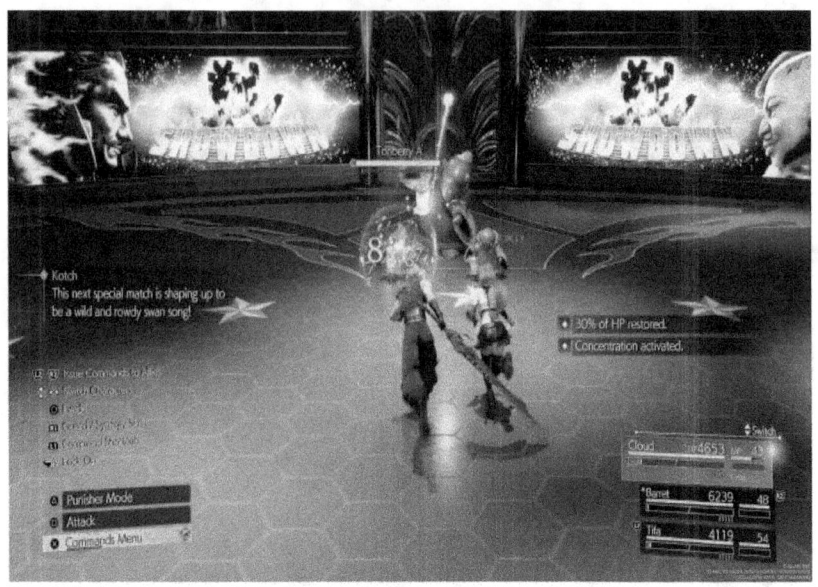

Round three introduces three Tonberries. Dodge their moves and focus on staggering them quickly. But your final challenge awaits: Corneo himself, riding Abzu. Fire spells are most effective against Abzu, so keep hitting him to wear him down. Maintain the pressure, and eventually, he'll fall.

Encountering Rude and Elena Again:

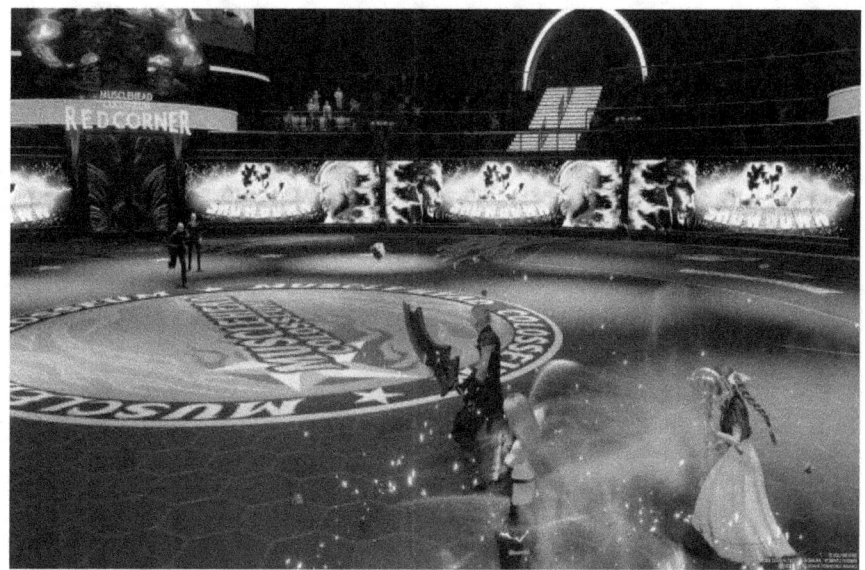

Your victory celebration is cut short by the sudden appearance of the Turks. Before facing Rude and Elena, Dio provides healing items. Their weaknesses remain the same: Rude uses Triple Shockwave, while Elena throws grenades. Dodge their attacks, heal as needed, and exploit their elemental vulnerabilities.

Defeating Rufus:

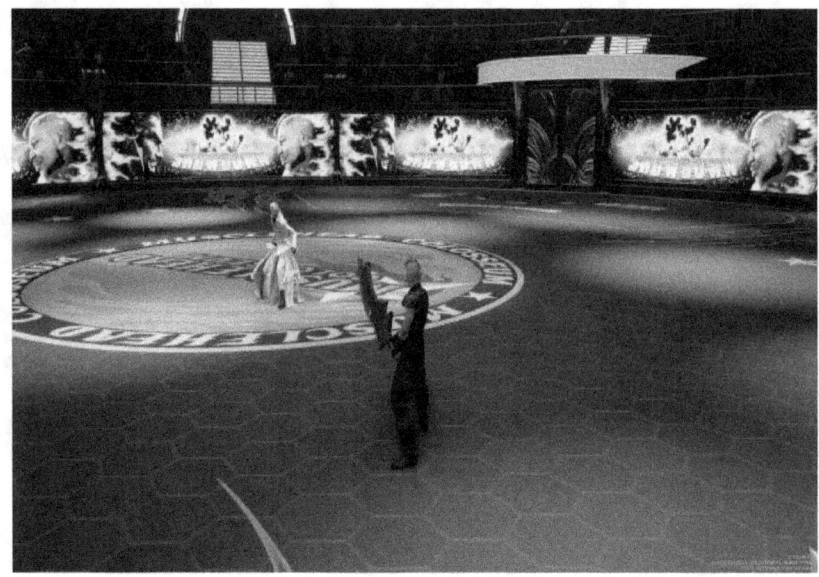

Rufus unexpectedly steps into the ring for a one-on-one showdown with Cloud, reminiscent of their encounter at the end of Final Fantasy 7 Remake.

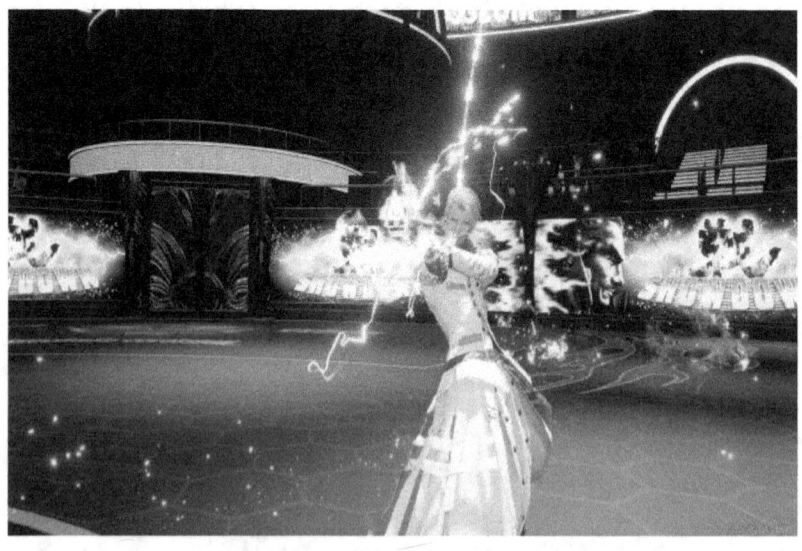

Rufus is a formidable opponent with no obvious weaknesses, skilled at blocking most attacks. Aim for moments when he's reloading or using abilities to land hits and apply pressure. Occasionally, hitting Rufus with an ATB ability while he's under pressure can stagger him.

When Rufus's health drops to 25%, Darkstar joins the fight to assist him. Like Rufus, Darkstar has no specific weaknesses. Rufus and Darkstar will occasionally team up, combining their attacks. Focus on Darkstar to build up your ATB gauge, then unleash abilities on Rufus to apply pressure and stagger him. Defeating Rufus means defeating Darkstar as well, regardless of its remaining health.

Finding Cait Sith:

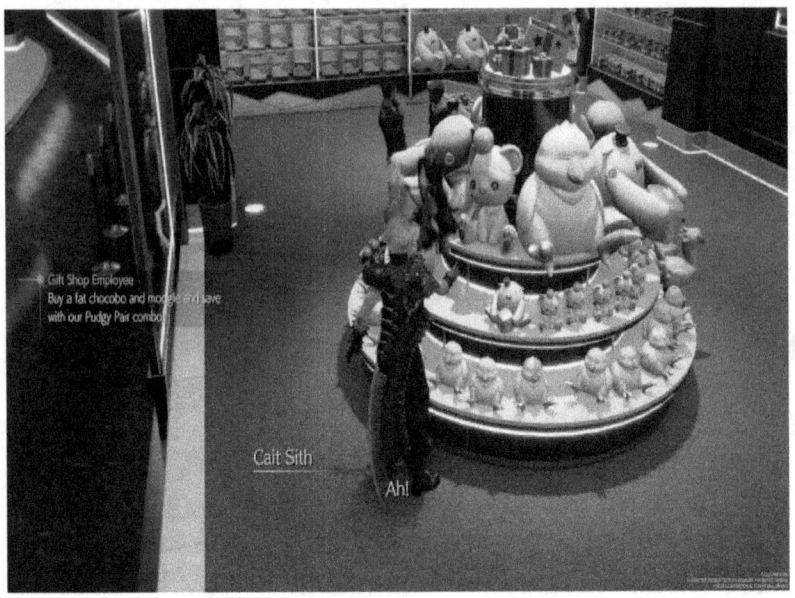

After the battle, your next objective is to locate Cait Sith. Approach Aerith at the hallway's end, then turn around to spot Cait Sith hiding among chocobo and moogle plushies. Press the Triangle button to make him flee.

Follow Cait Sith through a tunnel until you find Cid near the Ghost Square sign. As you approach, Cait Sith will dash off again. Head to the Event Square entrance, where Barret is standing. Once more, Cait Sith runs off, this time toward the Ghost Square.

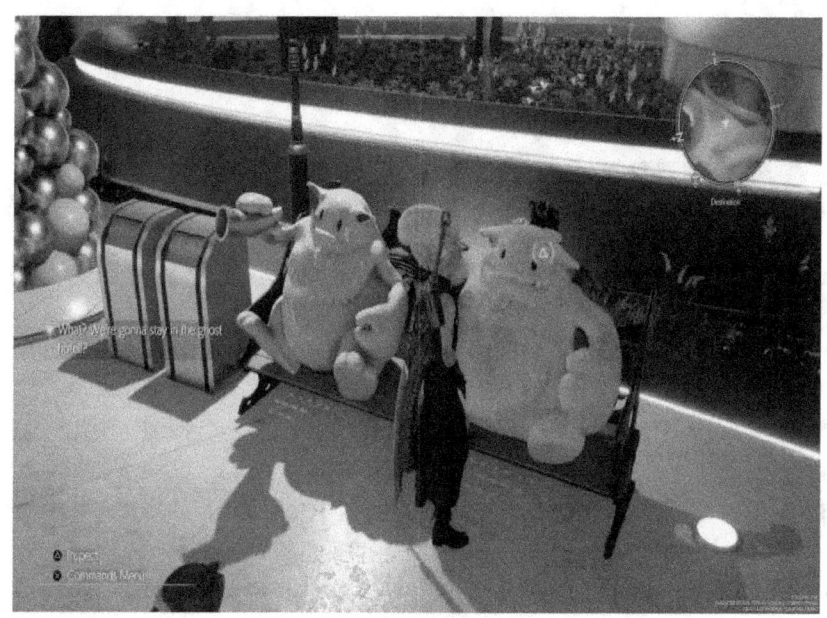

At the Ghost Square, you'll encounter Vincent, who hasn't seen Cait Sith. Descend the stairs to spot Cait Sith near a bench with a moogle statue. Interact with him, then follow him into a side room labeled "Authorized Personnel Only." While chasing Cait Sith, don't forget to grab the purple chest containing a weapon for Yuffie. Keep following Cait Sith until a cutscene triggers.

After the cutscene, speak to the Parking Attendant to leave the Gold Saucer. You can either drive back to Costa del Sol with the buggy or fast travel for convenience. Once you talk to Cid, the chapter will conclude.

CHAPTER THIRTEEN

WHERE ANGELS FEAR TO TREAD

In the last part of Final Fantasy 7 Rebirth, Cloud and his friends managed to find the Keystone, but Shinra double-crossed them and snatched it away. Luckily, Vincent intercepted some radio signals and uncovered the temple's location. Before heading north to the temple, it's a good idea to tackle any side quests or extra tasks you might have.

The Temple of the Ancients is the climax of the story. It's a tough dungeon, so get ready as you dive into Chapter 13: Where Angels Fear to Tread.

Setting Sail North:

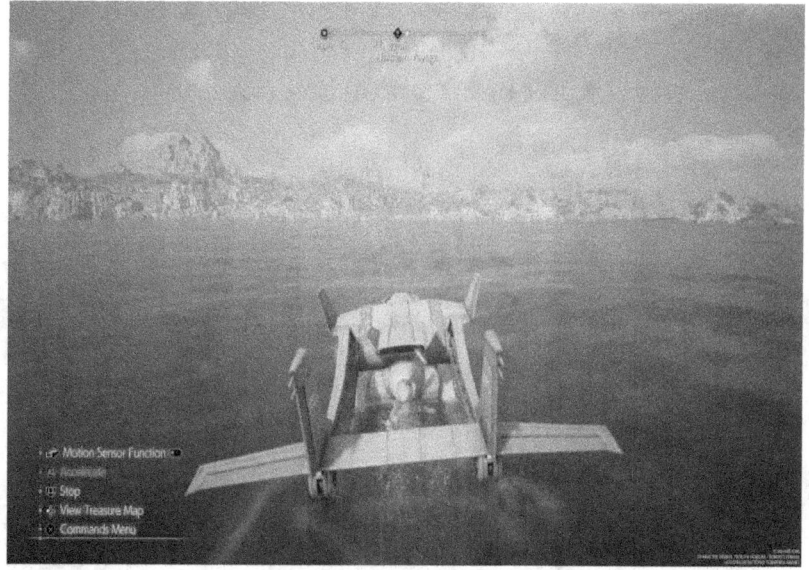

After the cutscene, head north by sailing. Along the way, you can break open boxes in the water to find useful items. Keep an eye out for spots where you can dock and explore further, like searching for pirate relics.

As you sail farther north, the sky gradually darkens. Once you get close enough, a cutscene will kick in. Keep moving towards the temple after the scene ends. Eventually, you'll reach a dock where you can disembark.

NOTE:

- Keep in mind that once you land here, there's no turning back. Make sure you're prepared before proceeding, as fast travel won't be an option anymore.

Journey to the Temple:

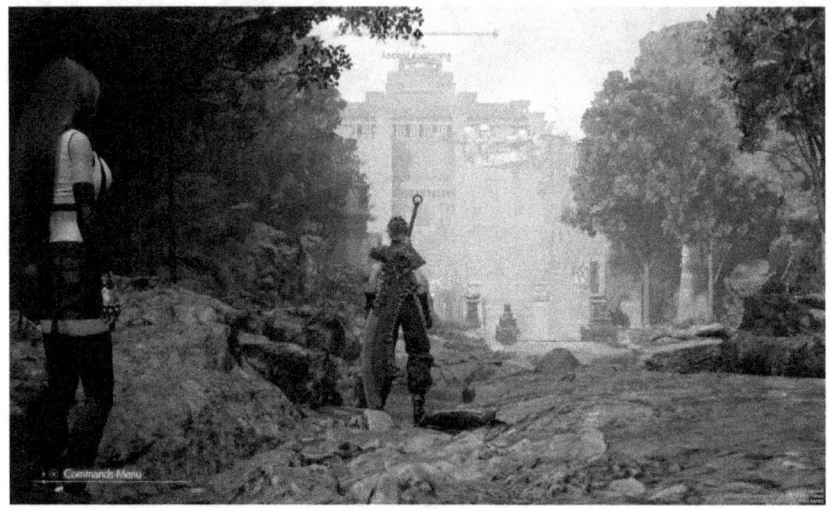

At the dock, you'll find vending machines and a rest area. Take advantage of these facilities, save your progress, and follow the path into the woods. It won't be long before the temple comes into view. Head towards it to trigger another cutscene.

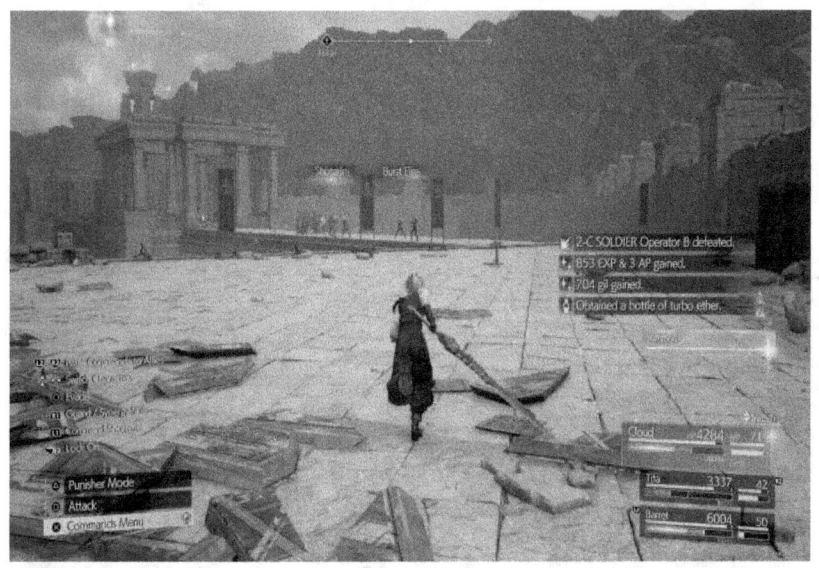

Upon reaching the Keystone Altar, grab the chest on the left before entering the temple. On the other side, you'll encounter a substantial group of Shinra forces, including 2nd Class SOLDIERS. After defeating them, proceed north towards the temple steps.

Inside the temple, move past the tree and through a partially open door. Deal with the Shinra Security forces inside and venture deeper into the temple. When the cutscene ends, head right and descend the stairs. Navigate through the square below, defeat the monsters, and proceed through the gate and up the stairs.

Here, you'll come across a floating green device. Interact with it to alter gravity. This allows you to walk on the ceilings and progress.

Navigating the Maze:

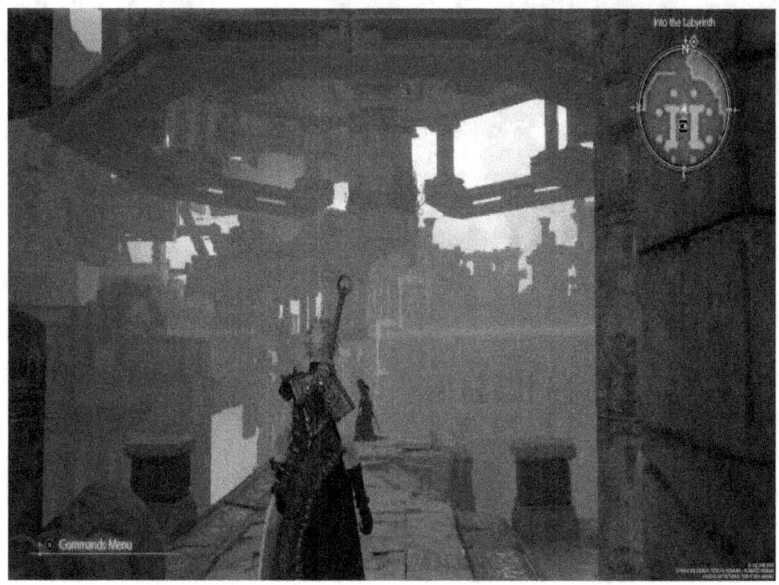

Pass the black-robed figure and go down the stairs. Follow the path, dealing with any enemies you encounter. Climb the ivy vines and reach the ledge on the right, where you'll find a chest containing a weapon for Cloud. Descend the ivy and continue across. In the small chamber ahead, you'll find another gravity-altering device. Use it, grab the chest outside, then continue where a group of fiends awaits. To the north, you'll see stairs leading up to another gravity device.

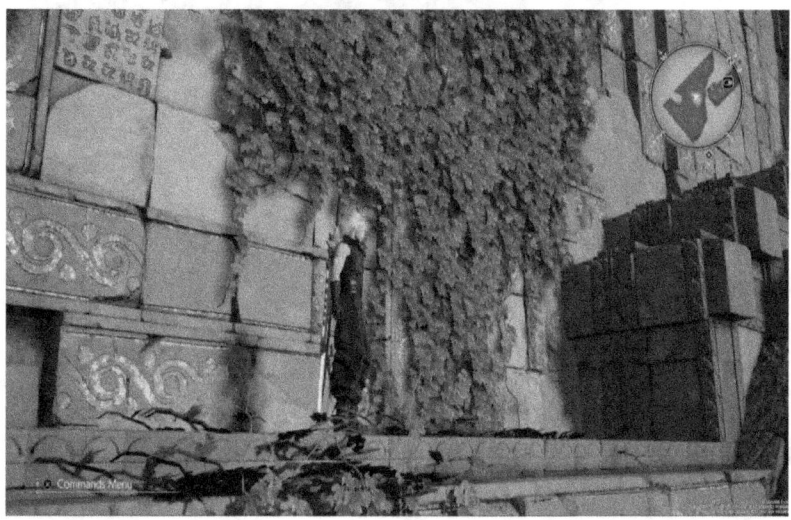

Now, things get tricky as you can flip the temple in three directions. Flip it to reveal two large walls of ivy vines to climb. At the top, pass through the gate and handle the small squad of Shinra forces.

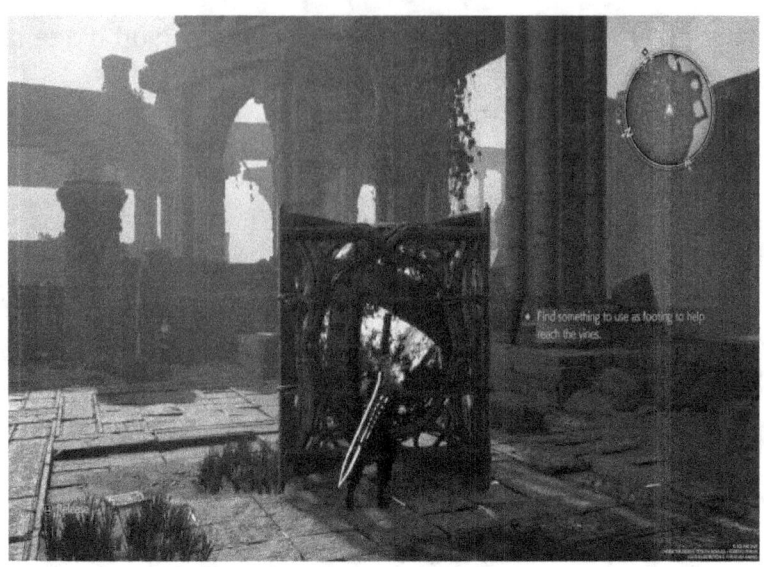

Next, push the box with the sphere toward the ivy vines. If done correctly, a blue icon will appear at the top of the box. Climb the vines and head towards the waterfall where two Shinra troops will jump down.

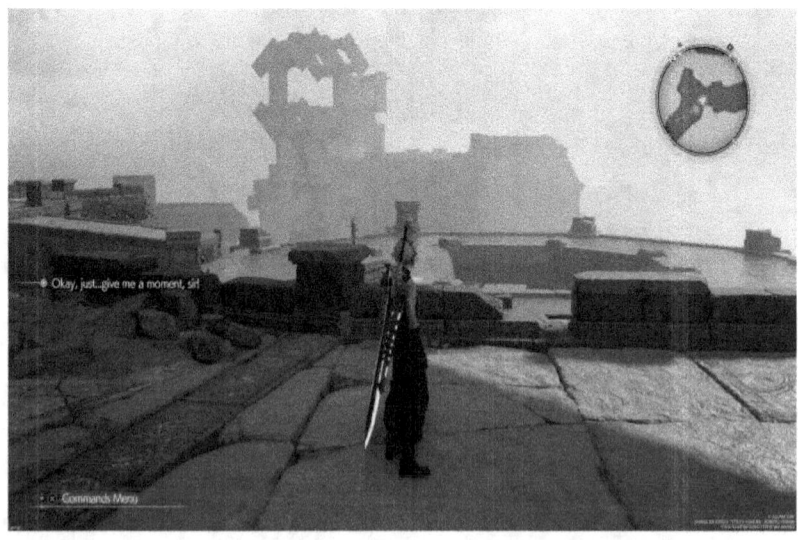

Before you go down, go west to find a chest at the edge. When you're ready, jump down the waterfall and climb out when you reach the bottom. This leads to an area with two gravity-altering devices. Rotate the device in the purple room, then climb the vines. At the top, there's a chest with a Cetra Bangle inside.

Head back to the purple chamber and rotate it again. Pass the black-robed figure, go down the stairs toward a group of Shinra troops. Defeat them and go through the door they were guarding. Even the Cetra had vending machines and rest stations, so use them if needed. When you're ready, go down the stairs ahead.

How to Defeat the Red Dragon:

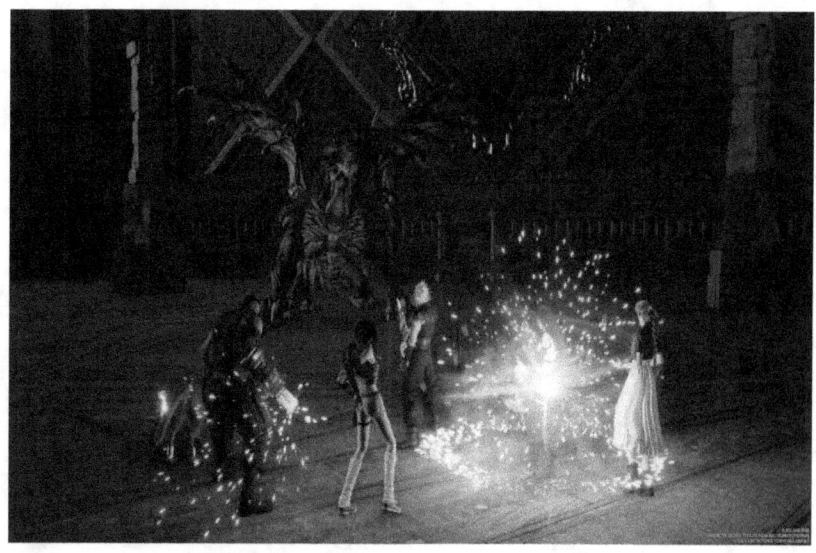

It's not surprising that a huge monster guards the labyrinth, and this one's a fire-breathing dragon. It's weak against ice attacks. At the start of the battle, target its head to weaken it and put pressure on the boss.

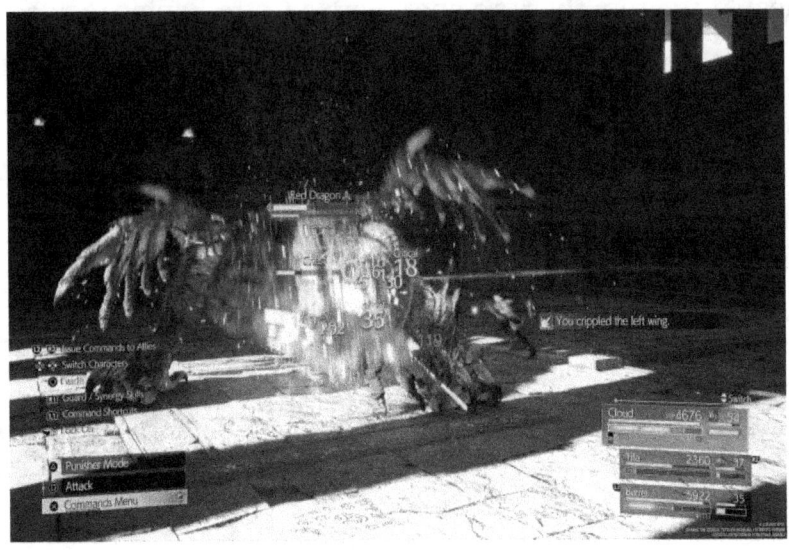

Once the boss's health drops to 50%, you can target its chest and wings. Focus on crippling the wings to bring it down to the ground. Quickly disable the chest to limit its range for the Crimson Breath attack.

The chest becomes active periodically. Disable it swiftly because if the Crimson Breath goes off with the chest active, it covers the entire arena in lava, which can be deadly if your party's health is low. Keep pressuring and staggering the boss, and victory will be yours. You can return to the rest station before moving forward.

Splitting Up the Party:

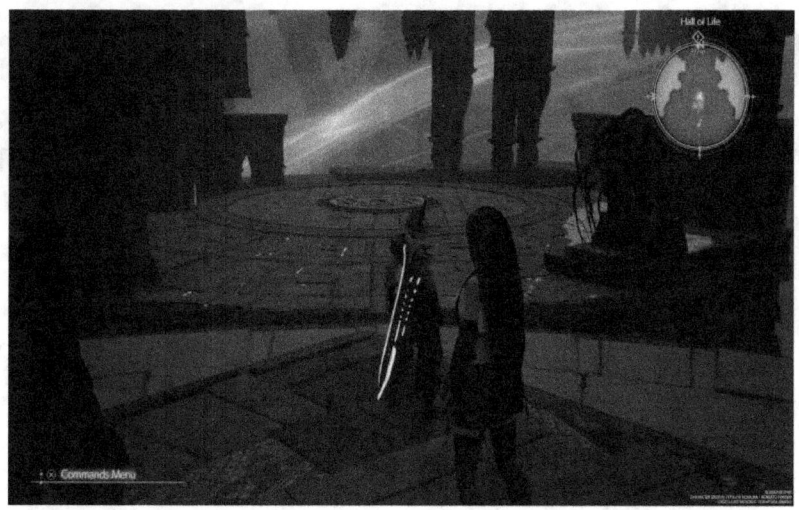

When you're prepared, go through the door guarded by the dragon. Head down the hall and activate the elevator to descend into the Hall of Life. After the cutscene, the party splits up. Keep moving forward, defeating any fiends along the way.

You'll encounter another group of Shinra troops besides the fiends. After defeating them, keep going north and find a chest containing a weapon for Tifa. Go down the nearby stairs and climb onto the vines to reach another platform.

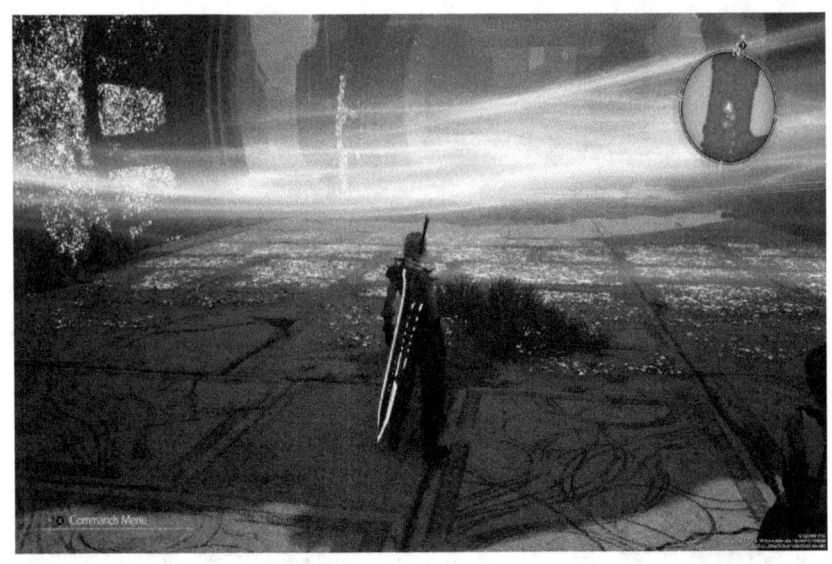

Carefully navigate a narrow edge and walk across a beam to reach stable ground. As you head north, watch out for sudden gusts of wind. Wait for them to clear before proceeding.

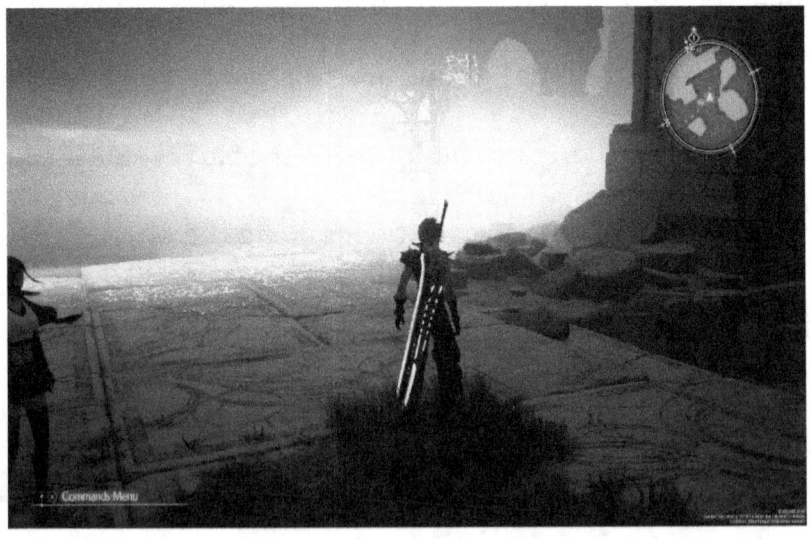

After crossing two sections, you'll face a never-ending gust of wind. To pass through, backtrack and go through when the wind clears. Push the nearby box towards the third gust directly ahead. Once it's in place, the box will block the wind, allowing you to continue.

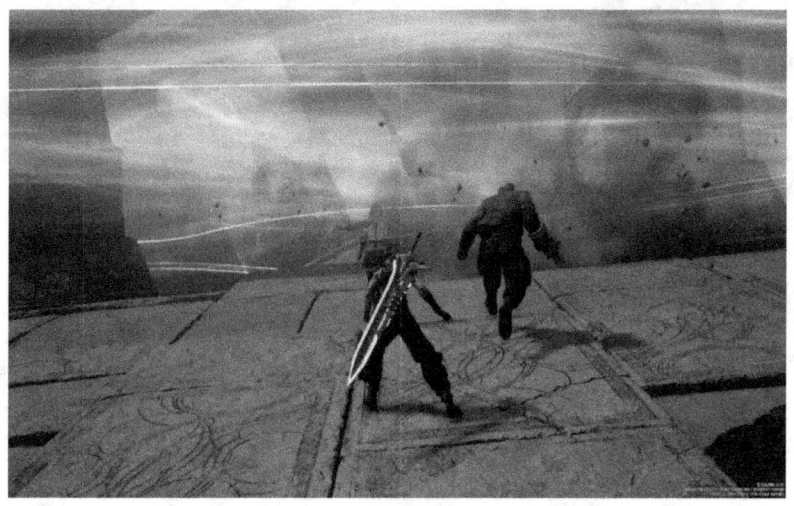

Moving ahead, take a left at the dead end. There, you'll find vines to climb up and reach another room. Enter through the door and dash across the platform as it gradually crumbles from the storm. When you hear voices nearby, duck under the rubble and enter a circular room. Defeat the special forces, and soon Rude and Reno will appear.

The Other Half:

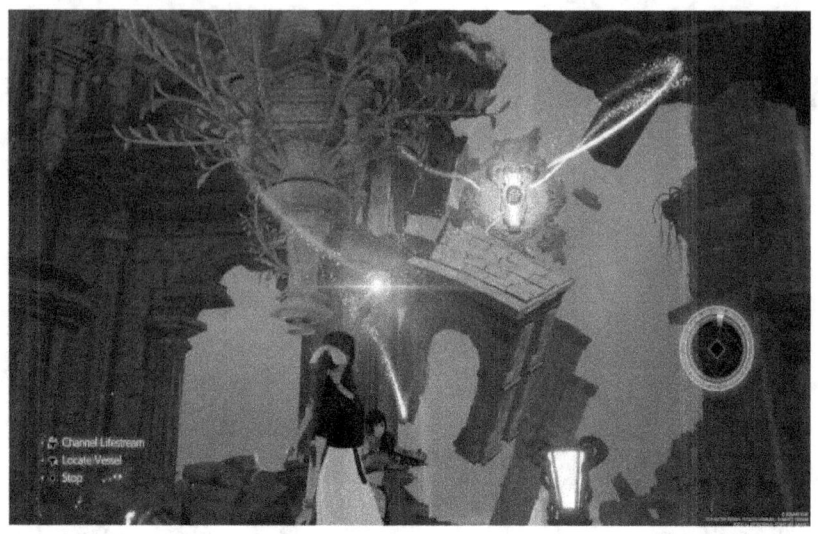

Now, the game focuses on Aerith, Yuffie, and Red XIII. Go through the door and approach the pool of water. You'll receive a tutorial on Aerith's new power. Look up at the rift and rotate the left stick until the area stabilizes.

In the next area, destroy crystals and pray around the small glowing green wisps to gather energy. Once you have enough, use it to open new pathways. Aerith gains various buffs at the start of combat when she absorbs more lifestream.

To gather enough lifestream, defeat the lurking fiend in the small circular room. If you've collected all available lifestream, you'll have enough to open both paths. The eastern path contains a chest, while the western one allows progress. Descend the stairs and turn left at the bottom to find a chest with a weapon for Aerith.

In this area, there's a glyph with four spots opened by lifestream. Gather lifestream from both containers, destroy crystals, and stabilize the vessel on the right first. Move to the new area to gather more motes of lifestream, then return to the glyph and stabilize the vessel on the left.

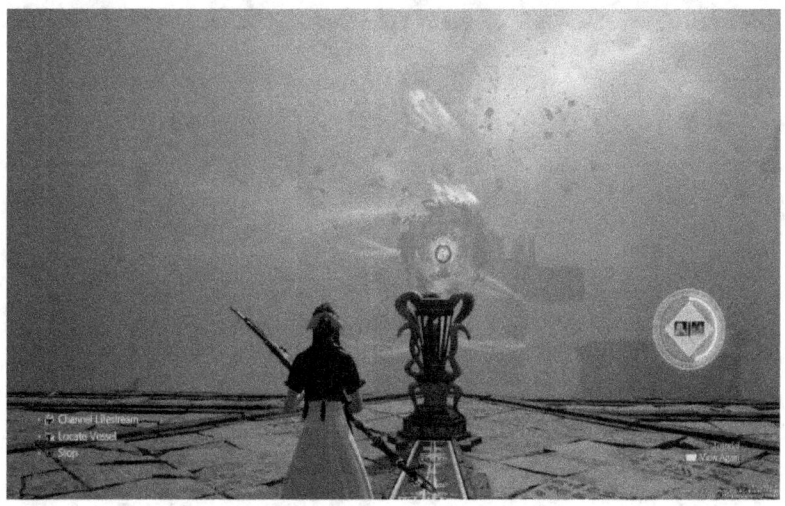

Explore the newly restored area, defeat lurking fiends to gather more lifestream, then return to the glyph and use lifestream on the distant vessel to trigger a cutscene. After this, you switch back to Cloud and the others dealing with fiends. Leave the arena and head down to the rest station. Follow Rufus and the Turks' trail.

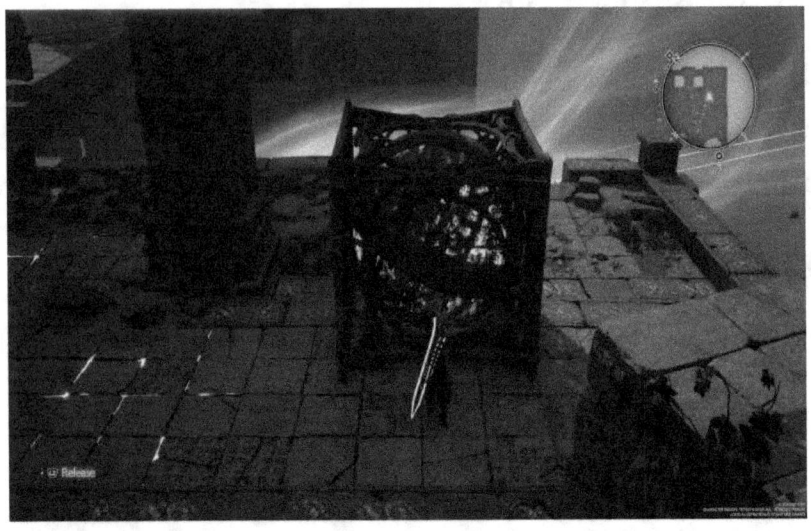

Eventually, you'll come across a gap in the platform. Push the nearby box to the edge until it falls into the wind. Walk across your newly formed bridge and go up the stairs. Just past this point is a small room with a chest containing a weapon for Barret. Beyond that is another gap in the floor. Go up the nearby stairs and push another box off the edge to form part of another bridge. Go up the next set of stairs to find a tower with a turnable crank at the bottom.

Approach the crank, hold down L2, and trigger a cutscene followed by a boss fight.

How to Defeat Ironclad:

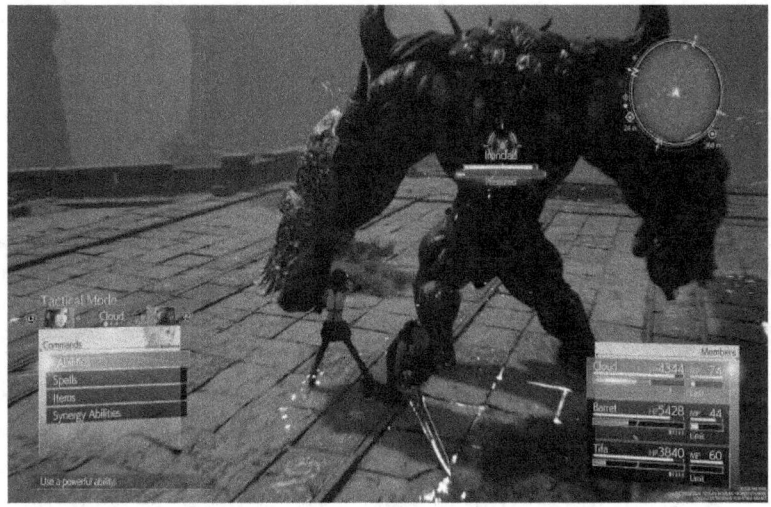

In this battle, avoiding Condemned is crucial—it's an instant kill, even if you have Safety Bit equipped. This towering metal foe is vulnerable to lightning damage. You'll want to steer clear of unblockable attacks, as they deal massive damage.

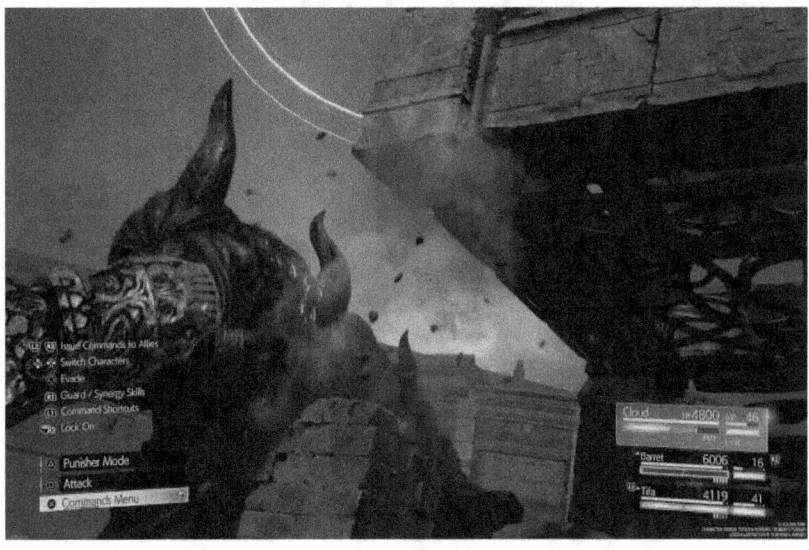

This fight is peculiar because simply defeating the boss isn't sufficient. To win, you must stagger the boss. It becomes easier to stagger after using Sharpen, which puts pressure on itself. Stagger it quickly, but be cautious not to deal too much damage, or you'll defeat it before staggering. Failing to stagger before defeating means you'll need to redo the fight.

After dealing with the boss, push the box off the ledge and return to your makeshift bridge. Cross the narrow ledge and enter the nearby room patrolled by two large fiends. Proceed onward to find another rest station.

How to Defeat Rude and Reno:

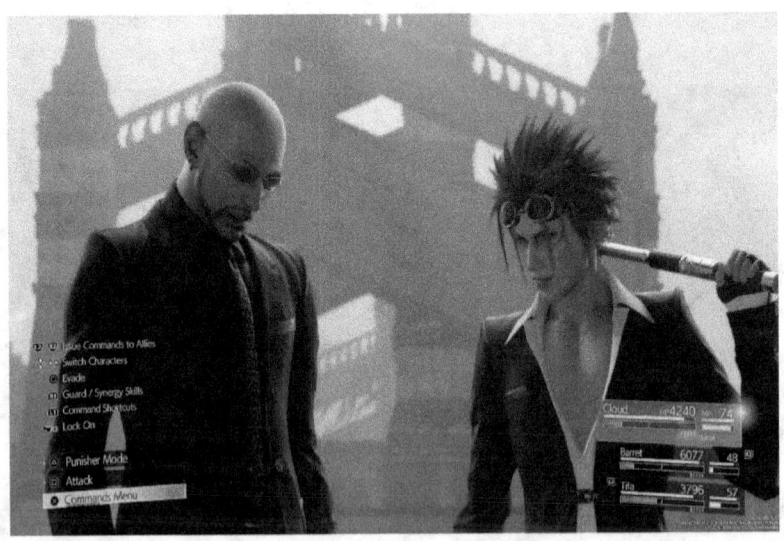

Soon after the rest station, you'll encounter Rude and Reno battling fiends. Assist them in clearing out the fiends, then prepare for a boss fight against the iconic Turk duo. Reno is vulnerable to fire, while Rude remains weak to wind.

Unlike Elena, Reno is in perfect sync with Rude, faster, and adept at dodging attacks. He'll intermittently release EM Mines that roam the battlefield. If possible, focus on defeating Reno first, then concentrate on Rude.

Back to Aerith:

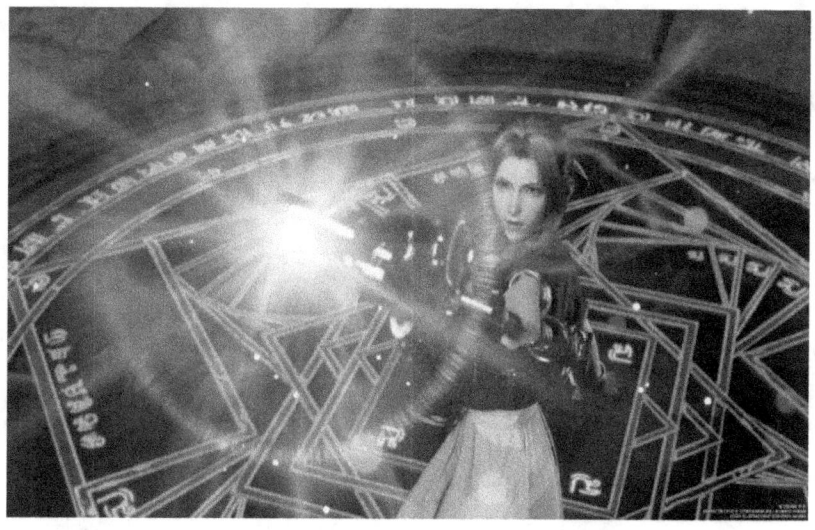

Once the group is back together, the game rewinds a few hours earlier. Remember to collect Lifestream from defeated enemies as it will come in handy later. Approach the nearby rest station and destroy any crystals you come across. Once you've gathered enough Lifestream, stand on the glyph.

Unfortunately, fiends interrupt the process, feeding on nodes supplying the vessel. Head right and deal with the first group. The flying fiend periodically becomes invincible except to magic, while Hecteyes can only be damaged with physical attacks.

Next, cross the floating debris towards the next group to the west. The second beam is guarded by two Hecteyes instead of one. Don't forget to gather Lifestream as you clear the obstructions. Return to the glyph and use the Lifestream to create a path forward. Descend the stairs into the reconstructed area, prepared for a fight.

How to Beat Elena and Tseng:

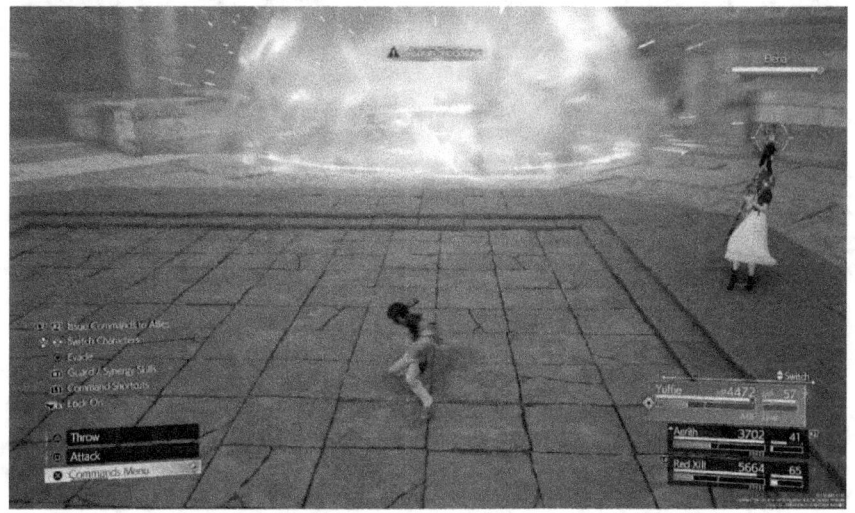

By now, you know what to expect from Elena, having fought her twice before. Focus on Tseng, moving away when he casts Asuran Shockwave. He's weak to ice damage, so keep that in mind. Since most of his attacks are unblockable, focus on evading them. Blocking or evading his attacks can build pressure on him.

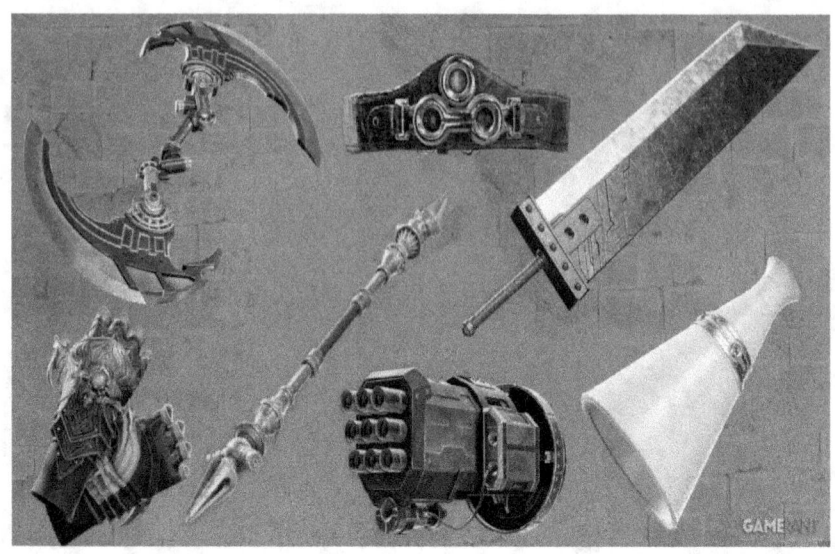

Have Yuffie switch to Lightning or Ice Ninjutsu to make it easier to pressure whichever boss you want to focus on first. Then switch to the Ninjutsu matching the other boss's weakness after defeating the first one. Focus on one boss at a time to defeat this duo efficiently.

A Series of Trials:

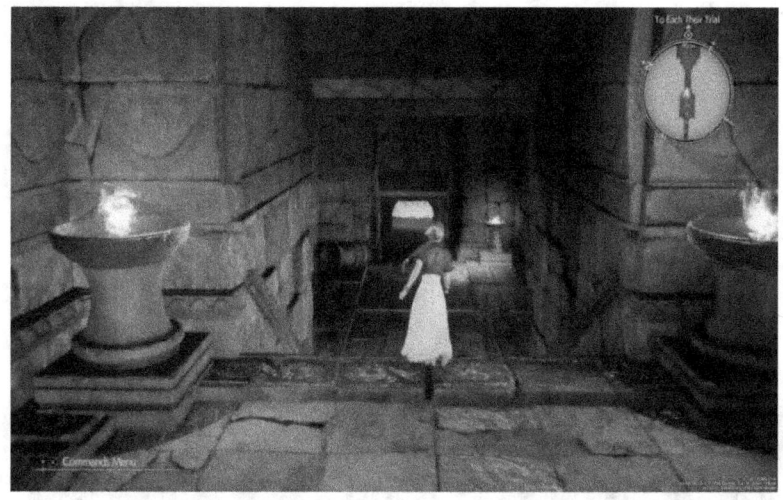

After the battle, proceed down the hallway and use the device to descend further into the Temple of the Ancients. Trigger a cutscene by approaching Tseng, then interact with the altar. To progress, every party member (except Cloud) must complete a special trial alone.

Enter the chamber ahead and approach the statue, holding down the Triangle button. Starting as Red XIII, climb the walls and run while avoiding illusions of Shinra troops shooting at you. Despite being illusions, their bullets cause damage, so keep moving.

When prompted in the lab, hold down L2, R2, or both. Eventually, you'll switch to Tifa's trial. Head up the hill toward the water tower, climb the ladder, and trigger a cutscene. Descend the ladder, chase young Cloud, open the metal door, and proceed through the hallway to find another door at the end.

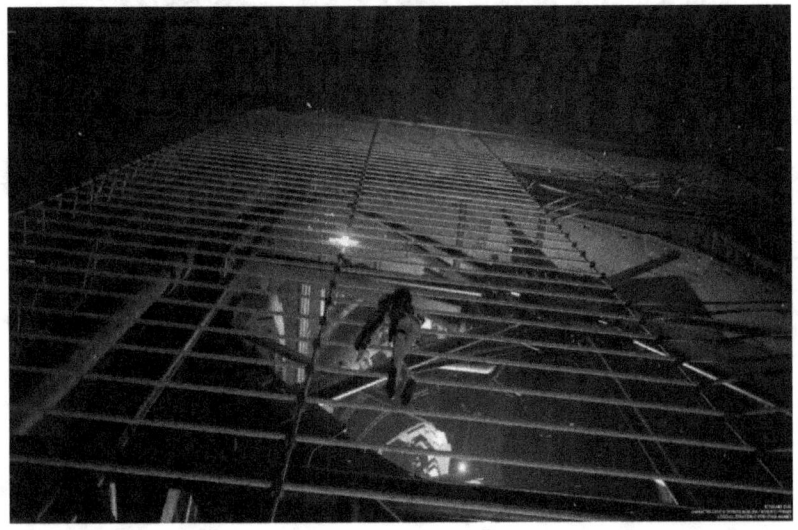

Once you pass through this door, Yuffie's trial begins. Descend the stairs to trigger a cutscene, then start climbing the wall. Navigate through the glowing shurikens, climbing upward and to the right while collecting them. Follow the specter until you reach the top, then drop down and enter the doorway. In the next area, use the grappling hook to traverse the miasma-covered ground. Interact with the elevator to switch to Barret's trial.

As Barret, proceed down the narrow path toward the stairs leading up. Traverse the village and approach Myrna. After a brief cutscene, move toward the hole in the rubble and go through it. Take a left toward the gate blocking your path. Press the Triangle button and then L2 whenever prompted to knock down the gate.

For Aerith's trial, interact with the butterfly on the ground, repeating the process with the next three butterflies. Shortly afterward, you'll play as a younger Aerith searching for a doctor. Approach people in the area and press L2 to interact with them. Keep moving forward and seeking help until you trigger a cutscene. Return to Ifalna, and the game will switch to Cloud. Proceed through the opened door and along the long hall to trigger Cloud's trial.

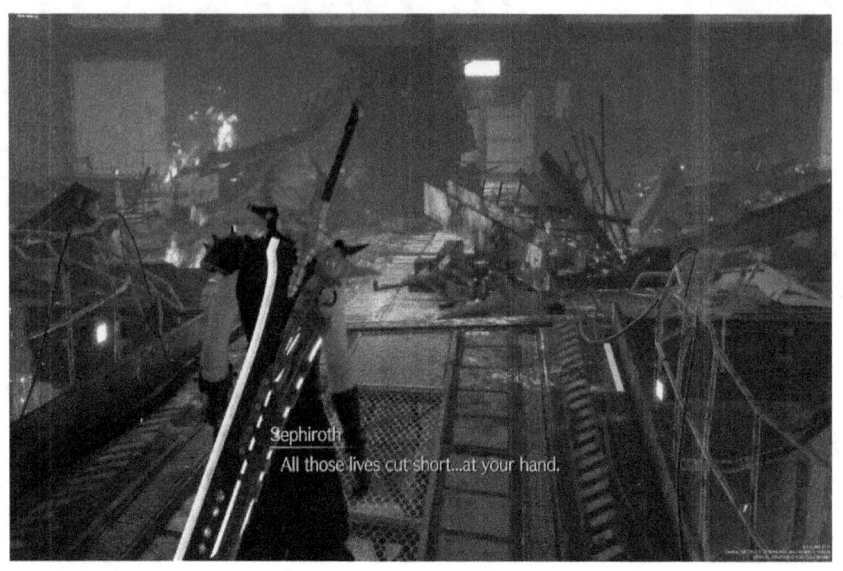

Sephiroth
All those lives cut short...at your hand.

Cross the hall toward Biggs and ascend the flight of stairs. After the cutscene, you'll find yourself back in the Temple of the Ancients. Proceed through the door at the hallway's end and descend the spiral staircase until reaching a dead end. Enter the room to the right, dispatch the fiends, and proceed through the door on the other side. Descend the stairs and find a platform to the left with a chest containing a weapon for Yuffie. From here, choose between two paths.

To the right, stairs lead to a large room with a Floating Death guarding a chest containing a Cetra bracer. Straight ahead, stairs descend to a room with a large fiend. While you can fight it, you can also sneak past along the room's edges to reach a lower part of the earlier spiral staircase. Before descending, head upward to find a chest containing an elixir.

Continue downward on the spiral staircase to reach the bottom. Enter the next area to trigger a cutscene, then proceed down the hallway. Deal with the two fiends blocking the way forward, then confront the next pair of fiends. Utilize the rest station you encounter, as you'll need it.

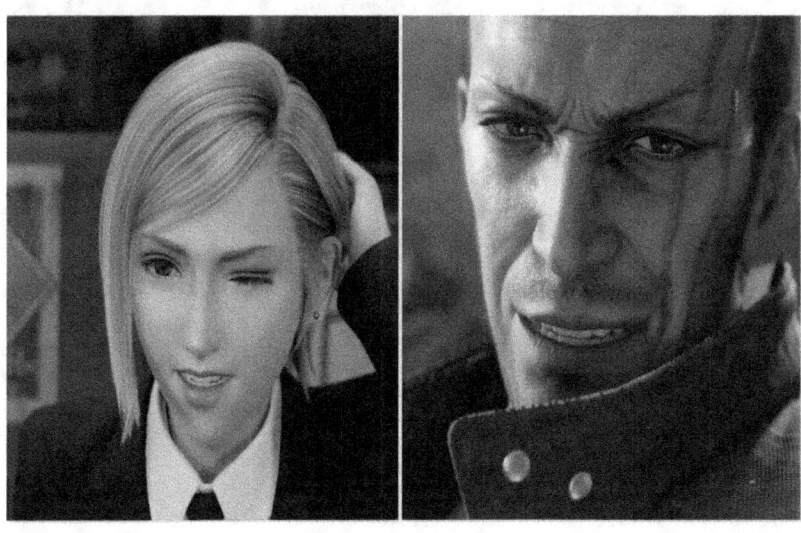

How to Defeat Demon Gate:

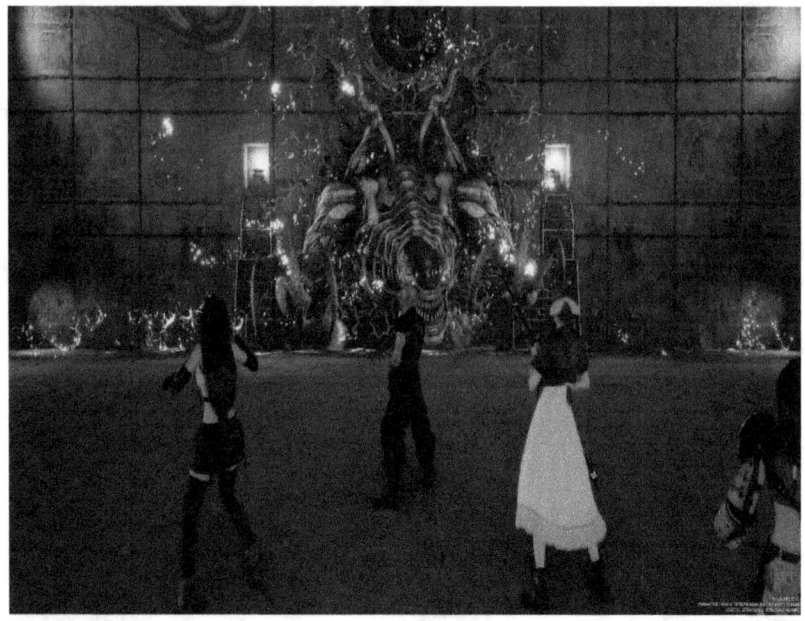

As a recurring boss in the Final Fantasy series, Demon Gate offers a tough battle, especially as the fighting space gets smaller. Deal enough damage to stop this process and keep up the pressure. Adding to the challenge, a second Demon Gate appears when the first one reaches about 60% health.

Concentrate on defeating the first Demon Gate while staying alert for the attacks of the second one. Watch out for squares appearing on the ground—they signal incoming damage. Save your Limit Breaks for when a Demon Gate is staggered to deal maximum damage.

When the first Demon Gate's health drops to zero, it unleashes Final Throes and moves faster towards you. Dodge this attack and continue attacking until it's defeated. Once the first Demon Gate is down, focus on the second one. Dealing with just one makes the fight easier. Repeat the process to clear the path to the Black Materia.

Run:

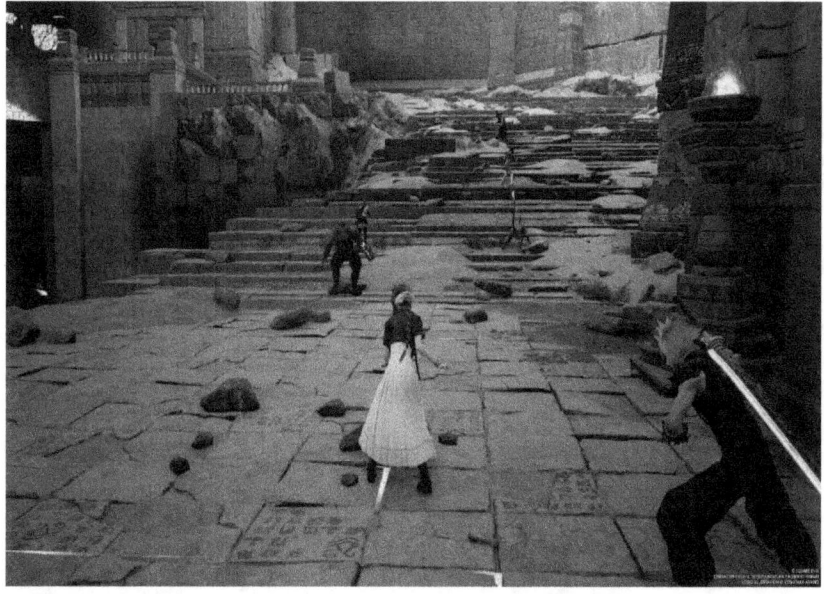

After the cutscene, you'll control Aerith. Follow Cloud as he heads towards the Black Materia. Once the cutscene ends, start running. Stick to the path and sprint as fast as you can, as if your life depends on it. Luckily, Vincent found a shortcut, so you won't need to go through the whole temple again to escape.

Once you're outside, calmly move towards Sephiroth. Another cutscene will follow, then a chase after Aerith. When you catch up, this chapter ends, leading into the final chapter.

CHAPTER FOURTEEN

END OF THE WORLD

In the previous part of Final Fantasy 7 Rebirth, Cloud and his friends ventured into the Temple of the Ancients to find the Black Materia, but Sephiroth ultimately seized it. This fourteenth chapter marks the conclusion of the second part of the Final Fantasy 7 Remake trilogy. Although it's shorter than other chapters, the final boss fight presents a real challenge. Here's what unfolds in Chapter 14: End of the World.

The Illusion of Choice:

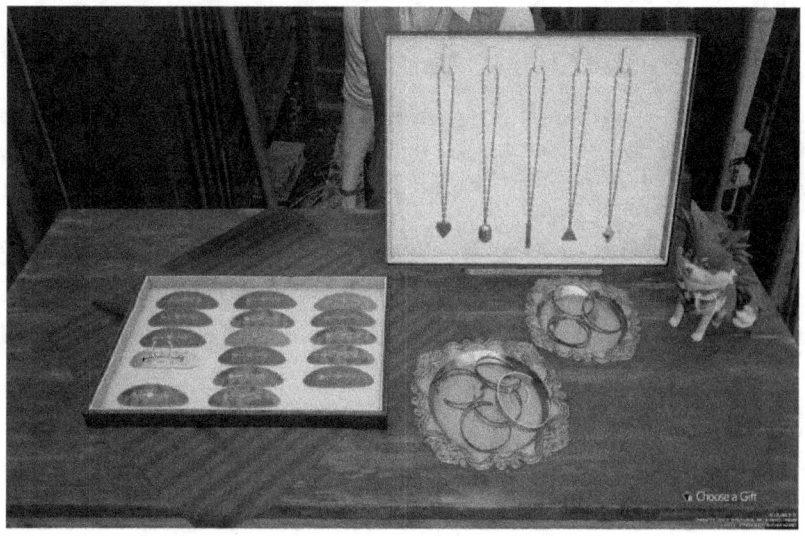

After the cutscenes, follow Aerith downstairs to witness another scene. Then, you'll need to choose a gift for Aerith, but your choice doesn't seem to affect much. At a snack stall, your options seem inconsequential once again. After more scenes, you'll pose for a photo, but once more, your choice doesn't matter. Stick with Aerith, and you'll end up back at the Sector 5 church.

Follow Aerith:

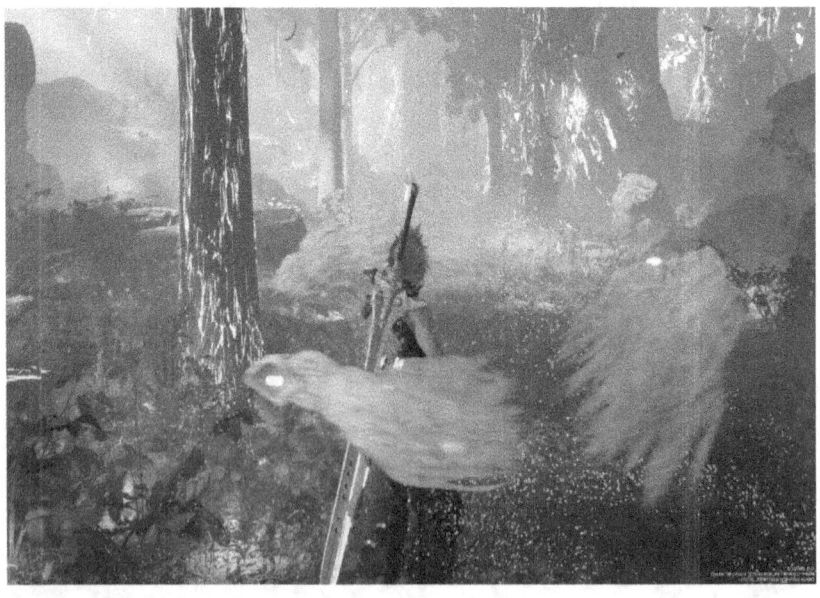

After a peculiar cutscene, you'll find yourself in a new area facing three Whispers. This battle feels more like a story scene, so don't fret about health or abilities. Defeat the Whispers and continue following Aerith as she moves away, ignoring the Whispers around you. When prompted, hold L2 or R2 for another scene.

Follow the Whispers:

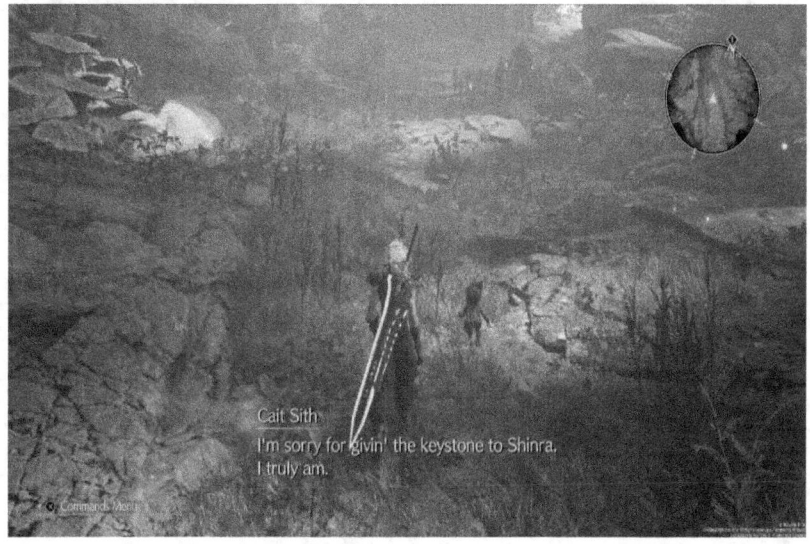

As you search for Aerith, you'll reunite with your party. Follow the path the Whispers took, listening to your friends' conversation. Eventually, you'll reach the Forgotten Capital. Save your game when you regain control. Jump down to confront Sephiroth and engage in a real battle against the white Whispers. They're tough opponents, so be ready. After defeating them, Cloud will proceed alone. Head down and catch the elevator.

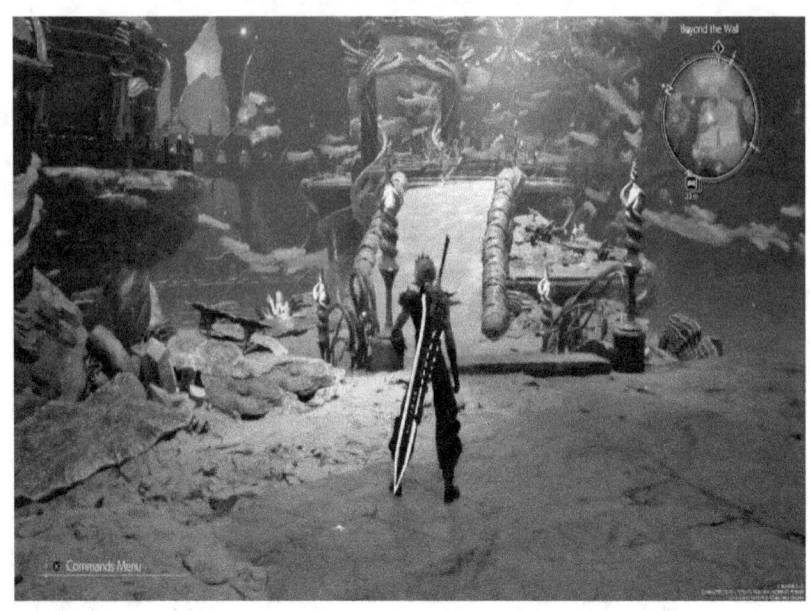

You'll be warned that this is your last chance to rest before finding Aerith. Prepare yourself by saving, resting, and buying what you need. When ready, head east towards Aerith, pushing through the Whispers along the way.

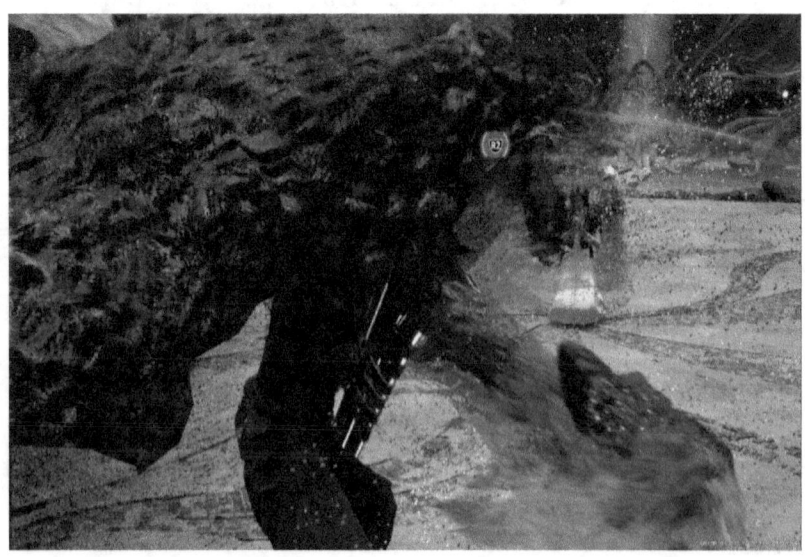

At a certain point, you'll need to quickly press both L2 and R2 buttons together on the PS5 controller, which will make the haptic triggers reach their maximum resistance.

How to Defeat Jenova Lifeclinger:

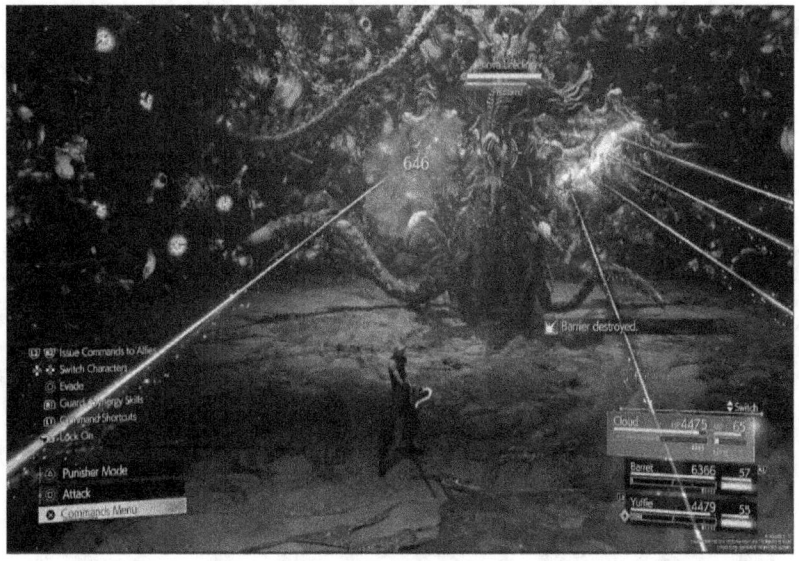

Jenova Lifeclinger doesn't have any specific weaknesses and is resistant to ice and wind attacks. When the boss uses Eye of Providence, move away from the blue sphere it generates to avoid damage. Soon after, Jenova Lifeclinger will put up a barrier to defend against physical attacks. Use magic attacks to break the barrier. This will pressure the boss, but watch out for her

Vengeance attack. Avoid the purple beams to stay safe. If you're aggressive, you might stagger the boss after breaking the barrier.

During the stagger, deal as much damage as you can to Jenova Lifeclinger. When she casts Contaminant Expulsion, quickly move away to avoid being banished from the battlefield (except for Cloud, who stays). Luckily, your party members return shortly after.

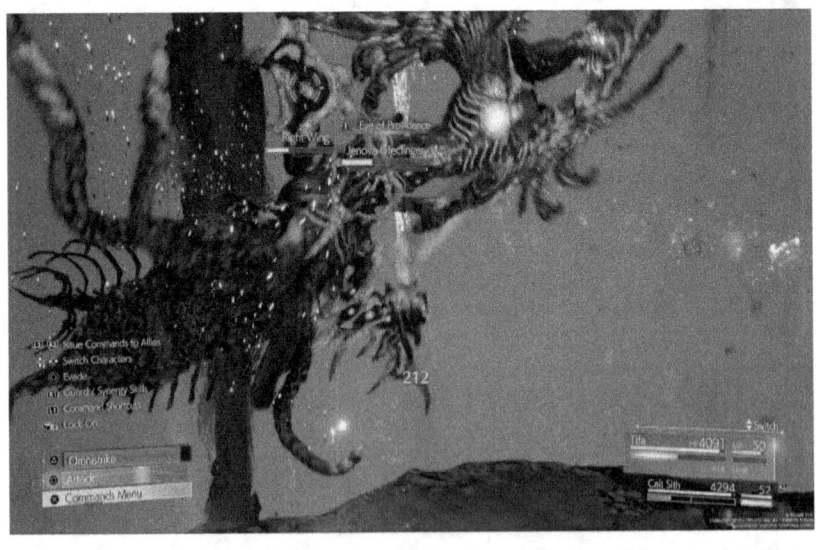

When Jenova Lifeclinger uses Desecration, position yourself directly beneath her to dodge the red beams she fires. When her health drops to about 33%, your party will change. You'll continue with Tifa and Cait Sith. Focus on destroying the right wing, then switch to Barret and Red XIII.

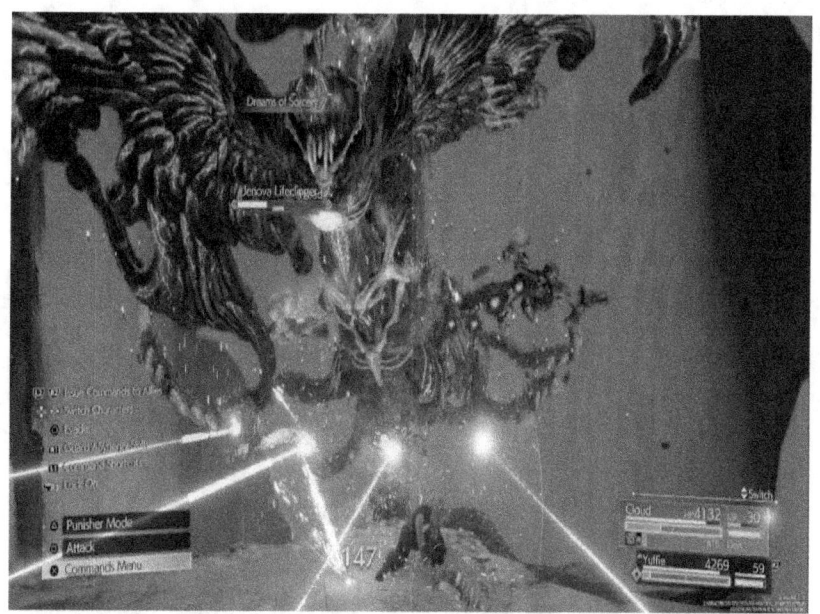

Concentrate your attacks on the left wing while dodging Jenova Lifeclinger's assaults. After destroying the left wing, switch to Cloud and Yuffie. Target Jenova Lifeclinger's head to enter the final phase.

Now, the only target is Jenova Lifeclinger herself. Move away when she summons a storm of fireballs. After a while, she becomes immune to physical damage. Use magic until the shield drops. If you can stagger her once more, seize the opportunity to unleash any Limit Breaks you've saved up and defeat her.

How to Defeat Sephiroth:

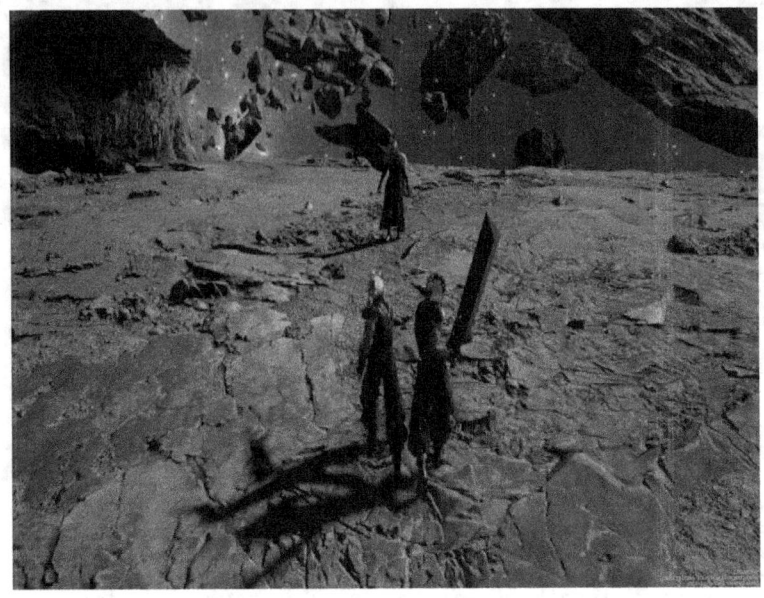

After Jenova Lifeclinger's defeat, Zack jumps into the fray against Sephiroth. Analyzing Sephiroth won't reveal much except that he's resistant to everything, has less health than the previous boss, and can't be debuffed. When Sephiroth initiates Skewer, step back to dodge the attack. Surprisingly, he's quite susceptible to being staggered with abilities. As his health diminishes, watch out for Octaslash and avoid its follow-up. When Sephiroth's health depletes entirely, Zack leaves the battle.

How to Beat Sephiroth Reborn:

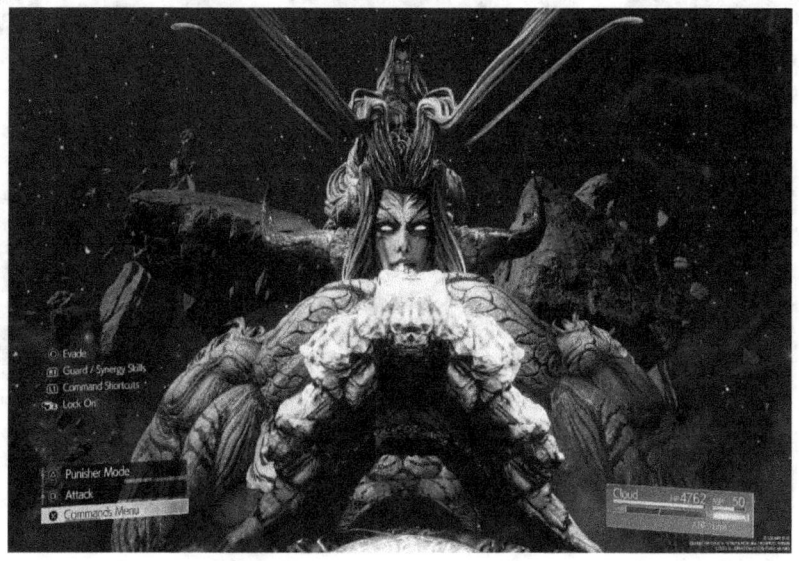

In classic Final Fantasy style, the final boss, Sephiroth Reborn, comes in multiple forms. He boasts a hefty 54,240 HP and no particular weaknesses. At the start of the battle, wait for the Whisper tornadoes to dissipate. Then, position yourself beneath Sephiroth Reborn and concentrate your attacks on his body, his weak spot. After landing several hits, he'll knock you back, but once the Whispers clear, resume your assault.

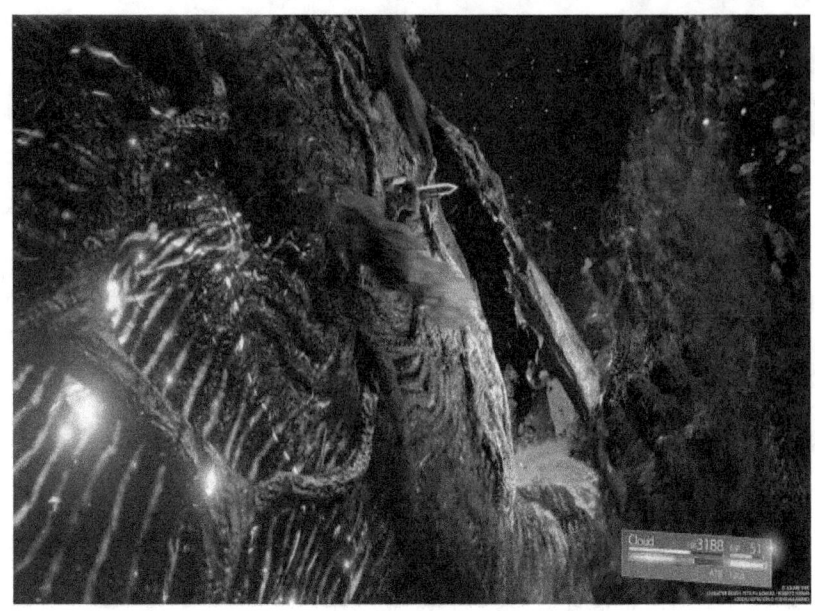

After dealing enough damage to the body, you'll ascend Sephiroth, advancing to the next phase where you'll confront his upper torso. While his attacks aren't overly powerful here, stay vigilant and try to evade or block whenever possible.

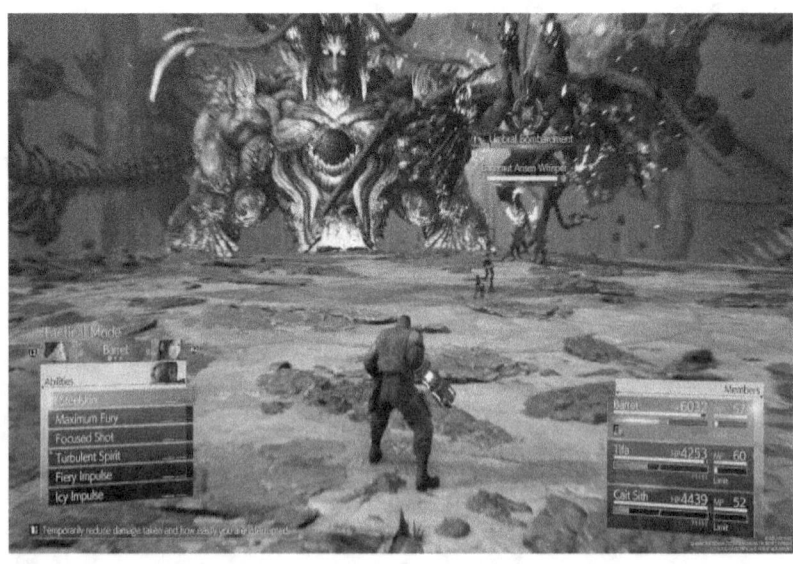

As you damage Sephiroth sufficiently, the battle transitions, and the party must confront Bahamut Arisen Whisper. Watch out for its devastating Gigaflare attack and ensure your party is well-prepared with healing or buffs. After defeating Bahamut Arisen Whisper, Sephiroth Reborn's wings become vulnerable. Disable them and then deal with Bahamut Arisen Whisper again as it resurrects. Once both wings are incapacitated and Bahamut Arisen Whisper is vanquished for the last time, the final phase commences.

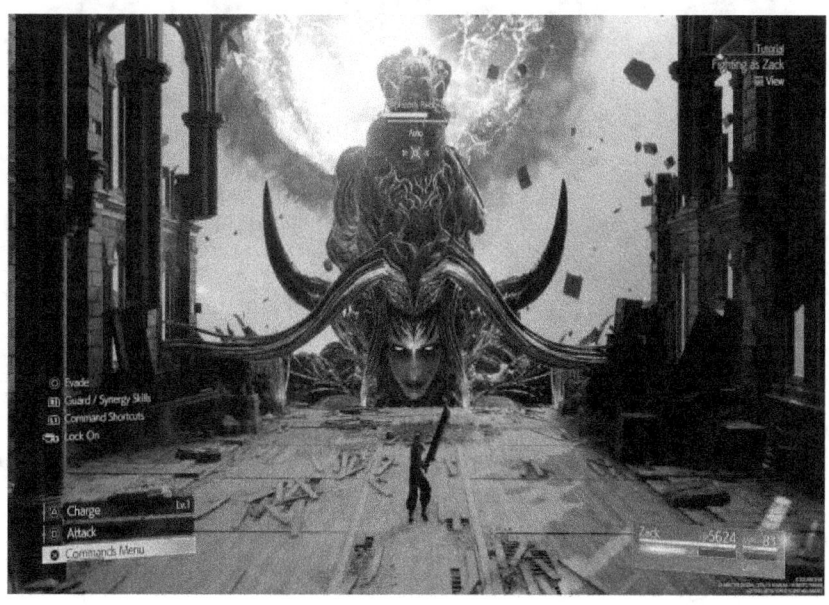

In this phase, you take control of Zack against Sephiroth Reborn. Focus on the face that manifests on Sephiroth to apply pressure.

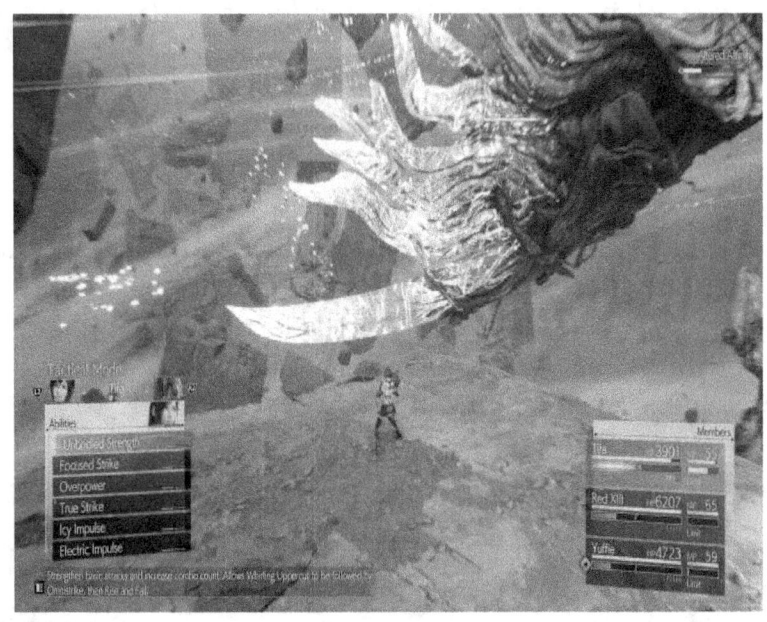

As the battle shifts back to Tifa, Red XIII, and Yuffie, concentrate on crippling the wings to damage the core. Be mindful of the wings' changing elemental affinities and target them with the opposite element. Once the wings are demolished, focus your attacks on the core.

NOTE:

- Be cautious of Sephiroth's devastating Heartless Angel attack, which reduces party members' HP to 1. Keep an ATB command saved to immediately use a Mist Potion afterward to heal the party.

As the final battle escalates, Aerith joins the fray. When Sephiroth summons a tornado of Whispers, utilize magic to damage his sword from a distance. Breaking it increases pressure on Sephiroth.

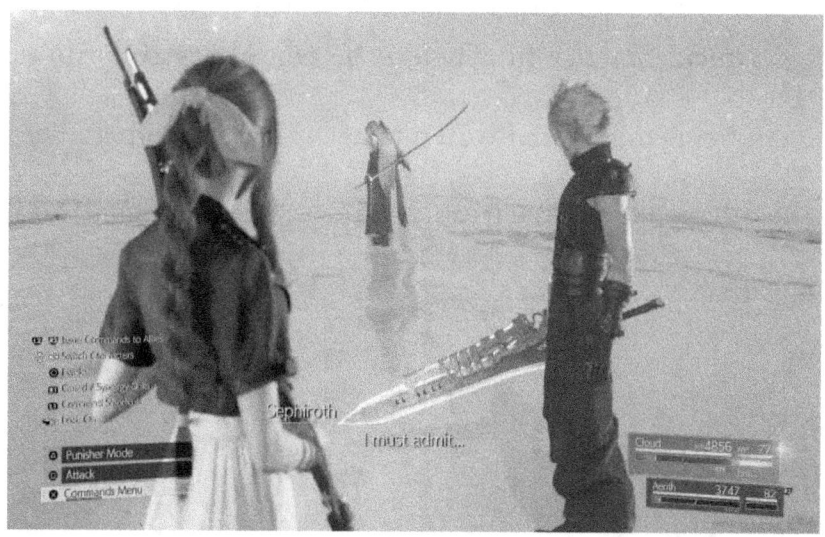

Be cautious of Sephiroth's Skewer attack and Errant Whisper, and avoid the emerging Whispers from the ground. Stay ready for frequent Heartless Angel assaults, using items or Aerith's Limit Break to counter them.

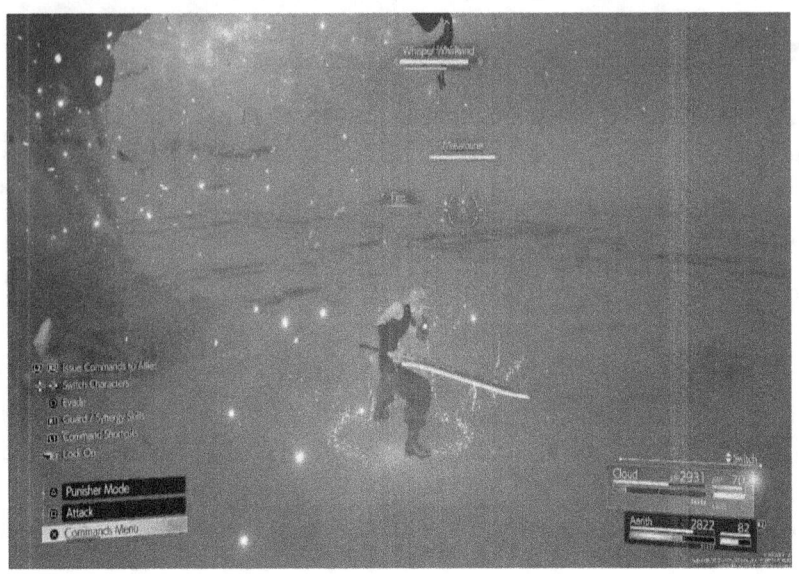

As Sephiroth's health decreases, he launches a devastating beam attack. Stagger him before he completes this move to prevent being defeated. If you manage to stagger him and drain his health, you'll emerge triumphant, concluding Final Fantasy 7 Rebirth.

www.ingramcontent.com/pod-product-compliance
Lightning Source LLC
Chambersburg PA
CBHW071205240526
45470CB00018B/1502